UNIVERSITY OF NORTH CAROLINA AT CHAPEL HILL
DEPARTMENT OF ROMANCE LANGUAGES

NORTH CAROLINA STUDIES
IN THE ROMANCE LANGUAGES AND LITERATURES

*Founder:* URBAN TIGNER HOLMES

*Distributed by:*

UNIVERSITY OF NORTH CAROLINA PRESS

CHAPEL HILL
North Carolina 27514
U.S.A.

NORTH CAROLINA STUDIES IN THE
ROMANCE LANGUAGES AND LITERATURES

Number 175

## MOLIÈRE'S *TARTUFFE*

AND THE TRADITIONS OF ROMAN SATIRE

# MOLIÈRE'S *TARTUFFE*

AND THE TRADITIONS OF ROMAN SATIRE

BY
JERRY LEWIS KASPAREK

CHAPEL HILL

NORTH CAROLINA STUDIES IN THE ROMANCE
LANGUAGES AND LITERATURES

U.N.C. DEPARTMENT OF ROMANCE LANGUAGES

1977

I.S.B.N. 0-8078-9175-4

# PREFACE

In the belief that the most meaningful literary criticism must combine the methods of textual criticism with the historical approach, this book attempts an evaluation of Molière's *Tartuffe* which in many ways is a return to the scholarly attempts of the early 20th century to come to an understanding of this intriguing play. It is my hope that this book will provide a better understanding of Molière in respect to the literary traditions within which he lived and wrote, and that further research on these traditions will be stimulated by my findings.

My indebtedness to the critical work of the hundreds of writers on Molière and on the Classical Tradition is obvious as well as great.

It is my pleasure to thank for their aid on my book in its various stages of development: Dr. James Patty and Dr. Phillip Rhein of Vanderbilt University; Dr. John Zarker of Tufts University; Dr. Robert Sears and Dr. David Gadziola of Ball State University.

For a grant-in-aid toward publication of this book, I am grateful to Ball State University.

TABLE OF CONTENTS

Chapter                                                                                                    Page
I. INTRODUCTION ................................................... 1
    Introduction (1)
    Review of Criticism (4)
    Molière's Background and Association
      with Classical Literature (11)
    The Relationship of Comedy and Satire (23)
    The Comic Element in *Tartuffe* (30)

II. THE SATIRIC ELEMENT IN *TARTUFFE* ............................... 46

III. MOLIERE'S *TARTUFFE*: AN INTERPRETATION BASED ON
    SIGNIFICANT PARALLELS WITH THE TRADITIONS OF
    ROMAN SATIRIC LITERATURE ...................................... 67
    Introduction (67)
    Sophrosyne and Sapientia (68)
    The Hypocrite (102)
    Parasite, Client and Friend (112)
    Sejanus and the Corruption of Political Power (127)

IV. CONCLUSION .................................................... 168

APPENDIX. ADDITIONAL PARRALLELS BETWEEN *TARTUFFE* AND
          CLASSICAL LITERATURE ..................................... 178
SELECTED BIBLIOGRAPHY


Library of Congress Cataloging in Publication Data

Kasparek, Jerry Lewis.
  Moliere's Tartuffe and the traditions of Roman satire.

  (North Carolina studies in the Romance Languages and literatures; no. 175)
  Bibliography: p.
  1. Molière, Jean Baptiste Poquelin, 1622-1673. Tartuffe. 2. Latin-drama (Comedy)—History and criticism.
I. Title. II. Series
PQ1842.K3      842'.4
ISBN 0-8078-9175-4

I

INTRODUCTION

None of Molière's plays has provoked more scholarly controversy than has *Tartuffe*. The divergence of opinion centers on the meaning of the play itself and of its protagonist, Tartuffe. Although the "new critics" have turned their backs on such considerations, the questions of the sources of, and influences on, *Tartuffe* were among the primary considerations of Molière scholarship until the work of Alméras, Michaut and Lancaster, who sifted through and summed up the theories on sources and influences.[1] Their findings indicate that *Tartuffe* and its protagonist were either drawn from the recent history of France and actual characters whom Molière may have known or known about or were based upon the literatures of France, Italy, and Spain, which were available to Molière. These both seem plausible answers at first, and much scholarly effort has been spent in attempts to validate them, as I shall show later in this chapter. Acceptance of either of these theories in its strict applications to single personages or literary influences, however, severely limits any appreciation of Molière as an artist. Although it is possible that any one historical individual or group may have been preeminent in his mind in some period of his creation of *Tartuffe*, or even that some play or novel may provide the major outlines of Molière's plot, it is more likely that he availed himself of the elements of character from dozens of examples of hypocrisy drawn both from history and literary tradition. Molière himself rejected ready conclusions, remarking in the *Impromptu* that "si quelque chose étoit capable de le dégoûter de faire des comédies, c'étoit les ressemblances qu'on y vouloit toujours trouver," and further that "son dessein étoit de peindre les moeurs sans vouloir toucher aux personnes." The meaning of *Tartuffe* is implicitly bound to the total literary tradition which affected Molière. Certainly the French, Italian and Spanish literatures provide keys to an understanding of Molière's play and protagonist. Perhaps any one of the proposed sources was the primary impetus for Molière to write *Tartuffe*. This, however, would not mean that there could not have been other sources or influences as well. Moreover, one must remember that the literatures of France, Italy, and Spain, which were part of the literary heritage available to Molière, were not isolated phenomena, but were themselves the common heirs of a lengthy and fertile literary patrimony. These literatures were the exponents of a continually evolving but continuous tradition drawn from the culture of Rome, and particularly from Latin literature. Therefore, although it may seem easier and even more justifiable to search for the answers in the more immediate of proposed sources, it is possible that a better understanding of the meaning of the play can be provided when its relationships to the original works of literature, within the traditions of which it was created, have been elucidated.

Before attempting to show the relationship of Molière's *Tartuffe* to classical literature, one should be aware of certain facts which must affect the method used in the study: throughout the Roman Empire and the countries that developed therefrom, there was a diffusion of the classical spirit, especially as exemplified in Latin literature; much of the classical culture, again through Latin literature, reentered the European literary stream in the Renaissance, as was the case with Plautus and Terence, so that there existed in the time of Molière a stock of literary commonplaces; finally, the restrictions of the dramatic genre make originality in plot elements so difficult that there are bound to be resemblances from one drama to another in methods, materials and devices.[2] Since comparative literature studies are used to indicate *affinity*, which consists of resemblances in style, structure, mood, or idea between works which have no other connection, *tradition*, or *influence*,[3] it becomes obvious how difficult it must be to determine which of the three relationships is indicated. As I shall show later in this chapter, Molière was well acquainted with Latin literature, which fact removes the possibility of a study based on affinities. The determination whether Molière's *Tartuffe* was influenced, in spite of the rejection by many of the "new critics" of source and influence studies,[4] by classical literature or merely represents parallels in a continuing tradition can only be determined by a study of Molière's play in relation to Latin literature. Such a study is very much a part of comparative method according to one critic, who has noted that any serious study of an author should consider how the component parts of a work were suggested to that author, and what they mean to him in his work.[5] Studies of parallel manifestations, when the relationship of two authors is in question or when there is some question of direct borrowing, because comparable materials are available in other works, often are necessary to determine if there are "sufficient exclusive parallels" to determine if, in part or as a whole, the two works can justifiably be labeled "source" and "borrowing."[6]

> The value of the study of parallels . . .is in the light they cast on the qualities and merit of the individual works; they may also be of interest in indicating similarities and differences in national literary traditions. When one studies parallels in this sense, he nevertheless should consider the possibility of direct relationships.[7]

We see, then, that a study of parallel manifestations may lead to an influence study. If influence is present, it

> must be manifested in an intrinsic form, upon or within the literary works themselves. It may be shown in style, images, characters, themes, mannerisms, and it may also be shown in context, thought, ideas, the general *Weltanschauung* presented by particular works.[8]

Such a study, which begins as a consideration of parallels, and works toward a consideration of the possibility of influence, must "adduce satisfactory external evidence that the hypothetically influenced author *could* have been influenced by the influencing author ... But the essential test must be within the works themselves."[9] Ultimately the influence study should consider what qualities were taken and how they were transmuted. The primary intention of such a study should be to show what the borrowing or influenced author does with what he takes, and what effect the earlier work has upon the finished literary work.[10]

My attention was first drawn to the possibility that classical literature in general and Roman satire in particular provided bases of Molière's *Tartuffe* by a footnote in Gilbert Highet's *Juvenal the Satirist* (Oxford, 1954), p. 325, in which Mr. Highet states: "Mr. Vincent Pascucci has suggested to me that the character of Tartuffe is partly built on the greedy Greeky of Juv. 3 ..." One purpose of this study, then, is to examine the relationship of Molière's comedy *Tartuffe* to the traditions of classical literature, especially those of Roman satire. The study will center on the protagonist of Molière's play, Tartuffe, his characterization and meaning as determined by his actions and relationships with the other characters. On the basis of this information, I shall determine to what extent Molière's play and protagonist reflect the traditions and themes of Roman satire. Necessity will limit the consideration of classical literature to the two greatest Roman satirists, Horace and Juvenal, and Seneca, who, living after Horace and before Juvenal, wrote within the same moral tradition, if not always the genre. Other classical sources will be employed to show the continuity or latitude of the traditional themes and subject matter which were available to Molière.[11]

The remainder of the Introduction will consider these matters: the scholarship on the proposed sources and influences for *Tartuffe*; the background of Molière, with emphasis on his association with classical literature, and the Roman satirists Horace and Juvenal especially; the relationship of comedy and satire; and the comic nature of *Tartuffe*. Chapter two will consider the satiric nature of Tartuffe, noting the satiric element in the play and the satiric intent of the author as expressed in the words of Molière and implicit in the play. It will consider the possibility that *Tartuffe* should be interpreted as a satire written within the structures of comedy. It will not attempt to disprove the comic nature of *Tartuffe*, which will already have been shown in the Introduction, but rather will determine if Molière's play should be designated a satiric comedy. Chapter Three will be an interpretation of the characterization and meaning of Tartuffe based on significant parallels in classical literature, especially in Horace and Juvenal. It will be determined in this chapter to what extent the elements of the characterization of Tartuffe reflect the classical traditions present in Roman satire. Chapter Four will summarize the findings of the previous chapters and draw conclusions therefrom.

## Review of Criticism

France in the time of Molière must have had her fair share of hypocrites, many of whom specialized in religious hypocrisy. Accordingly, much time and effort have been spent in trying to ascertain the character or characters who provided Molière with the incentive to write a play on the subject of religious hypocrisy, and on whom the character of Tartuffe could have been based. Many men have been proposed, among them a certain père Joseph, of whom it is said an incident occurred in which it was remarked of him: "Le pauvre homme!"; an abbé de Pons who made a declaration of love to Ninon de Lenclos; Desmarets de Saint Sorlin, who confessed in his book *Les Délices de l'Esprit* that he had exercised casuistry in his seductions; and the abbé Gabriel de Roquette, Bishop of Autun, who achieved great advancement by his talent for intrigue and his ability to court the rich and powerful.[12] All these have been considered as sources for Molière's *Tartuffe* in an exacting study by Henri d'Alméras, *Le Tartuffe de Moli*ère (Paris, 1928), pp. 41ff., but have been rejected as providing far too limited aspects of the figure of Tartuffe and as unlikely figures for Molière to have heard of or known. There are, however, historical figures who were known to Molière and who have been suggested as prototypes of Tartuffe. Such was Charpy de Sainte-Croix, who is generally conceded to be the most likely of all the proposed avatars of Tartuffe, since he had lived but a short distance from Molière,[13] and since his career provides far the closest resemblances to that of Tartuffe. Tallemant des Réaux gives the following account of Charpy in his *Historiettes*.

> Il s'est mis la dévotion en tête ...Or, un jour qu'il était dans l'église des Quinze-Vingts, Madame Hansse, veuve de l'apothicaire de la reine, y vint; elle loge dans les Quinze-Vingts mêmes. Il l'accosta et lui parla de dévotion avec tant d'emportement qu'il charma cette femme, qui est dévote. Elle le loge chez elle. Lui, qui est si charitable qu'il aime son prochain comme

# INTRODUCTION 5

lui-même, s'est mis à aimer la petite Mme Patrocle, la fille de Mme Hansse: elle est femme de chambre de la reine, et son mari est aussi à elle (la reine). Charpy se met si bien dans l'esprit du mari et s'impatronise tellement de lui et de sa femme qu'il en a chassé tout le monde, et elle ne va en aucun lieu qu'il n'y soit, ou bien le mari. Mme Hansse qui a enfin ouvert les yeux, en a averti son gendre; il a répondu que c'étaient des railleries et prend Charpy pour le meilleur ami qu'il ait au monde. Souvent les maris font leurs héros de ceux qui les font cocus ...Mme Hansse, enfin, n'a plus voulu qu'ils longeassent avec elle. Charpy n'est plus en même logis que la dame: mais il la voit toujours de même. Quand il prie Dieu, il dit: Seigneur, je me résigne à ta volonté: si tu m'envoies des bénéfices, je serai ecclésiastique; si tu ne m'en envoies point, je me résoudrai à la retraite. Par ces façons de faire, il a attrapé le prieuré de X sans le demander; même le cardinal l'a prié de [le] prendre en attendant mieux; il prétend avoir donné de bons avis à Son Eminence.[14]

The resemblance of Charpy to Tartuffe was commented on by Adolphe Brisson[15] and Gustave Michaut. Paul Emard published a book, *Tartuffe, sa vie, son milieu* (Paris, 1932), on the subject of Charpy's life. It fails, however, to provide any incentive beyond Tallemant's account for accepting Charpy as a prototype of Tartuffe. One is restricted to the obvious similarities: that Charpy met a lady, as Tartuffe met Orgon, at a church; that he, as Tartuffe, was lodged in his benefactor's house; that he had sexual designs on a married woman of the household, just as Tartuffe had designs on Elmire (and was a threat to Mariane); that Charpy was on friendly terms with the husband, as Tartuffe was with Orgon.

Another hypocrite of whom Molière may have known is Jacques Crétenet, a barber who became a dévot, who gained a reputation for having hypocritically rebuked himself for being a sinner, who was a director of intention, and who was accused of forming a cabal. He is the subject of a chapter in Francis Baumal's book, *Tartuffe et ses avatars (de Montufar à Don Juan)*, published in Paris in 1925.[16] Crétenet was brought to trial in Lyon in 1652, at the time when Molière's troup was in Lyon.[17] He was found guilty only of an excess of zeal and of a usurpation of functions.

Since several passages in *Tartuffe* allude to the casuistry attacked by Pascal in the *Provinciales*, the assumption has been commonly made that Molière was attacking the Jesuits. This theory is considered by Gustave Michaut, who finds that Molière did use the *Provinciales* in the creation of *Tartuffe*, since Tartuffe is an expert in "direction of intention," and a master of "mental restrictions."[18] Michaut finds that the passages revealing these Jesuitic practices leave no doubt that *Tartuffe* is, in fact, written partially against the Jesuits. This theory, however, has been countered by those who point out that the Jesuits offered little opposition to the theater of Molière's time, and that they participated but rarely in the proscription of actors. Furthermore, Molière seems to have been on very good terms with a number of Jesuits, such as Jean Maury, who addressed his Latin *Theatrum universae vanitatis* (1664) to the "illustre Molière, prince du Théâtre comique," with an admiring panegyric and an endorsement of Molière's position at court.[19] Other Jesuits of note such as Vavasseur, Bouhours, and Huet wrote eulogies of Molière after his death.

*Tartuffe* has also been seen as a blow against Jansenism. This theory was summed up by Louis Lacour in his *Tartuffe par Ordre de Louis XIV* (1877), in which Roquette is Tartuffe, the Prince de Conti is Orgon, and the play was written at the command of Louis XIV expressly against the Jansenists. This theory develops from such lines as:

> Il m'enseigne à n'avoir affection pour rien,
> De toutes amitiés il détache mon âme ...(II. 276-277)

in which Orgon is heard speaking in definite Jansenist terms. As noted in a recent work on Molière, "few spectators in the better seats could fail to recognize the accents of Port-Royal here."[20] The author of this comment, D.B. Wyndham Lewis, further finds that "Tartuffe more or less represents Jansenism ..." (p. 116).

Those who see in the Jesuits and the Jansenists the object of Molière's satiric attack are no doubt partly right, but there are other religious groups who have been seen as sources of the figure of Tartuffe; those are the "cabale dévote" which flocked around the queen-mother of Louis XIV, Anne of Austria, and the Compagnie du Saint-Sacrement. Antoine Adam has shown that the "cabale" surrounding Anne of Austria was full of men like Berryer, Pussort, and Poncet, "tous ces 'gueux' qui se poussent vers les hautes charges par la bigoterie."[21] Adam states that it was this "cabale," which Molière had before his eyes, that is the source of Molière's satire in *Tartuffe* (p. 309).

It is even more likely, however, that the religious group against which Molière particularly directed his satire was the Compagnie du Saint-Sacrement. This is the opinion of the majority of critics, most of whom will admit the likelihood of occasional satire against Jesuits, Jansenists and others.[22] There is a general agreement, however, that Molière had excellent reasons for looking at the Compagnie with the satirist's eye. This organization developed rapidly away from whatever ideals first motivated it, becoming spies and moral censors with their own police system. They opposed the stage in particular, and are partially credited with the failure of the Illustre

Théâtre. There can be little doubt that Molière was personally familiar with their activities, and studies of the Compagnie and *Tartuffe* suggest this knowledge. The work of Raoul Allier especially shows the justification of the belief in the influence of the Compagnie on *Tartuffe*: Tartuffe goes to see prisoners, just as the members of the Compagnie do; Tartuffe gives a handkerchief to Dorine, just as the Compagnie denounces immodesty in clothing; Tartuffe warns Orgon of men who eye his wife, just as the *confrères* warned certain husbands of their wives' debauchery; Orgon placed his friend's papers in Tartuffe's hands, even as the Compagnie directed its member chapters to have a box to put their books and papers in, with this note: This box and everything in it belongs to Mr. N . . ., who has the key and gave it to me in trust.[23] Francis Baumal confirms the findings of Allier, attesting the likelihood of the basis of the character of Tartuffe on that of certain members or a composite of the membership of the Compagnie du Saint-Sacrement.[24]

After careful consideration of the proposed historical sources of the character of Tartuffe, one must agree with Michaut that one can conclude nothing definite about Molière's intentions; one can only deduce that he studied, observed, and utilized contemporary reality in such a way that the verisimilitude of his depictions has presented ample opportunity for the malicious search for allusions and "clefs."[25]

The literary sources of *Tartuffe*, as considered by the critics, fall into two categories: works which supplied (or could have) Molière with substantial material for his plot or characters; and works that could have provided the idea for a few lines in Molière's play. Since by far the more important of these is the first category, it will be necessary to consider in some detail the sources proposed for Molière's plot and characters.

Following the work of Maurice Magendie,[26] the establishment of a hypocrite in a household where he wins the heart of the husband by means of his excessive piety and then tries to seduce the wife is found in d'Audiguier's *Amours d'Aristandre et de Cléonice* (1624). The novel tells of Hiparque, a dévot and preacher, who calls himself a sinner. Hiparque falls in love with Eurigène, the wife of Lycidas, who frequently entertained Hiparque. Trying to seduce Eurigène, Hiparque says, "Je suis sujet à l'amour comme les autres." She rejects his offer, but, when her husband comes in, does not tell him about Hiparque. Later, when she tells her husband of Hiparque's seduction attempt, he does not believe her. To convince her husband, she pretends to be willing, but tells Hiparque to wait until night. When he comes, she calls on her husband to help her, but he has been put to sleep in his hiding place by a magic charm. When he does not appear, she is forced to stab Hiparque.

The conclusion is markedly different from that in *Tartuffe*. However, this variation has been explained by Henry Carrington Lancaster,[27] who proposes that d'Audiguier's novel was combined with *Les Trahisons d' Arbiran* by Le Metel d'Ouville. In *Arbiran*, a wife, whose husband has been accused of crimes by a hypocrite, attempts to reveal the character of the hypocrite (and thus frees her husband) by persuading the king to hide in a place from which he can hear the confession into which she hopes to trick Arbiran. Lancaster feels that Molière created the main outline of his plot by combining the accounts of d'Audiguier and d'Ouville.[28]

It has also been considered likely that Molière was familiar with *Les Hypocrites* of Scarron.[29] This novel depicts the career of a Spanish impostor, Montufar. At Seville, with his two female accomplices, Montufar uses the same methods as Tartuffe:

> Montufar ... se fit faire un habit noir, une soutane et un long manteau ... [et] se fit voir dans les rues ... marchant les bras croisés et baissant les yeux à la rencontre des femmes. Il crioit d'une voix à fendre les pierres: 'Béni soit le saint-sacrement de l'autel et la bien heureuse conception de la Vierge immaculée,' et plusieurs autres dévotes exclamations de la même force.[30]

Like Tartuffe, Montufar devotes himself to charities:

> Il ne bougeoit des prisons, il prêchoit devant les prisonniers, consoloit les uns et servoit les autres, leur allant quérir à manger et faisant bien souvent le chemin du marché à la prison, une hotte pesante sur le dos.

Montufar is capable of self-depreciation and humility:

> Si on lui demandoit son nom, il répondit qu'il étoit l'animal, la bête de charge, le cloaque d'ordures, le vaisseau d'iniquités, et autres pareils attributs que lui dictoit sa dévotion étudiée.

He lives royally thanks to his pious gulls:

> Leur porte, en hiver, se fermoit à cinq heures, et en été à sept, avec autant de ponctualité qu'en un couvent bien réglé; et alors les broches tournoient, le gibier se rôtissoit, le couvert se mettoit bien propre, et l'hypocrite triumvirat mangeoit de grande force et buvoit valeureusement à leur propre santé et à celle de leurs dupes.

One scene from Scarron's work which has been seen as providing the germ of Tartuffe's self-denunciation and forgiveness of Damis (Act III, scene 6) presents Montufar set upon by a gentleman from Madrid, who, having been one of his dupes, recognizes him, denounces him, and begins to slap him. Montufar's followers attack the assailant:

> Tout le peuple se jeta sur lui ... Il fut porté par terre, roué de coups, et y auroit perdu la vie si Montufar, par une présence d'esprit admirable, n'eut pris sa protection, le couvrant de son corps, ... 'Mes frères, s'écrioit-il ... laissez-le en paix pour l'amour du Seigneur, apaisez-vous pour l'amour de la sainte Vierge' ... il le releva de terre où on l'avoit jeté, l'embrassa et le baisa tout plein qu'il étoit de sang et de boue, et fit une rude réprimande au peuple. 'Je suis le méchant, disoit-il ...je suis le pécheur, je suis celui qui n'ai jamais rien fait d'agréable aux yeux de Dieu. Pensez-vous ... parce que vous me voyez vêtu en homme de bien, que je n'aie pas été toute ma vie un larron, le scandale des autres et la perdition de moi-même' ... il s'alla jeter avec un zèle encore plus faux aux pieds de son ennemi, et, les lui baisant, non-seulement il lui demanda pardon, mais aussi il alla ramasser son épée, son manteau, et son chapeau .... Il les rajusta sur lui, et, l'ayant ramené jusqu'au bout de la rue, se sépara de lui après lui avoir donné plusieurs embrassements et autant de bénédictions.[31]

Following the suggestion of Gabriel Gueret, in *La promenade de Saint-Cloud* (1669), that *Tartuffe* was not the original, but that Molière had followed Aretino, Louis Moland[32] in particular has shown the resemblances between Molière's play and *Lo Ipocrito* of Aretino.

> Les analogies et les dissemblances entre l'œuvre de l'Aretin et l'œuvre de Molière sont très-sensibles. Le personage principal de la comédie de *lo Ipocrito* a de commun avec Tartuffe non seulement l'hypocrisie, mais encore la gourmandise et la sensualité. Il emploie les mêmes moyens pour conquérir son prestige et son influence: simagrées pieuses, humilité feinte, jargon de la dévotion. Il est placé dans un millieu pareil, au sein de la famille, où il exerce une autorité dangereuse. Une égale débilité d'espirit caractérise les deux chefs de maison, et les valets de Liseo n'ont pas l'œil moins clairvoyant ni la parole moins impertinente que la servante Dorine.[33]

It has also been suggested that Molière's play is indebted to Charles Sorel's *Polyandre* (1648),[34] especially for the opening scene. In *Polyandre*, the principal characters are at the home of Aurélie when the old grandmother is announced. The gallants exit; the granddaughters hide their romantic novels, get out the *Introduction à la vie dévote*, and take up their sewing. Mme. Ragonde enters, scoffs at their mock piety, and scolds them for their life full of carriages and footmen, of gallants and wine, while there is waste in the kitchen. Polyandre, the hypocrite, enters and reinforces her words. Mme. Ragonde is enchanted with his pious words and begs him to come often so that the household can profit from his words. As she leaves, she finds her servant asleep at the door and rousts the girl roughly.

The works of d'Audiguier, Scarron, Aretino, and Sorel provide the most acceptable literary sources for Molière's plot and the characters in *Tartuffe*. There are, however, a number of further sources which have been proposed as providing limited influence, and these should briefly be considered.

Renart le Contrefait has been seen as providing Molière an incentive toward satirizing religious hypocrisy.

> Pour renard qui gelines tue,
> Qui a la rousse peau vestue,
> Qui a grand queue et quatre piés,
> N'est pas ce livre commenciez,
> Mais pour cellui qui a deux mains,
> Dont il sont en cest ciecle mains,
> Qui ont la chappe faulx samblant,
> Qui va les coeurs des gens emblant ...[35]

Here we see that for Renart the road to royal preferment is in the mantle of the Jacobin and the *frère menu*.

Boccaccio's *Decameron*, the eighth tale of the third day, has been proposed as a source of Tartuffe's statement:

> Ah! pour être dévot, je n'en suis pas moins homme ...(l. 966)

Boccaccio had his character state:

> For being an abbot, I am not less a man.[36]

Regnier's Macette, in his Satire XIII, had the same attitude, dress, behavior, and type of life as Tartuffe.[37] Her morals resemble Tartuffe's in that, for her, there is no sin except in the scandal. Lines 995 and 1502-1506 of *Tartuffe* have been seen as possibly furnished by Regnier.[38]

Critics have also seen the possibility of the influence of Pascal on *Tartuffe*. The theory of the direction of intention was stigmatized in the Seventh *Provinciale*, mental restriction in the Ninth. It has been said that "Molière's debt to his predecessor is primarily philosophical rather than literary or dramatic."[39]

Ultimately one comes to the works of Molière himself, for there are a number of comic devices in *Tartuffe* which Molière had used in his previous plays: a double kneeling occurs in *Le Dépit amoureux*; brusque manners (of Orgon) in *L'Ecole des maris*; a consultation about a marriage (with Mariane) about which the father had already decided in *Le Mariage forcé*; the introduction of Chrysalde (of Mme. Pernelle) at the beginning and then toward the end of *L'Ecole des femmes*; and suspicions of one's sweetheart (Valère's) in *Sganarelle*.[40]

The consideration of the historical and literary sources suggested for *Tartuffe* leads one to no definite knowledge on Molière's method. Indeed the best approach may be to follow the critical attitude that, "with his great familiarity with satirical literature of all the ages, Molière like Poe mistook memory oftentimes for invention."[41] It is with that idea in mind that, after examining Molière's background and his association with classical literature, considerations of the relationship of satire and comedy and of the comic nature of *Tartuffe* will be made. These will be followed by a chapter on the satiric element in *Tartuffe*, and that by an examination of the relationship of Molière's *Tartuffe* to classical literature, especially satire, through a study of significant parallels.

## Molière's Background and Association with Classical Literature

The question of sources must, in the case of most of Molière's works, and specifically *Tartuffe*, be an elusive one. There can be no doubt that Molière drew from many divergent works of literature and historical occurrences. He himself disclaimed originality, saying, "Je prends mon bien où je le trouve."

To gain an understanding of why it is necessary to look at the Latin writers as a possible source of the elements of the character of *Tartuffe*, it is necessary only to look at the education of Molière. His earliest years are quite undocumented, but one may follow the assumption of one scholar that, although his mother died when Molière was quite young, she set him on the course that he was to pursue: a moral training drawn particularly from the Bible and the classical authors.[42]

As a young boy, probably at the age of nine or ten, Molière was sent to one of the celebrated Jesuit schools of his day, the Collège de Clermont. There Molière would have followed the *Ratio Studiorum*, a plan of studies designed by Loyola to endow the students with "Christianas costumbres."[43] This was achieved largely through the exacting study of classical authors, particularly the Latin, who had been a sourcebook for moral teaching since the time of Augustine.[44]

The Jesuit system of education, although it always allowed for modifications,[45] had as its dominant purpose the preparation of apostles of Christ.[46] It was through the coupling of learning and goodness that Loyola hoped to get men to work for the betterment of others. "If education is to be employed generously, a man has to be both good and learned. If he's not educated, he can't help his neighbors as effectively as he might. If he's not good, he won't help them or at least he can't be relied on to do so consistently."[47] This then is the underlying purpose of Jesuit education — to "acquire learning so as 'to be of benefit to [one's] neighbor'."[48] The education provided by the Jesuit schools was intended to prepare the young scholars in self-knowledge, expressed in the maxim *Nosce teipsum*. With this understanding of oneself, a man could then "understand the characters of others and deal with them successfully."[49] The motivation is clearly once again that of being properly prepared to help one's neighbors. Accordingly, that he might set a good example, the young student at a college of the Jesuits was taught the necessity not only of self-knowledge, but also of self-control and self-sacrifice.[50] This followed the teachings of Loyola, who often employed not only *Nosce teipsum*, but *Vince teipsum* as the keys to training the characters of men.

Loyola established a plan of studies from which the students could obtain the desired self-knowledge and good morals while gaining a scholarly education. The decision to base his *Ratio Studiorum* on classical literature follows his consideration that

> la jeunesse reçoit et garde si facilement les premières impressions bonnes ou mauvaises et que les premières notions, les exemples bons ou mauvais qu'on lui donne, quand je considère, d'autre part, que les livres, surtout les classiques qu'on a coutume d'expliquer aux jeunes gens, Terence par exemple, Virgile et d'autres, avec beaucoup de choses utiles pour l'enseignement et pour la vie en renferment d'autres qui sont très mauvaises et très dangereuses...[51]

The *Ratio Studiorum* states that the subjects taught to those attending the Jesuit colleges should be, in general, the humane letters of the various languages, logic, natural philosophy, moral philosophy, metaphysics, scholastic theology, positive theology, and the sacred scriptures.[52] The humane letters were understood by Loyola to signify "what pertains to rhetoric, poetry, and history."[53] Loyola specified that the pagan books should be purged of their immoral content, but what remained could "be used by the society like the spoils of Egypt."[54] Accordingly, nearly all the Latin and Greek authors were taught in the Jesuit schools.

Molière, following the traditional outline of the *Ratio*, would have studied the majority of classical Latin authors and some of the Greek, as the Jesuits de-emphasized Greek literature in order to stress the literature of the Latin writers. Among the standard authors read were Aristotle and St. Thomas Aquinas, Cicero, Caesar, Sallust, Ovid, Livy, Tacitus, Suetonius, Quintilian, Seneca, the poets from Horace to Juvenal, as well as Plautus and Terence.[55] All of these were rich in character studies and moral precepts, and no doubt Molière gained much of his ultimate knowledge of self and philosophy of life from them. It is, however, to three authors that this study will particularly look — the satiric poets Juvenal and Horace and the Stoic philosopher Seneca.

These three authors are represented in the curricula of many of the Jesuit colleges of the age of Molière. Horace, for instance, was read throughout the last four years of the Jesuit system, the *Satires* and *Epistles* being recommended for the Fourth Form, although, typical of the adaptability of their system, he was sometimes read earlier.[56] Juvenal, because of his difficulty both in style and subject matter (he was read in expurgated editions), was usually studied in the last years of the Humanities or the first years of the Rhetoric. He was employed, however, at all levels as a sourcebook of exempla.[57] Seneca was read in all but the earliest year. He was particularly stressed in the later years and in the course of Philosophy, which Molière took, although his works also were carefully selected so as not to present deleterious concepts.[58] The works of these three authors contain, as will be shown, many of the moral principles which are seen reflected in the character of Tartuffe. This is not, however, to say that they alone can be considered as possible bases of *Tartuffe*.[59] All the literature that Molière read and all that he saw of life provided him with his understanding of character and of moral principles. Classical literature was but one of the many sources of Molière's knowledge, but it was certainly an important and influential one.

During his last years at Clermont, Molière is asserted to have studied with Gassendi,[60] who had rehabilitated Epicurus for seventeenth-century France. Any direct association with Gassendi is unlikely, but Molière was subject to a strong indirect influence toward Epicureanism. For a number of years, and throughout the 1660's, when he was writing and rewriting *Tartuffe*, Molière was on intimate terms with two men, Chapelle and Bernier, who were the pupils of Gassendi. It is further known that Molière translated Lucretius' *De Rerum Natura*, probably in the 1660's.[61] It cannot be said, however, to what extent the Epicureanism of Gassendi, or the work of Lucretius influenced Molière's personal philosophy. Very likely, just as Gassendi had adapted Epicureanism to Church doctrine and his personal feeling, so did Molière. All of what Molière learned from Gassendi's pupils or Lucretius, however, was not contrary to the moral education he had received from the Jesuits. It has been noted that "Gassendi catalogued Epicurean virtues, and a new understanding of Epicurean ethics was achieved: *temperantia, continentia, fortitudo circa metum mortis, iustitia* . . .[and] *amicitia* were found to reside within Epicureanism."[62] The particular virtues stressed were related to those that Molière had learned from the Jesuits: *temperantia* and *amicitia* are basic to the Jesuits' teaching on neighborliness. Lucretius is important to our consideration of Molière's relationship to classical literature since Molière's association with his work shows first of all that Molière exhibited a strong interest in Latin literature in the 1660's, and, furthermore, that interest was directed notably at works of a philosophic and moral nature.

It would be easy to find in Lucretius a motivation for the writing of *Tartuffe*, for in the *De Rerum Natura* Molière could have found the germ of the spite that was to grow in his breast for the malignant and destructive thing that religion could become and the evils that it could educe or commit. Lucretius is probably a source of Molière's attitude toward certain aspects of religion and morality, but it is not the most significant source of classical parallels for the character and actions of Tartuffe.

Rather it is to three phases of classical writing that we can look for meaningful parallels for the various aspects of Molière's plot and his depiction of the main characters of *Tartuffe*. One was character-writing, which extended to practically every phase of literature and had its foremost representative in Theophrastus, who made of it a distinct genre. A second was the moral or ethical literature — an abiding element in the Greco-Roman tradition. A third basis, and one encompassing both character and moral traditions, was that of satire. The first two must be understood in order to appreciate the third.

Doubtless many earlier writers composed sketches of character-types, endowing them with traits which were universal in those particular types. There are such types obvious in Greek literature from Homer to Aristophanes. One of the most important attempts at "character-writing" was by Aristotle in Book IV of his *Ethics*. There, in order to actively demonstrate his theory of the "golden mean," he depicts his idealized Magnificent Man and Great-minded Man by showing the virtues which exist midway between the vices, which are all extremes. Aristotle continued writing in this vein in his *Rhetoric*; there he lists the typical "actions, motives, and passions of young men, old men, men in their prime, well-born men, rich men, men of power, and men of good fortune."[63] These are not characters, but disquisitions.[64] They do, however, along with the literature that preceded, form an influential basis for the study and writing of the character, a genre best represented by one of Aristotle's pupils, Theophrastus.[65]

Theophrastus based his *Characters* on Aristotle's doctrine of the mean, "according to which one may see three states or degrees in respect to any moral quality and according to which also one may pick out three types of people, the central virtuous type and the two extremes of excess and defect."[66] Theophrastus' *Characters* are all depictions of the vices, not of the virtues. Rather it is the point of the "Letter Dedicatory" to the *Characters* that the man who is willing to avoid the flaws shown in the characters depicted can direct himself on the right path — the mean.

What Theophrastus left behind him for the world to profit from and the writers of later ages to draw from was a series of depictions of "types of moral characters ... fashioned by means of an accumulation of suggestive, characteristic actions and words, and representative of a group of similar individuals."[67]

Latin authors were among those to borrow from the traditions of the *Characters*. One has but to read any of the plays of Plautus or Terence to be aware how dependent the humor is upon the vivid depiction of the traits and habits of certain classes of humanity.[68] Horace sees the Character as a rich source of meaningful information. When in the *Ars Poetica*, he delineates the universal conduct and character of the boy, the young man, the man in his prime, and the old man, Horace does so by means of brief pictures which are directly in the tradition of Aristotle and Theophrastus.[69] The *Satires* of Horace are a particular mine of character-depictions, succinct and vivid.[70]

In Seneca one finds as part of the Stoic teacher's repertoire a variation on the Character, e.g., in his forty-fifth and eighty-first epistles. Here one finds a picture of the *beatus vir*, the Stoic wise man, "self-judging, steady, just, his reason ever controlling his passions." One may see in the following statement from Seneca the strength of the character-writing tendency in his works:

> If you mark them carefully, all acts are always significant, and you can gauge character by even the most trifling signs. The lecherous man is revealed by his gait, by a movement of the hand, finger, by the shifting of his eye. The scamp is shown up by his laugh; the madman by his face and general appearance. These qualities become known by certain marks; but you can tell the character of every man when you see how he gives and receives praise.[71]

It is unlikely that Molière was personally acquainted with Theophrastus' *Characters*, although the work of Casaubon had brought them to the attention of the seventeenth century.[72] Theophrastus was taught in the Jesuit schools.[73] But as Greek was deemphasized in favor of Latin, Molière probably did not study his works. Rather it is possible that in the continuing tradition of the *Characters*, as represented in the many phases of Latin literature beginning with Plautus and Terence and extending thorough Cicero, Horace, Martial, Seneca and Juvenal, Molière found a particularly meaningful method of revitalizing the moral lessons which had been so deeply impressed on him by the Jesuits.

In Molière's time there was much literature written with ethical and didactic purposes. This is also true of the ancient world, for throughout the span of classical literature one may constantly find literature which contains moral and ethical principles. This is so in Homer, in Aeschylus, in Aristotle, and in countless others of the Greek authors. The Roman authors were aware of this tradition, and many of them wrote within it. So important, in fact, was this tradition that, when Horace wrote his treatise on the art of poetry, he designated as the function of poetry *delectare* (to give delight) and *prodesse* (to benefit). The idea of this word, *prodesse*, is, for instance, the benefit one can obtain from the inspiration to courage and the teachings of wisdom, particularly moral precepts, which one can find in the poets. Horace put into concrete terms the didactic nature of "so much of the best that was written in Latin."[74]

The first century B.C. was a time in which there occurred in the upper classes especially a "decline of religion . . . accompanied by a corresponding and inevitable decline of morality. The old simplicity of Roman manners, which had helped to build up the greatness of Rome, seemed dead beyond recall, and wealth, luxury, and license had followed the wake of Empire."[75] Augustus, aware that such conditions could not but work against his attempts at a settled government, initiated a general moral reform and religious revival. To add greater meaning to his policies, he enlisted the aid of a number of the prominent authors of his day, Vergil, Horace, and Livy, to actively promote the reform within the scope of their publications.[76]

So it is that one finds a strong strain of moral criticism running through Horace and the other Augustan authors who supported the policies of the new regime. This is not, however, to assert that moral literature would not have been produced without Augustus. The Roman people for centuries were of a moral, even a puritanical, nature.[77] Their literature strongly reflects this quality. Augustus was but one influence, then, towards this moral strain in Augustan literature. Another was philosophy and Stoicism in particular.

Stoicism permeated the literature of the late Republic and early Empire. Not only authors such as Vergil and Livy, who are accepted as having embraced the tenets of the Porch, but even those who were not adherents of Stoicism wrote under its influence, as was the case with Sallust and Tacitus.[78]

Roman literature found in the Stoic philosophy particularly, and also in a number of other philosophies such as Epicureanism, Platonism and neo-Pythagoreanism, tenets which were easily utilized, sometimes in slightly adapted form, in its ethical considerations.

The central doctrine of Stoic physics — that there is an essential harmony in matter, directed by a material god immanent in it — is thus surveyed from the viewpoint of ethics; and the man who follows reason and virtue, being in harmony with the universe, inevitably succeeds, whereas he who espouses rashness and vice inevitably fails.[79]

Many an author, such as Livy, following his Stoic physical doctrine, stressed the idea that "the reader should look to the moral qualities of the early Romans, and that the causes of decline [of religion, and thus the state] are the vices which the Stoics condemn — greed and soft-living, lust and base ambition ..."[80]

The traditions of character and moral writing were merged in the satiric genre (as they were in history and epic) from its earliest important manifestations — notably in the work of Lucilius. Fiske shows that to some extent (the fragmentary nature of Lucilius' extant works limits judgment) Lucilius used "popular methods of character delineation," in the tradition of Theophrastus.[81] Lucilius utilized the character as part of his "miscellaneous criticism which always retained a considerable element of ethical tone. This tone was in general Stoic."[82] The Satiric authors added little to the genre of character delineation. "A stock of moral and social types of men had been ticketed and succinctly described; the description could be concrete and dramatic."[83]

Molière was doubtless aware of the use of character delineation from Roman drama. There was, however, also available to Molière in the works of the classical satirists a rich and abounding source of images, allusions, and characters, with their particular traits, all drawn up with an underlying tone of criticism, often moral, directed toward reform. Satire was available to Molière; if he used it, the character of Tartuffe should be formed along traditional guidelines.

It has been shown that part of Molière's Jesuit schooling consisted of the reading of selected passages from Latin authors, among whom were Horace, Juvenal, and Seneca. But was this early encounter influential enough to make an author look back to his school days some decades later and recall vividly the character and lessons of the satiric poets? Considering the quality of Jesuit education, this author believes that it is possible. Henri Peyre, commenting on the influence of classical literature on the French literature of the seventeenth century, stated, with obvious appreciation of the effects of Jesuit education, that Molière was among a large number of writers in whose memories there was a wealth of material from Tacitus and Seneca, Cicero and Plutarch.[84] It is possible, however, that what Molière gained at the feet of the Jesuits was an impetus — an interest in certain aspects of the satiric literature, the potentialities of which he would not fully see for a number of years. His school lessons could have instilled in Molière an abiding interest in, and a firm knowledge of, classical satire. We know that Molière read Roman satire in his days at Clermont, but were there any further influences toward satire in Molière's life?

Molière, like most writers of his time, read widely and deeply in the literatures of many countries. He was familiar with much of the recent drama of Spain, Italy and his own country. It has been shown that he read a good deal outside of his chosen genre of drama;[85] in the process he encountered his old acquaintance of school days, satire. Many authors of the Middle Ages and Renaissance wrote satire in the tradition of Juvenal and Horace. Molière no doubt encountered any number of these. He is known to have read, in particular, the satires of Regnier and of Francisco Quevedo, the Spanish Juvenal.[86] But Molière's reading of the works of Regnier and Quevedo, although it shows that he was aware of satire and the satiric tradition, does not show that he was consciously thinking of Roman satire or moral literature during the 1660's when he was writing *Tartuffe*. The likelihood of such an awareness, however, can be shown by a review of certain details of Molière's life after 1660.

Molière in 1658 returned with his troupe to Paris, having toured the provinces, where their presentations were primarily farces. In 1659 Molière presented *Les Précieuses Ridicules*, with instant success. In 1660 the first *Satires* of Boileau were published, and no doubt came to the attention of Molière. It was not, however, until 1663 that Molière actually entered into relations with Boileau. In 1664 Molière offered the first version of *Tartuffe*. But, under the influence of the "dévots," the King interdicted the public presentation of the play. Molière and his wife, Armande Béjart, whom he had married in 1662, decided to live separately in 1667. At that time Molière took an apartment in the village of Auteuil, where he withdrew in the company of a number of friends, the most noteworthy of whom were Chapelle, the pupil of Gassendi, and Boileau, the satirist. It was later in the same year that Molière presented his second version of *Tartuffe*, under the title of *L'Imposteur*. This version too was forbidden. Ultimately, Molière was allowed to play *Tartuffe* in its third version, after the King removed his interdiction. Four years later, in 1673, Molière died.

Molière's period of withdrawal at Auteuil, occurring as it did at the same time as his rewriting of *Tartuffe* in the second and third versions, must particularly be of concern to us for our understanding of Molière's ultimate version of *Tartuffe*. Molière and his wife Armande agreed that, because of her consistent infidelities, they should cease to be husband and wife. Armande stayed in Paris, while Molière moved to his bachelor retreat at Auteuil. "He was at that moment fatigued and discouraged by his long struggles on behalf of *Tartuffe*. He was in bad health, scandalously overworked, and living on a milk diet. He needed tranquility...."[87] At

## INTRODUCTION 19

Auteuil Molière was joint tenant with Chapelle, his friend from school days. Molière's life there, however, was far from "idle solitude."[88] During his "retirement" Molière wrote three of his finest plays, *Amphitryon, George Dandin,* and *L'Avare.* Besides having the companionship of his housemate Chapelle, Molière was frequently visited by a number of his friends, including Boileau and La Fontaine. Palmer comments that "this chapter in the life of Molière is traditionally devoted to his friendships."[89] He continues by stating: "Their association had been constant from the early days of the comic war. La Fontaine had been one of the first to proclaim Molière to be 'his man', and Boileau was the first of the critics to appreciate his genius correctly. Upon the outbreak of the comic war, Molière had found Boileau by his side, first and most generous of his supporters in the controversy over *L'Ecole des Femmes:*

> En vain mille jaloux esprits,
> Molière, osent avec mépris
> Censurer ton plus bel ouvrage;
> Sa charmante naïveté
> S'en va pour jamais d'âge en âge
> Divertir la postérité.
>
> . . . . . . . . . . . . . . . . . .
>
> Ta muse, avec utilité,
> Dit plaisamment la vérité;
> Chacun profite à ton Ecole;
> Tout en est beau, tout en est bon;
> Et ta plus burlesque parole
> Vaut souvent un docte sermon."[90]

We do not know exactly on what basis the friendship of Molière and Boileau started and grew. Initially one assumes that the basis must have been the fact that they were both literary men, and that Boileau had early esteemed Molière's ability. This is no doubt part of the answer, but a lasting relationship between two intelligent and sensitive men will usually grow from more than an appreciation of talent. Although it is impossible to say what caused Boileau's affection for Molière, we do know the kind of qualities that Boileau appreciated in a man. Describing a friend of his, Boileau wrote: "C'était un homme d'un savoir étonnant, et passionné admirateur de tous les bons livres de l'antiquité . . . ."[91] Boileau also noted other qualities in his friend: generosity; sincerity; personality; but the first and most important characteristics of his friend, one observes, are knowledge and admiration for the good books of antiquity. One wonders if Boileau did not, in fact, look for these two characteristics in all his friends. Boileau's life, after all, was constructed on a meaningful reapplication of classical literature to his own times. Between 1660 and 1674 he wrote satires based on Horace's and Juevenal's satires, epistles based on those of Horace, and the *Art Poétique* based on Horace's *Ars Poetica*.[92] Would not his friends have been especially those men who enjoyed, as did Boileau, spending their time in "relisant Juvénal, refeuilletant Horace"?[93]

Friends of Molière's had been accustomed to meet even before Molière went to Auteuil. Their meetings took place two or three times a week at Boileau's flat in the rue du Vieux Colombier. La Fontaine described their association in his *Psyché*:[94]

> Four friends, whose acquaintance had begun upon Parnassus, came together in a species of society which I would call an academy if the numbers of its members had been greater, and if they had shown as much regard for the muses as for their diversion. The first thing they did was to banish any conversations conducted by the rules and anything which suggested an academic conference. When they were met together, if by chance they happened, in recounting their experiences, upon any point of literature or science, they profited by the occasion, without, however, dwelling too long upon the same matter, but proceeding lightly from one subject to another in the manner of bees who happen upon various kinds of flowers. Nothing malicious or envious or in the nature of scandal was ever heard among them. They adored the works of the ancients, and did not refuse a tribute to those of modern authors to whom praise was due. They spoke of their own works with modesty, and they exchanged their views in all sincerity when by chance anyone of them happened to contract the malady of the age and produce a book. But that was a disaster which but rarely occurred.

From this statement by La Fontaine, it is possible to see a strong influence toward the reading of the classical authors, since the friends "adored the works of the ancients." But what classical works did Molière read during this period of repose? There is no definite answer to this question. However, on the basis of certain points of information, it is possible to supply the names of the authors most likely to have been read. First, one must consider the prevailing attitude of Molière while at Auteuil. *"He lived like a philosopher* — such is the impression which the contemporary gossips, as reported and embellished by Grimarest, almost unanimously emphasized in their references to Molière...".[95] An example of Molière's philosophic tendencies is provided by Grimarest, who tells of a discussion in which Chapelle and Molière discussed the merits of Descartes and Gassendi.[96] Obviously such philosophic studies would lead Molière to the Roman works which dealt with philosophy, and especially those which presented views on ethics, for Molière's chosen field was mankind. Among the Latin works which included ethical statements were the satires of Horace and Juvenal and the moral writings of Seneca. We have seen that, according to the traditional course of study at the Jesuit Collège de Clermont, Molière would have read the works of Horace, Juvenal and Seneca in his schooldays. But is there any evidence that Molière ever read them again?

When Molière died in 1673, an official inventory was taken of his goods. It is in this inventory that one can find proof of Molière's reading habits, for there among his possessions, some thirty years after he had completed his education, were copies of the works of Horace, Juvenal and Seneca.[97] There were more than 350 books in Molière's private library, many of them French, Italian, or Spanish plays for which no title is given. The other classical authors noted are Herodotus, Thucydides, Plutarch, Lucian, Diodorus the Sicilian, Terence, Caesar, Livy, Vergil, and Ovid. Furthermore, although the contents are not listed, an eighteen-volume dictonary of philosophy was found, along with a number of unnamed treatises on philosophy.[98] Notably absent from the list are the comedies of Plautus, suggesting either that the inventory does not contain the total library of Molière, or that Molière had ready access to a library capable of filling the gaps in his own.

It is impossible to assess the full importance of the association Molière had with Boileau. One scholar who has touched on the subject states concerning that relationship:

> On trouve l'écho émouvant d'une profonde amitié et même d'une communauté de vues philosophiques, d'influences communes subies sur lesquelles nous aurons à revinir. Sans doute Boileau a-t-il reproché sévèrement à Molière ses farces, indignes de son talent, lui semblait-il. Scapin lui paraissait inacceptable, après le *Misanthrope*. Le Satirique se refusait à tenir compte de deux nécessités qui s'imposaient à Molière: le goût du public, les ordres du Roi "commandant" des farces, comédies-ballets et divertissements à l'auteur comique qu'il pensionnait et qu'il considérait donc comme à son service. Mais, à part cette critique qui, du point de vue du seul goût littéraire, est parfaitement admissible, on voit Boileau toujours dévoué à Molière et à son œuvre.[99]

Discussing with Molière the many subjects which are typical of professionals considering their trade, its purposes, meanings, bases, etc., it would have been only natural for Boileau to bring the discussion around to the subject of satire, his particular interest, and the writing of which he practiced.[100] When he criticized Molière for writing works unworthy of his talent, Boileau would no doubt have suggested to Molière the possibilities of satire. But, even if Boileau made no such suggestions, Molière was aware of Roman satire from his days at the Collège de Clermont. Furthermore, on the basis of the inventory taken after Molière's death, it is reasonable to believe that sometime in his later years, perhaps in the 1660's at the encouragement of Boileau, Molière read the satires of Horace and Juvenal as well as the philosophic works of Seneca. This reading could well have led Molière to the realization that his comedies were in fact satirical comedies, and that, for his art to come to fruition, as Boileau had suggested, he must become intimate with the satiric traditions in which he, perhaps unaware, had been writing. Accordingly, he would have read the satires of Horace and Juvenal, pondered their content in relationship to the moral lessons he had been provided by the Jesuits, thinking always about their dramatic potential.

The subject of Molière's play, hypocrisy, as we are told in the *Préface* of 1669, could first have occurred to him in any number of ways: through his reading of one of the numerous works of literature which involve hypocrites, such as Scarron's *Les Hypocrites* and Aretino's *Lo Ipocrito*; or through his knowledge of the events surrounding such infamous hypocrites of his day as the abbé Roquette or Charpy de Sainte-Croix.[101] Whether the idea came from one of these or another work or historical occurrence, it did come to Molière, and he acted according to the advice of Boileau and his own natural inclinations. One critic, writing on *Tartuffe*, has suggested the line of action which Molière took:

> Quand il se décida à mettre sur la scène un hypocrite, il traça d'abord les grandes lignes du caractère, l'étudia chez les écrivains qui avaient décrit des personnages de même espèce, puis, à tous les hypocrites intéressants, utilisables, placés par le hasard sur sa route ou recherchés par lui pour sa documentation, il demanda un trait de moeurs, un mot, une expression de visage, un simple geste.[102]

It is, however, impossible to say exactly how, or even if, Molière researched hypocrisy. If he did, it is logical to assume, on the basis of his personal library, that Molière turned to the French, Italian and Spanish literature involving hypocrites, and also to classical literature. Moreover, in consideration of his relationship with Boileau, it is reasonable to believe that one genre of classical literature that he would have reread was satire. There was available to Molière in the works of Horace and Juvenal a sourcebook on characters and morals upon which he could base a play. By a consideration of parallels in character and action, we shall be able to determine the extent to which the traditional materials of satire and the moral literature of Rome are reflected in Molière's *Tartuffe*. On the basis of this consideration, it may be possible to ascertain whether Molière actually employed the works of Horace, Juvenal and Seneca in his creation of *Tartuffe*.

## The Relationship of Comedy and Satire

Although comedy and satire are distinct literary genres, there is a relationship between them that was first noted for posterity by Horace, who emphasized the dependence of Lucilius, his predecessor in satire, on Aristophanes and other poets who wrote Old Comedy.

> Eupolis and Cratinus and Aristophanes, true poets, and the other good men to whom Old Comedy belongs, if there was anyone deserving to be drawn as a rogue and thief, as a rake or cut-throat, or as scandalous in any other way, set their mark upon him with great freedom. It is on these that Lucilius wholly hangs; these he has followed . . .[103]

Horace states that he is a follower of Lucilius, whereby he proclaims himself a follower of Old Comedy as well. A few decades later Persius, the Stoic satirist, continued the acceptance of this relationship by claiming that his satires were designed for those who enjoyed the Old Comedy of Greece.[104] Similarly Juvenal "looks back to Lucilius as his model."[105]

> But when Lucilus roars and rages as if with sword in hand, the hearer, whose soul was cold with crime, grows red; he sweats with the secret consciousness of sin.[106]

It is obvious that the great satirists of Rome saw an affinity between comedy and satire. This affinity, however, is not always clear even to the scholar who studies comedy or satire. Therefore, since much of the difficulty in interpreting *Tartuffe* arises from confusions as to the nature of comedy and its relationships to satire, it will be of profit to consider how the two genres are related and how satire is employed as one of the elements of comedy. This consideration will be directed toward an understanding of the comedies of Molière, and *Tartuffe* especially.

Since Plato and Aristotle first treated the essence of comedy and the nature of laughter, these subjects have been considered and reconsidered. Thus, our examination of theories of comedy must be limited to those opinions which are especially important in the history of literary theory or are revealing for our study of *Tartuffe*.

Although one can find theories of comedy and the nature of laughter before Plato,[107] it is Plato, who, for Western man, begins the considerations of comedy which continue to our day. He found the ridiculous or laughable to be associated with that which is morally or physically flawed, eliciting laughter by comparison with serious things (*Laws* 7, 816). Plato's most important comments are in the *Philebus:*

> And are you aware that even at a comedy the soul experiences a mixed feeling of pain and pleasure? . . .
>
> The ridiculous is in short the specific name which is used to describe the vicious form of a certain habit; and of vice in general it is that kind which is most at variance with the inscription at Delphi (''Know thyself'') . . . .The ignorant may fancy himself richer than he is . . . . And still more often he will fancy he is taller or fairer than he is, or that he has some other advantage of person which he really has not . . . . And yet surely by far the greatest number err about the goods of the mind; they imagine themselves to be much better men than they are . . . . Those of them who are weak and unable to revenge themselves, when they are laughed at, may be truly called ridiculous . . . .
>
> When we laugh at the folly of our friends, pleasure, in mingling with envy, mingles with pain, and laughter is pleasant; and so we envy and laugh at the same instant.[108]

Here it can be seen that, in Plato's opinion, comedy was especially a depiction of those vices which are in opposition to the admonition to ''Know thyself''; that the comic character has a false appreciation of himself, and that the most truly ridiculous man is he who is weak and cannot avenge himself. Moreover, the last paragraph suggests that Plato ''is speaking of innocent, almost sympathetic, humor rather than personal satire and ill-natured ridicule.''[109]

Aristotle's discussions of comedy are a development from the ideas of Plato. In the *Poetics* he states:

> As for Comedy, this, as we have said, is an artistic imitation of men of an inferior moral bent; faulty, however, not in any or every way, but only in so far as their shortcomings are ludicrous; for the Ludicrous is a species or part, not all, of the Ugly.[110]

Aristotle finds in comedy an expression of a moral truth, which he also considers in the *Nicomachean Ethics*, according to which the weaknesses and shortcomings of men are seen as contrasts with the ideal, which, as I shall discuss in a later chapter, he calls the ''mean.'' Accordingly, Aristotle, following Plato, feels that comedy is concerned with the basic and enduring flaws in mankind rather than with personal satire.

The fundamental nature of comedy is suggested by its etymology (*Komoidia*: revel song), which indicates the descent of ancient Greek comedies from fertility rituals, dramatizing the joy of renewal, of triumphing over obstacles, the joy of being reborn.[111] Comedy contains a movement from disaster to prosperity within a social context. Comedy is, in fact, inseparable from society. This point has been stressed by critics of comedy since the time of Meredith, who tend to agree that the final standards of comedy are "always social,"[112] and that the vision of comedy is toward the establishment of a desirable society.[113] Accordingly, in comedy it does not matter whether a character is good or bad; if he is unsociable, he is capable of becoming comic.[114] Thus, as Allardyce Nicoll points out,[115] a character is not comic through any individualizing element of his personality unless the character or his eccentricity is opposed to, or contrasted with, a norm, which, in comedy, is society.

Comedy's concern is with human imperfection; one of the recurring indications of a man's imperfection in comedy is his failure to meet his own or the world's conception of excellence. Often irony, the "heart of the comic on the stage,"[119] exists in the difference between a character's self-concept and that known to the audience. Irony develops from incongruity, which has been called the keyword of comedy; "it is the inconsistency of our own natures that keeps us doing the deeds that appear 'funny' to others. The real incongruity springs from character. It implies a deviation between aim and accomplishment."[120] Accordingly, as Bergson noted, the comic character is comic in proportion to his ignorance of himself.[121] Comedy works toward dispelling the false and revealing the true. It has been said that comedy is always seeking the flaw in man. This is because "all comedy tends to be skeptical and says in effect, 'The absurdity of it' — that in spite of his fine talk or noble resolution, a man is the mere creature of pettiness and vanity and folly."[122]

The function and viewpoint of comedy, which looks for incongruity and other comic effects, are decidedly critical. But the questions arise: are all comedies critical and what is the significance of the term "critical" in a consideration of the relationships of comedy and satire?

Critics have divided comedy into Old and New Comedy, classical and medieval comedy, high and low comedy, farcical, pastoral, sentimental, laughing comedy, comedy of manners, comedy of humours, comedy of the absurd, and so on. It would appear that almost every author of comedy must have produced a distinctive kind of comedy. However, without establishing an infinite number of sub-categories of comedy, one can follow a pattern which is accepted by most critics of comedy: comedy is either critical or non-critical (judicial or non-judicial).[123] Non-critical comedies are "an escape from reality, and intend to be so."[124] They tend to present no problems because the events on the stage are not "wholly related to the actual conditions of life."[125] Accordingly, in this genre we are not asked to think, nor to pass moral judgment on the characters, but rather to laugh kindly at them and sympathize with them. We are not expected to feel superior to the characters. We are placed in a world where "no values count. There are no rules of conduct, hardly laws of nature."[126] Among the many examples of non-critical comedy are the farce and the Commedia dell'Arte.

It is in the division we have termed critical comedy, however, that most critics find what for them is the essence of comedy. Critical comedy includes social and satiric comedies, and such high comedy as the comedy of manners. The purpose of the author of a critical comedy is "to arouse our critical judgment, and to make us laugh at the follies, affectations, or vices of the characters."[127] It intends definitely to correct manners by laughter, its end being especially the repression or even suppression of eccentricity, exaggeration, or deviation from the normal.[128] It may be noted that the comedy of manners, although it is inseparably linked with ideas and satire, does not necessarily forego the traditional elements of other kinds of comedy. But it is never written without the satiric or critical elements which are part of the essential character of the comedy of manners. Critical comedy may be further subdivided into "explicit criticism, which exposes definite follies or abuses to contempt and ridicule, and implicit, which is the natural result of revealing nature as it is."[129] Accordingly, critical comedy is associated with a definite social order, as compared with the world of farces which, as we have seen, tends to be an escape from reality. There is, furthermore, a suggestion of a universality of character in critical comedy. Nicoll states that in the higher types of comedy "the characters are not the characters peculiar to one age or to one place; and, second, that the comedy as a whole is but a part of, or a mere symbol of, the larger world of society beyond it."[130] A comedy thus can be seen as a microcosmic view of the world at large, intended to elicit that "thoughtful laughter" which Meredith saw as the product of comedy.[131]

Discussions of the relationship of, and differences between, comedy and satire have as often led to confusion as to enlightenment. In the former category is the statement of Meredith, who says that the comic "is the perceptive, is the governing spirit, awakening not giving aim to these powers of laughter, but is not to be confounded with them; it enfolds a thinner form of them, differing from satire in not sharply driving into the quivering sensibilities, and from Humor in not comforting them and tucking them up, or indicating a broader [sic] than the range of this bustling world to them."[132] More helpful is the statement of Gilbert Highet that comedy is one of those forms of literature which are "particularly close kinsmen and near neighbors of satire," often exchanging with it "both costumes and ideas."[133] Accordingly, comedy can be satire, just as nearly every satire contains comic elements. But, as Highet indicates, the difference between the comic and the satiric is that the comic is kind, that it does not hurt, that it is generally inoffensive, wishing always "to evoke laughter, or at least a smile of pure enjoyment."[134] Also helpful is the statement by J. Wight Duff, who finds that "there must, indeed, always be a kinship between satire and comedy. They are linked on the ground of social outlook . . . ."[135] Northrop Frye maintains that comedy lies midway between satire and romance and is influenced by both of them.[136] This position is followed by James Calderwood and Harold E. Toliver, who find that there is a line of satiric descent from Old Comedy which includes the plays of Machiavelli, Ben Jonson, Molière, Congreve, Sheridan, and Shaw.[137]

The interrelationship of comedy and satire in classical literature is a natural result of the fact that both genres sprang from the same source — ritual.[138] Accordingly, there must have been mutual borrowings and influences between comedy and satire from their earliest manifestations. It is no wonder, then, that critics often prefer to call Aristophanes a satirist rather than a writer of comedies. Their justification arises partly from Aristophanes' episodic structure, suggestive of the original meaning of satire (*lanx satura*: a mixed dish);[139] it arises more, however, from an understanding of the purpose and effects of the satirist. Commenting on Aristophanes, Robert W. Corrigan states: "First and foremost, the writer of satire must have the gift of turning our eyes inward in hilarious scorn of ourselves. But his purpose is always corrective. In showing us the immensity of our follies, the satirist is either seeking to restore values and patterns of behavior that he believes have been lost, forgotten, or debased, or he is urging us to discover new ideals and ways of living. Therefore, all of his jibes — no matter how bitter — are ultimately directed at the restoration or preservation of the social order."[140] In contrast with Aristophanes, who wrote works generally known as comedies, satirists are sometimes referred to as comedians. Such is the case of Horace and Petronius, who are included in James Feibleman's study of comedy. He notes: "There were the urbane writings of the poet Horace, whose comedy was based on the detection of small faults and the celebration of amusing pleasures rather than on the higher criticism which we have come to expect from the great comedians. Petronius, a more uproarious comedian than Horace, is yet like him in urbanity, and specialized chiefly in the *Satyricon* in satirizing the *nouveau riche* of the Roman provinces. The comedy of Horace and Petronius and their kind is not profound; it dances over the surface of manners and customs in a critical mood, yet remains deeply approving of the fundamental moral and social structure of the day. It calls for little improvement of any radical kind."[141] Horace's satire contains a union of humor and deep seriousness which is the essence of his work.[142] This union is a development from the Greek tradition of *to spoudaiogeloion* (jesting in earnest), which finds its expression in Horace's *ridentem dicere verum* (telling the truth with a laugh). Horace's type of satire can be seen as indirectly related to the comedy that developed in accordance with the motto *castigat ridendo mores* (chastening manners with ridicule).[143]

The function of satire is accepted to be connected with the reformation of manners and morals. This is a development from the didactic and moralistic tone of such Latin satirists as Persius, Martial and Juvenal, who helped fix the tone of satire for later ages.[144] Renaissance dramatists, influenced by the Latin satirists as well as comic writers, learned that comedy had a moral purpose and that virtuous actions should be praised and vicious actions blamed.[145] The method of comedy was the depiction of examples of folly and vices so that the fools and evildoers would be exposed to ridicule and led away from their sins.[146]

The didactic element in comedy is well represented in the works of Ben Jonson. In the prologue to *Every Man in His Humour*, Jonson says he will treat

> deeds, and language, such as men do use:
> And persons, such as comedy would choose,
> When she would show an image of the times,
> And sport with human follies, not with crimes.

This statement, applicable to comedy and satire as well, is merely a starting point for Jonson, for in his next play, *Every Man Out of His Humour*, Jonson indicates the satiric heritage of his purpose by paraphrasing Juvenal's Satire I:

> Who is so patient of this impious world,
> That he can check his spirit, or rein his tongue?
> Or who has such a dead unfeeling sense,
> That heaven's horrid thunders cannot wake?
> To see the earth crack'd with the weight of sin,
> Hell gaping under us, and o'er our heads
> Black, ravenous ruin, with her sail-stretch'd wings,
> Ready to sink us down, and cover us.
> Who can behold such prodigies as these,
> And have his lips seal'd up? Not I: my soul
> Was never ground into such oily colours,
> To flatter vice, and daub iniquity:
> But, with an armed and resolved hand,

# INTRODUCTION

> I'll strip the ragged follies of the time
> Naked as at their birth ...(I,i)

He continues to show his Juvenalian attitude, his indignation, stating:

> I will scourge those apes
> And to these courteous eyes oppose a mirror
> As large as is the stage whereon we act;
> Where they shall see the time's deformity
> Anatomised in every nerve and sinew,
> With constant courage, and contempt of fear. (I,i)

Here we see Jonson establishing for comedy a natural ending with a sort of poetic justice, wherein vice and folly are properly scourged and punished. But he draws this purpose clearly from satire, for this is the purpose of satire.[147]

Jonson's comedies may also be used to consider a further problem — to what extent is humor or the laughable necessary for comedy? This problem comes to bear particularly in *Volpone*, which has been found "not wholly laughable."[148] Jonson's *Volpone* may elicit laughter, but his object in writing the play was not primarily to raise a laugh or entertain his audience, if we are to believe him, but rather to satirize some person or thing by casting ridicule on them. This derision appears to be the product of a moral viewpoint, but, in the same sense that the "true moralist appeals nearly always to the feelings and not to the intellect, and the satirist rarely plays upon the emotions,"[149] Jonson's play is the work of the satirist and not of the moralist, nor of the author of uncritical comedy, who, it will be remembered, appeals to the emotions rather than the reason. Jonson follows a satiric tradition wherein vice is not to be attacked because it is morally wrong, but because it is a form of folly. Furthermore, when follies are exaggerated, they become vicious and immoral, so that the writer of satire, by attacking the follies, takes on the function of the moralist.

The differences between critical comedy, and uncritical (pure) comedy, although they are often very slight, have been discussed by Allardyce Nicoll. "Satire may be so mild that it can barely be detected under its mask of laughter ... Still, the fact remains that we do not laugh at the satirical as such; we laugh at the purely comic qualities with which it is accompanied or in which it is enclosed. The purest of comedy, however, usually rules satire in any form out of its province. The appeal of this pure comedy is solely to the laughing force within us."[150] It is obvious, then, that Jonson's *Volpone* fits into a special category of comedy wherein the critical element is expressed in terms drawn particularly from classical satire, and wherein the purpose is precisely that expressed in, and developed from, classical satire. That category was entitled appropriately "satirical comedy" by Jonson himself.

Satire in comedy is inseparable from the critical element, for, in fact, it can be said that the criticism in comedy is achieved through satire, the extent and severity of which varies with the intent of the author as surely as Horace's satire was "laughing" and Juvenal's was "indignant." Satirical comedy, which holds up a mirror to the real world so that it may reform itself closer to the ideal, follows a typical pattern: a protagonist, who is often a jealous husband, a demanding father, or an elderly suitor, interferes with the movement toward a happy outcome; near the end of the play the characters who serve as contrasts to the normal characters of the society of the play and who have impeded the progress toward the happy ending — nearly always a wedding — are summarily dismissed. The movement of the satirical comedy is suggestive of the rituals from which comedy and satire are sprung — "from conflict to social harmony, joy, and abundance."[151]

### The Comic Element in *Tartuffe*

There has been much discussion of the exact type of comedy which Molière wrote in *Tartuffe*. There are references to the serious, the satiric, and even the tragic elements which fill the play. One scholar states that "Tartuffe is first and foremost a sociological study of the corrosive influence, not of religion, but of a decadent religiosity on the life of the community . . ."[152] Although this critic, Martin Turnell, does treat *Tartuffe* as a comedy, his attitude makes it especially a "study." This opinion develops from his belief that Molière was a great comic writer, who "realized that comedy is essentially a serious activity."[153] This opinion was also held by Percy Chapman, in whose estimation Molière's *Tartuffe*, in spite of the comic elements, was serious in its total effect.[154] His explanation for this seriousness was that

> to the sense of the comic is now added the sense of life, and the sense of life, constantly threatening to become dominant, tends to merge the comic with the serious.[155]

The serious and satiric elements of Molière's play have been remarked on by numerous critics, but equally worthy of note are the comic elements in *Tartuffe*, for ultimately one must consider what there is in a play which has been admitted to be serious and even somber which admits it into the ranks of comedy. Assuredly, if anyone were to classify Molière's dramatic works, it would be as comedies in accordance with critical tradition.[156] However, in order to understand better the nature of *Tartuffe*, it will be necessary to consider what elements therein combine to justify the title comedy.

Comedy, especially critical comedy, as we have seen, is primarily concerned with the social. The comedy arises from a conflict of the unsociable element with society. The normal comic plot opposes its major characters, who are usually young lovers, with an impediment (often overcome by a sudden reversal) so that a happy ending occurs where defeat was expected. Accordingly, all who oppose the social integration function as the impediments and cause the conflict that results in the comic. Thus, as Hubert notes, "Tartuffe by his hypocrisy, Orgon by his stupidity and his selfishness, practically exclude themselves from humanity or at least society."[157] The comedy develops from the attempts of the family to break down the influence of the unsociable Tartuffe and Orgon. Northrop Frye has analysed the characters who are impediments to the maintenance or establishment of a moral norm and social bond: they are "people who are in some kind of mental bondage, who are helplessly driven by ruling passions, neurotic compulsions, social rituals, and selfishness .... People who do not know fully what they are doing, who are slaves to a predictable self-imposed pattern of behavior."[158] The conflict that results has been noted by Lancaster who states of *Tartuffe* that "Molière's theme is hypocrisy in conflict with a family."[159] Nicoll finds concerning the comic conflict that "the laughable element is increased by the direct opposition of two eccentric individuals one to another, and by indirect opposition of both to a society as a whole."[160] Bergson, as we have seen, found that a character could become comical, if he were unsociable.[161] Writing of French comedy in general, and Molière in particular, one critic states: "French comedy applies to human nature the test of sanity and common sense, and ridicules, from an emotionally detached standpoint, human beings who do not conform to the social norm."[162] Molière, he further finds, directs his shafts of wit at the people who depart from the rules and moral conventions of society — such men as the hypocrite, the miser and the misanthrope.

It is obvious that, from the consideration of the social element in comedy, there must develop also a consideration of the morality of comedy. In the case of Molière's comedy, Chapman found that "its broadest principle is the necessity of accepting society."[163] His conclusion is, in fact, that for Molière social and moral are identical. This attitude is also present in Meredith, who, employing his concept of comedy as an intellectual activity, states that Molière's comedy "appeals to the individual mind to perceive and participate in the social."[164]

There are, of course, set within the basic comic structures (theme, character, plot) numerous comic devices which are used to intensify the comic effect. Although these are too numerous to list in total, a number of the more important comic devices may be considered.

Bergson lists two comic devices which appear in Tartuffe: repetition and reversal or inversion. A good example of repetition, the word or sentence repeated by an individual, as selected by Bergson, is the "le pauvre homme" scene.[165] The inversion in *Tartuffe* has been discussed by Gossman, who finds that a double inversion, in fact, occurs: Tartuffe and Orgon exchange roles as tricker and dupe; and as master of Orgon's household and underling.[166] Bergson further considers automatism a condition of the comic character. He states:

> what is essentially laughable is what is done automatically. In a vice, even in a virtue, the comic is that by which the person unwittingly betrays himself — the involuntary gesture or the unconscious remark ...
>
> Take any other [than Don Quixote] comic character: however unconscious he may be of what he says or does, he cannot be comical unless there be some aspects of his person of which he is unaware, one side of his nature which he overlooks; on that account alone does he make us laugh. (p. 155)

For many critics, following the lead of Brunetière,[167] this aspect in Tartuffe is his sensuality. It is Tartuffe's sensuality, of which he is unaware, which leads him astray, and which, by contrast with his ascetic mask, makes him comic.

There are many other comic devices to be found in *Tartuffe*. One such device is comic irony. One of the many varieties of comic irony shows how a fool or dullard fails to recognize the obvious truth. An equally common device is "the improbable, the reversible, the redemption that comes from nowhere (deus ex machina). Nothing in *Tartuffe* prepares us for the officer of the suddenly omniscient king ..."[168]

Eugène Rigal has particularly commented on the comic in *Tartuffe*. He states that Tartuffe is comic because he is put into comic situations such as the seduction attempts with first Damis, then Orgon in hiding.[169] Tartuffe "est comique incontestablement," says Rigal.

> Il l'est d'abord, parce que son masque d'honnête dévot le gêne singulièrement pour s'expliquer et qu'Elmire feint longtemps de ne pas le comprendre. Il l'est ensuite, parce que, toute sa casuistique étante percée à jour par Elmire, plus il s'efforce de la gagner, plus il

## INTRODUCTION

> l'éloigne et se compromet lui-même. Il l'est enfin, parce que lui, le dupeur de profession, va être trompé par une âme sincère, droite, à qui la fourberie répugne et qui n'y a recours qu'en désespoir de cause.[170]

Implicit in the preceding statement by Rigal is the concept of comic contrast. The comic author, by establishing a divided world, imposes upon the judgment of the reader or audience the obligation of seeing the contrast between the two sides. Molière himself, in the *Préface* of 1669, points out that he has followed this practice by depicting the character of a wicked man, Tartuffe, which brings out in sharp relief the character of the truly good man, Cléante. Molière's employment of this comic convention, however, is not limited to Tartuffe and Cléante, for every character in the play fits into one of the two sides. Guicharnaud, who has seen this comic contrast, finds that Tartuffe himself is the "metaphor of a divided universe," with the family of Orgon representing "an incarnate norm" and Tartuffe "incarnate aberrations."[171] He sees the idea of comedy developing from the contrast between the one side struck by blindness or vice, and the other side by good sense and lucidity. He notes particularly that it is with respect to the morals of Cléante and Elmire that Tartuffe and Orgon are judged.

Two of the ways that this comic contrast is emphasized are exaggeration and distortion. Accordingly, a comic character often appears to have certain facets of his character and behavior stressed. Such is the case with both Tartuffe and Orgon. A study of the character of Tartuffe reveals that he is, as one critic phrased it, "all black." This aspect has been observed by Turnell, who states:

> Tartuffe is a superb comic creation; he possesses the same life and vitality as the Wife of Bath or Falstaff and his character is perhaps more varied. He is a composite figure. He represents all the main varieties of contemporary religious abuse and is the channel through which they infect the sane, balanced life of the family and almost bring it to disaster.[172]

Tartuffe is presented as all bad, a virtual synthesis of vices; and certain of these vices, developing from his sensuality, are emphasized. Molière's total depiction of Tartuffe stands in constant contrast to that of Cléante. This was, as Molière says in his *Préface*, part of his intention, and accordingly, it was part of his method.[173]

It is possible to list many elements of Tartuffe's character which are exaggerated or distorted — his sensuality, pride, ambition, deceit. Hubert, who has seen the importance of exaggeration to the character of Tartuffe, finds him "a histrionic criminal who overplays his part."[174] Following this viewpoint, Hubert considered *Tartuffe* as a "spectacle." He notes that by repeated use of the dramatic devices of "the show within a show," Molière stresses the literal as well as figurative mask that Tartuffe wears.

> The author so consistently puts his impostor, present or absent, in the limelight, that all the other personages are more often than not reduced to the state of spectators. Indeed, we can regard as spectators Cléante, Damis, Orgon, Madame Pernelle, Mariane, and even such active characters as Elmire and Dorine, or so lofty a person as the King, who sends the Exempt to Orgon's house in order to bring the whole performance to a close. Of course, several of these characters emulate Tartuffe by putting on shows of their own. In the interest of poetic justice, Tartuffe must indeed be defeated by performances more successful than his own. Elmire stages two of them and the Sun King a third ...Thus Tartuffe the actor is, to everyone's edification, thrice transformed into a spectacle which he had never intended to show. (pp. 91-92.)

Among the comic devices used by Molière in *Tartuffe* is *incongruity*, which for some literary critics is the essence of the laughable.[175] "The incongruous in space is the disproportionate, asymmetrical, in time the unexpected," says Calderwood, who notes that it is often seen as "anticipation set up and reversed, or fulfilled explosively ..."[176] In *Tartuffe*, the incongruity, "the forced linkage of disparate categories," as Calderwood defines it (p. 163), is seen in the opposition of Tartuffe's real self and his pretended character (his mask), and in the opposition between Orgon's Christian ideals and his selfish motives. Bergson, who considered *Tartuffe* in his treatise on "Laughter," finds that disguise is a form of comic incongruity:

> A man in disguise is comic. A man we regard as disguised is also comic. So, by analogy, any disguise is seen to become comic, not only that of a man, but that of society also, and even the disguise of nature.[177]

Nicoll finds that "mental incongruity is another prime source of merriment, either incongruity within one character (inner conflict) or between two characters (outward conflict)."[178] Bergson has provided good examples of the inner-conflict incongruity. "It is not uncommon for a comic character," he says, possibly thinking of the description of Tartuffe given in Act I, "to condemn in general terms a certain line of conduct and immediately afterwards afford an example of it himself ..." (p. 155). In the case of Tartuffe, the essence of his incongruity is observed, when, in Bergson's words, "we are shown the soul *tantalized* by the needs of the body ..." (p. 93).

# INTRODUCTION

Moore, too, finds incongruity a (if not the) basic device in Molière's comedy. He finds that except for his gross sensuality, Tartuffe would be completely inhuman. He states:

> The conception of humanity would seem to me to be the key to that of the comic. The comic figure is redeemed from complete inhumanity by the fatal irruption into his ingenious scheme of his unsuspected *natural* qualities. Laughter arises only when the contrast between these two comes to the surface, but the contrast itself lies deep in human nature.[179]

Incongruity, in the case of Orgon, is combined with another comic device, that of showing the absurdity of man's ideals. By placing the idealist in a series of improbable situations, the dramatist demonstrates the absurdity of the ideal, at least as it is represented in the life of the idealist. Thus, Orgon is revealed to be the antithesis of the ideal which he professes, and which could no doubt work to the benefit of many men, but which merely establishes him as an example of incongruity, an absurdity which is laughable. There is another aspect of Orgon which complies with the concept of incongruity: he is one of Bergson's characters who "thinks he is speaking and acting freely, and consequently, retains all the essentials of life, whereas, viewed from a certain standpoint, he appears as a mere toy in the hands of another, who is playing with him."[180] Orgon, then, is further incongruous, in the comic sense, in his estimation of himself and his abilities in relation to Tartuffe: he plans to use Tartuffe, but is used instead. He is a supreme example of Bergson's "dancing-jack."

In our consideration of incongruity and other comic devices, we must ultimately come to the realization that all these devices are adaptable to drama in general. What is it, however, that makes them comic in certain instances? The answer to this important question can be found again in Bergson's study of laughter and the nature of the comic. Since this material is important to our understanding of the nature of Molière's comedy, it will be necessary to quote Bergson *in extenso*.

> When a mental state is depicted to us with the object of making it dramatic, or even merely of inducing us to take it seriously, it gradually crystallises into *actions* which provide the real measure of its greatness. Thus ... the pious hypocrite, though pretending to have his eyes fixed upon heaven, steers most skillfully his course here below. ...To prevent our taking a serious action seriously in order to prepare us for laughter, comedy utilises a method, the formula of which may be given as follows: *instead of concentrating our attention on actions, comedy directs it rather to gestures*.

> By *gestures* we here mean the attitudes, the movements and even the language by which a mental state expresses itself outwardly without any aim or profit, from no other cause than a kind of inner itching. Gesture, thus defined, is profoundly different from action. Action is intentional or, at any rate, conscious; gesture slips out unawares, it is automatic. In action, the entire person is engaged; in gesture, an isolated part of the person is expressed, unknown to, or at least apart from the whole of the personality.[181]

Of the three divisions of gesture, it is especially movement that one should note, for herein lies much of the essence of any comedy. It is when a play is put onto the stage in the hands of competent actors that its comic nature really comes to the fore.

Knowing the traditions of literary criticism which proposed a didactic approach to comedy, Molière himself considered *Tartuffe* "un poëme ingénieux qui par des leçons agréables reprend les défauts des hommes..." (*Préface*). It is obviously intended, then, to be a critical comedy (whether Molière thought of it in such terms or not). This is further demonstrated by the fact that an analysis of *Tartuffe*, especially of the words of Cléante and the actions of Tartuffe and Orgon, reveals that Molière's comedy does exactly what Dobrée says critical comedy does: "It supports the happy mean, the comfortable life, the ideal of the *honnête homme*."[182] Molière's comic effect is achieved in *Tartuffe*, as he tells us in his *Préface* of 1669, by the juxtaposition of Cléante, who is almost an incarnation of the concept of the golden mean, and Tartuffe, who, as described by Turnell, is "a man, but a man whose natural instincts have been warped and perverted because he has strayed from the norm. For this reason he is an object of satire, is one of the varieties of perversion which are studied in [*Tartuffe*] ..."[183]

Guicharnaud, agreeing that a lesson is not inappropriate to Molière's comedy, finds the underlying (but dominating) idea in Molière's play to be: order is value.[184] His consideration of the lesson of *Tartuffe* develops from this concept.

> Il suffit d'un peu de bon sens et de discernement. Un bonheur est possible, une norme existe: celle d'un ordre où les hommes peuvent vivre en paix, avec une liberté suffisante ...Le désordre et le malheur viennent du dehors, de la présence de natures extrêmes.[185]

What makes Tartuffe and Orgon dangerous, according to Guicharnaud, "ce sont des corruptions de la nature, c'est la force des passions."

Furthermore, the solution which Molière provides for the impediments in *Tartuffe* is "non le rachat des âmes corrumpues, mais le rétablissement d'un ordre viable."[186]

We have seen earlier in this chapter that comedy is concerned primarily with the social. Michaut, remarking on *Tartuffe* in particular and Molière's plays in general, says: "Je n'y vois que la morale du bon sens et de la raison, de l'adaptation à la vie sociale et aux nécessités qu'elle impose, du juste-milieu."[187] Guicharnaud particularizes on Michaut's analysis: "Être soi-même — c'est-à-dire vivre sans masque et sans illusions—et l'être avec les autres: telle semble être la norme idéale de *Tartuffe*. Heureuse rencontre, qui est fondement de la société honnête."[188]

In spite of Molière's own words,[189] there are a number of critics who either see Molière's comedy as representative of that category of critical comedy known as Comedy of Manners, which "sets out to present a picture of society as the dramatist sees it, without any direct moral purpose in its satire . . .,"[190] or who, following René Bray, find moral problems irrelevant, since "comedy exists only to please, to make us laugh."[191] The majority of critics, however, agree with Michaut and Guicharnaud in finding a moral viewpoint an inseparable element in Molière's comedy.

It is generally acknowledged that there is a satiric element in *Tartuffe*, although the intent of the author and the extent of the satire are questioned. Guicharnaud finds that in *Tartuffe*, for the first time since Aristophanes, social satire became the material, support, and soul of comedy.[192] Since neither Guicharnaud nor any of the other critics who have commented on the satiric nature of Tartuffe have revealed the nature and extent of the satiric element in *Tartuffe*, this must be the function of the next chapter. There it will be shown that much of the confusion that has arisen over *Tartuffe* is a product of the failure to realize the extent and effect of the satiric element, which, as we have shown, is inseparable from the comic in critical comedy. The intention is not to deny that there are comic elements in *Tartuffe* or that *Tartuffe* is a comedy, but to clarify the nature of Molière's play by a consideration of his method and purpose as presented in the play.

---

[1]Henri d'Alméras, *Le Tartuffe de Molière* (Paris, 1928), pp. 41 ff.; Gustave Michaut, *Les Luttes de Molière* (Paris, 1925), pp. 65ff.; Henry Carrington Lancaster, *History of French Dramatic Literature in the Seventeenth Century*, III, ii (Baltimore, 1936), 620ff.

[2]John Wilcox, *The Relation of Molière to Restoration Comedy* (New York, 1938), p. 23.

[3]A. Owen Aldridge, *Comparative Literature: Matter and Method* (Chicago, 1969), p. 3.

[4]Aldridge, p. 225, notes that they do "justify the examination of major literary works in order to ascertain the elements which are traditional and those which are unique qualities."

[5]J.T. Shaw, "Literary Indebtedness and Comparative Literary Studies," in *Comparative Literature: Method and Perspective* (Carbondale, Ill., 1961), p. 59.

[6]*Ibid.*, p. 64.
[7]*Ibid.*, p. 65.
[8]*Ibid.*, p. 66.
[9]*Ibid.*, p. 67.

[10]*Ibid.*, p. 71.

[11]All quotations and references will be made in accordance with the following editions, unless otherwise noted:

Molière, *Œuvres complètes*, ed. Despois and Mesnard, Les Grands Ecrivains de la France (Paris, 1873-93), 13 vols.

Horace, *Satires, Epistles* and *Ars Poetica*, with an English translation by H. Rushton Fairclough, Loeb Classical Library (London, 1947).

*Juvenal and Persius*, with an English translation by G.G. Ramsay, Loeb Classical Library (London, 1918).

Seneca, *Ad Lucilium Epistulae Morales*, with an English translation by Richard M. Gummere, Loeb Classical Library, 3 vols. (New York, 1918-1925).

[12]He was generally considered to be the original of La Bruyère's Théophile in the chapter of the *Caractères* entitled "Des Grands." A biography of Roquette written by J. Henri Pignot (1876), according to Arthur Tilley, *Molière* (Cambridge, 1921), p. 114, rehabilitates his memory.

[13]Lancaster, p. 626.

[14]Cited by Gustave Michaut, *Les Luttes de Molière* (Paris, 1925), p. 66.

[15]*Portraits intimes* (Paris, 1899), IV, 223-233.

[16]See also, Gustave Charlier, "L'Original de Tartuffe," in *Flambeau*, IX (1926), 319-332.

[17]Alméras, pp. 78-79.

[18]Michaut, *Luttes*, pp. 93-94. See also Sainte-Beuve, *Port-Royal III*, where the moral consequences of the *Provinciales* are considered.

[19]This dedication is quoted at length by Louis Lacour, *Tartuffe par Ordre de Louis XIV* (Paris, 1877), pp. 28-32.

[20]D.B. Wyndham Lewis, *Molière: The Comic Mask* (New York, 1959), p. 115.

[21]*Histoire de la littérature française au XVIIe siècle* (Domat, 1952), III, 307-308.

[22]Michaut, *Luttes*, pp. 94-97.

[23]*La Cabale des dévots, 1627-1666* (Paris, 1902), pp. 384-410.

[24]*Tartuffe et ses avatars* (Paris, 1925), pp. 283ff.

[25]Michaut, *Luttes*, p. 93.

[26]"Une source inconnue du *Tartuffe*," *Revue des Deux Mondes*, LI (1929), 929-936.

[27]"Additional sources for Molière's *Avare, Femmes savantes*, and *Tartuffe*," *MLN*, XLV (1930), 154-157.

[28]*French Dramatic Lit.*, p. 625.

[29]This novel was adapted from the *Hyja de Pierres y Celestina* of Salas Barbadillo. It is believed much more likely that Molière read the French version of Scarron than the Spanish version by Barbadillo. See Alméras, pp. 36-38; Lancaster, *French Dramatic Lit.*, III, ii, 620-621, 625. A consideration of the relation of *Tartuffe* to the Celestina is given by E. Martinenche, *Molière et le Théâtre espagnol* (Paris, 1906), pp. 159ff.

[30]Burt Edward Young, ed. *Le Tartuffe: ou l'Imposteur* by Molière (New York, 1918), pp. li-liv, cites this and the following passages from Scarron's work for comparative purposes. See also, Léon Deffoux, "L'hypocrisie et Tartuffe," *Mercure de France*, CLXVII (1923), 222-225.

[31]Michaut, *Luttes*, pp. 87-88, notes the parallels between Montufar and Tartuffe, stating that Scarron's work doubtless provides a model for *Tartuffe*.

[32]*Molière et la comèdie italienne*, (Paris, 1867), pp. 210-223. See also Michaut, *Luttes*, pp. 88-89; Alméras, pp. 34-36, considers the possibility of other Italian plays as sources of *Tartuffe*, but dismisses them in favor of the *Ipocrito*, as does Michaut, *Luttes*, p. 89.

³³*Ibid.*, pp. 222-223. Moland also remarks on the differences between *Tartuffe* and *Lo Ipocrito:*

> D'autre part, quelle distance entre la conception de l' Arétin et celle de Molière! Dans l'Arétin, Ipocrito ne joue son jeu que pour soutenir son parasitisme. Il indique bien qu'il pourra faire pis; en attendant il se contente de peu. Il finit, chose étrange, par avoir le beau rôle; il pacifie la maison troublée. Il est vrai qu'on doit trembler pour la famille où cet intrus a pris un tel empire; mais rien ne donne encore à prévoir ces éventualités funestes.

³⁴Georges Monval, "Madame Pernelle, Flipote et Monsieur Tartuffe dans un roman de Charles Sorel," *Moliériste,* X (1888/9), 97-108, 129-140; E. Roy, *La vie et les œuvres de Charles Sorel* (Paris, 1891), pp. 191ff.

³⁵*Roman de Renart le Contrefait,* ed. Gaston Raynaud et Henri Lemaître (Paris, 1914), I, 1. 455-462, cited by Young, ed., *Tartuffe,* pp. xlvi-xlvii. See also Félix Hémon, *Cours de littérature* (Paris, 1893), II, 3. Hémon also considers Faux-Semblant from the *Roman de la Rose* a possible influence (pp. 3-4).

³⁶In *La Critique du Tartuffe,* Molière was charged with parodying line 1194 of Corneille's *Sertorius:*

> Ah! pour être Romain, je n'en suis pas moins homme.

³⁷Michaut, *Luttes,* p. 89.

³⁸Young, p. xlix; see also Hémon, pp. 5-6.

³⁹*Ibid.*, p. lviii. Young, in his notes to lines 16, 194, 235, 310, 596, 919, 966, 972, and 1502, discusses Pascal as a possible source of certain ideas in *Tartuffe.* See also Michaut, *Luttes,* p. 89; Lancaster, *French Dramatic Lit.,* III, ii, 625.

⁴⁰Lancaster, *French Dramatic Lit.,* III, ii, 626. One may note that other sources proposed as bases of or influences on *Tartuffe,* such works as Quevedo's *Buscon,* DuRyer's *Lucrèce,* Zabeleta's *El Dia de fiesta,* have been dismissed by Lancaster on the basis of the material available in the sources I have considered in the text (p. 625).

⁴¹In the inside cover of my copy of Alméras's study of Tartuffe, some student (or scholar) had scribbled: "Doubtful whether M. sought by reference to books, the traits of the character he wished to present; inevitably used reminiscences of his reading as well as observation of people about him, and stories he had heard."

⁴²Eudore Soulié, *Recherches sur Molière et sur sa famille* (Paris, 1863), p. 13, comments on the fact that Marie Cressé, Molière's mother, possessed a Bible and Plutarch. He submits in Document II, pp. 130ff., a record of the inventory made at her death. See also Madeleine Jurgens and Elizabeth Manfield-Miller, *Cent Ans de Recherches sur Molière* (Paris, 1963), pp. 41-63.

⁴³John E. Donohue, *Jesuit Education* (New York, 1963), p. 118.

⁴⁴It should be clearly understood that the purpose of the Jesuits was not to purvey information about classical civilization so much as to provide the students with good morals and an active sense of good rhetorical style. Cf. Donohue, *Jes. Ed.* p. 121.

⁴⁵André Schimberg, *L'Education Morale dans les Colléges de la Compagnie de Jésus en France sous l'Ancien Régime* (Paris, 1913), p. 140; Robert Schwickerath, S.J., *Jesuit Education* (St. Louis, 1903), pp. 120, 280.

⁴⁶Donohue, *Jes. Ed.* p. 119.

⁴⁷*Ibid.*, p. 131.

[48]*Ibid.*, p. 138.

[49]Schwickerath, *Jesuit Educ.*, p. 418.

[50]*Ibid.*, p. 419.

[51]P. Genelli, *Vie de Saint Ignace de Loyola*, tr. Sainte-Foy (Paris, 1857), II, vii, cited by Schimberg, *Ed. Morale*, p. 183.

[52]Part IV, Ch. V of the *Constitutions*, George E. Ganss, *Saint Ignatius' Idea of a Jesuit University* (Milwaukee, 1956), pp. 306-7.

[53]Part IV, Ch. XII, Clarification A; Ganss, p. 332.

[54]Part IV. Ch. V, Clarification E; Ganss, p. 308.

[55]Gustave Dupont-Ferrier, *Du Collège de Clermont au Lycée Louis-le-Grand (1563-1920)*, (Paris, 1921), I, 133.

[56]Schwickerath, *Jesuit Educ.*, pp. 119, 123, 373, 375, 391, 446; Schimberg, *Ed. Morale*, pp. 133, 149; L'Abbé Augustin Sicard, *Les Etudes Classiques avant la Révolution* (Paris, 1887), pp. 21-22.

[57]Schwickerath, *Jesuit Educ.*, 373, 374; Schimberg, *Ed. Morale*, 144, discusses the employment of Juvenal to emphasize a lesson in Cicero; also, 133, 149. Sicard, *Etudes Class.*, 21-22.

[58]Frederic E. Farrington, *French Secondary Schools* (London, 1910), 194-198; Schimberg, *Ed. Morale*, 133, 149; Schwickerath, *Jesuit Educ.*, 373, 374, 375.

[59]Since they will play an important part in a later chapter, it is necessary to see that Tacitus and Suetonius were also read according to the *Ratio:* For Tacitus, see Schimberg, pp. 133, 149; Schwickerath, pp. 373, 374, 383-4; for Suetonius, see Schimberg, p. 133; Schwickerath, p. 373.

[60]Grimarest, *La Vie de M. de Molière*, ed. Georges Mongrédin (Paris, 1955), p. 39. Gustave Michaut, *La Jeunesse de Molière* (Paris, 1922), pp. 67-77, attacks this theory. Antoine Adam, *Histoire de la littérature française au XVIIe siècle* (Paris, 1952), III, 214, n. 4, finds the association likely if it occurred between 1641 and 1643.

[61]This translation has been contested; however, the witnesses of Molière's day seem incontestable by their very number. L'abbé Marolles, in the prefaces to his translations of Lucretius in 1659 and 1677 mentions Molière's translation. Chapelain wrote to Bernier (April 25, 1662) that Molière had translated "la meilleure partie de Lucrèce." Brossette, *Avis sur la deuxième Satire de Boileau*, sets Molière's translation in 1664. J. Nicolas de Traflage, *Manuscripts de la Bibliothèque de l'Arsenal*, IV, 226, comments that the publisher Thierry "les trouva trop forts contre l'immortalité de l'âme."

[62]George D. Hadzsits, *Lucretius and His Influence* (New York, 1963), p. 311.

[63]Benjamin Boyce, *The Theophrastan Character in England to 1642* (Cambridge, Massachusetts, 1947), pp. 12-13.

[64]Boyce, *Ibid.*, p. 13, says, "They are more philosophical and in some cases more thorough and more complete than the compositions of Theophrastus; they mostly eschew humor and present only a modicum of concrete detail about dress and action and speech; and, most significantly, they investigate causes and explain emotions, interrupting the description at any moment with a generalization."

[65]G. M. A. Grube, "Theophrastus as a Literary Critic," *TAPA*, LXXXIII (1952), 60 finds that Theophrastus is "a disciple of Aristotle who repeats, develops, and elaborates the theories of his master..."

[66]Boyce, *Theophrast.*, p. 13. See also D. J. Furley, "The Purpose of Theophrastus's Characters," *Symbolae Osloenses*, XXX (1953), p. 60, who noted that "the *Characters* could be a handbook for rhetorical students on 'how to indicate Character' ..."

[67]Boyce, *Theophrast.* p. 22; Furley, "Purpose of Th. Char.," p. 60. I shall briefly discuss the *Characters* in relation to Tartuffe and Orgon in a later chapter.

[68]For a discussion of the comedy writers, including Menander, as representative of the "character" tradition, vd. Boyce, pp. 18, 38-39.

⁶⁹L1. 153-178. Boyce, *Theophrast*. p. 30.

⁷⁰Edward P. Morris, ed., Horace, *The Satires* (New York, 1909), pp. 12-13.

⁷¹"Omnia rerum omnium, se observentur, indicia sunt et argumentum morum ex minimis quoque licet capere: inpudicum et incessu ostendit et manus mota et unum interdum responsum et relatus ad caput digitus et flexus oculorum. Inprobum risus, insanum vultus habitusque demonstrat. Illa enim in apertum per notas exeunt; qualis puisque sit, scies, si quemadmodum laudet, quemadmodum laudetur, aspexeris." *Ad Lucilium Epistulae Morales* with an English translation by Richard M. Gummere, Loeb Classical Library (New York, 1930), LII, I, 350-351. (Hereafter referred to as *Epistles*.)

The employment of the Character is but one device in the Stoics' repertoire. See J.W. Duff, *A Literary History of Rome in the Silver Age* (New York, 1964), p. 182.

⁷²Between 1595 and 1612 Casaubon wrote a commentary on the *Characters*. See J.E. Sandys, *A History of Classical Scholarship* (New York, 1967), II, 208-209.

⁷³Schimberg, *Ed. Morale*, p. 133.

⁷⁴Duff, p. 44.

⁷⁵J.F. D'Alton, *Horace and His Age* (New York, 1917), p. 43. Arthur E. R. Boak, *A History of Rome to 565 A.D.*, 4th ed. (1921; rpt. New York, 1955), pp. 271-275, comments on the attempts by Augustus to revive the pristine ideals of Rome.

⁷⁶J. W. Duff, *A Literary History of Rome from the Origins to the Close of the Golden Age*, ed. A. M. Duff, 3rd ed. (1909; rpt. New York, 1960), p. 447. See also pp. 320, 321, 337, 342, 348, 380ff., 466, 467. See Boak, *History of Rome*, pp. 271-275.

⁷⁷J. W. Duff, *A Literary History of Rome from the Origins to the Close of the Golden Age* (New York, 1960), pp. 31-33.

⁷⁸Patrick Gerard Walsh, *Livy: His Historical Aims and Methods* (Cambridge, 1967), p. 51.

⁷⁹*Ibid.*, p. 50.

⁸⁰Walsh, *Livy*, p. 51.

⁸¹*Lucilius and Horace* (Madison, Wisconsin, 1920), pp. 172-173.

⁸²*Clarence Mendell, Our Seneca* (New Haven, 1941), p. 163. Mendell further states: "Epicureans would never have developed a vehicle for criticism and improvement, for they were not particularly interested in conversion or reform: it requires a dogma of duty to a supreme power to develop the missionary zeal of the reformer, and anyone whose sincere ideal is personal pleasure and freedom from pain can hardly undertake seriously to improve his neighbors.

"An Epicurean, like Lucretius, might offer joy and release from fear to anyone that cared to accept [his ideals], but he could never have attacked those who failed to listen. The Stoic not only taught virtue but tended to demand an audience."

⁸³Boyce, *Theophrast*, p. 97.

⁸⁴Herni Peyre, *L'Influence des littératures antiques sur la littérature française moderne. Etat des travaux* (New Haven, 1941), p. 40.

⁸⁵For the breadth of Molière's reading one may consider merely the influences on *Tartuffe* listed by Michaut, *Luttes*, pp. 55ff. He was well-read both in the novel and essay literature of his day, as well as in earlier writers such as Boccaccio. All of these, of course, are to be added to the various Latin authors whose works were found among his possessions at his death, among them Horace, Seneca, and Juvenal. See Jurgens, *Cent Ans de Recherches sur Molière, 554ff.*

⁸⁶Paul d'Estrée, "Une Origine Possible de Tartuffe," *Moliériste* X (1888/9), pp. 121-122.

⁸⁷Palmer, *Molière*, pp. 204-205.

⁸⁸*Ibid., p. 361.*

⁸⁹*Ibid.*, p. 361.

⁹⁰*Ibid.*, pp. 364-365.

⁹¹*Préface* to the edition of 1683, referring to President Lamoignon.

[92]During the next twenty years Boileau also published a translation of Longinus' *On the Sublime* and his own *Reflexions critiques sur Longin*.

[93]This line is from Boileau's epigram in reply to the attacks of the *Journal de Trévoux*, published in 1703. For the background of this epigram, see Pierre Clarac, ed., *Boileau* (Paris, 1936), p. 63.

[94]Palmer, p. 366. Although the "quatre amis" theory has been disputed, there is not any doubt that Molière was on familiar terms with both Boileau and La Fontaine. For a discussion of the problems involved, cf. Demeure, "Les Quatre Amis de Psyche," *MF*, CCI (1928), 331-66; "L'Introuvable Société des quatre amis," *RHLF*, XXVI (1929), 161-80, 321-36; and Adam, "L'Ecole de 1660: Histoire ou légende?" *RHPh*, VII (1939), 215-50.

[95]Palmer, *Molière*, pp. 370-371; Grimarest, *La Vie de M.*, p. 118. It should be noted here that Palmer's statement is justified by the life Molière led, not merely by the term "philosophe," which would not necessarily imply a study of philosophy.

[96]*La Vie de M. de Molière*, p. 101.

[97]Madeleine Jurgens and Elizabeth Maxfield-Miller, *Cent Ans de Recherches sur Molière* (Paris, 1963), present the inventory completely on pp. 554-584; Horace is cited on p. 576; Juvenal on p. 561; and Seneca on p. 560.

[98]*Ibid.*, pp. 561 and 572.

[99]Georges Mongrédien, *La Vie Littéraire au XVIIe Siècle* (Paris, 1947), pp. 138-139. Although Mongrédien debunks the popular "quatre amis" theory of French classicism, he strongly affirms, as here, the influence of Boileau on Molière.

[100]"There are no more typical French authors than Boileau the critic and Molière the comic dramatist. They had the same intense relish for veracity and the same disgust for the unreal, the inflated and the exaggerated... What Molière had already done in the drama and what he was to do, were precisely what Boileau was best fitted to enjoy. What Boileau attacked in his satires was what Molière naturally detested and what he was likely himself to assail on occasion. Both of them recognized the importance of the social bond and distrusted excessive individuality. They both sought to set forth a general view of life, rather than a particular view. They both had a high regard for reality and sobriety, for balance and order and proportion." Brander Matthews, *Molière, His Life and Works* (New York, 1910), p. 102.

[101]Charpy has been considered in detail as the basis for Tartuffe in Paul Emard's *Tartuffe, sa vie, son milieu, et la comédie de Molière* (Paris, 1932). The other influences on Molière are considered by Michaut in his book *Les Luttes de Molière* (Paris, 1925), pp. 55ff.

[102]Henri d'Alméras, *Le Tartuffe, de Molière* (Amiens, 1928), p. 83.

[103]*Satires*, I. 4. 1-6; Fairclough, p. 49. G. C. Fiske in his elaborate study, *Lucilius and Horace* (Madison, 1920), discusses Horace's relationship to Lucilius and to Old Comedy.

[104]*Satires*, I. 124.

[105]Louise E. Lord, *Aristophanes: His Plays and His Influence* (New York, 1963), p. 94.

[106]Juvenal *Satires* I. 165-167.
>    ense velut stricto quotiens Lucilius ardens
>    infremuit, rubet auditor cui frigida mens est
>    criminibus, tacita sudant praecordia culpa.

[107]M.A. Grant, *The Ancient Rhetorical Theories of the Laughable* (Madison, 1924).

[108]Plato, *Philebus* 48ff.; cited by George E. Duckworth, *The Nature of Roman Comedy* (Princeton, 1952), p. 306.

[109]Duckworth, *Roman Comedy*, p. 307. Passages dealing with comedy and laughter in Plato can be found in Lane Cooper's *An Aristotelian Theory of Comedy* (New York, 1922), pp. 104ff.

[110]Aristotle, *On the Art of Poetry*, tr. Lane Cooper (Ithaca, N.Y., 1947), pp. 13-14.

# INTRODUCTION 43

[111] Albert Cook, *The Dark Voyage and the Golden Mean* (Cambridge, 1949), p. 48. F. M. Cornford, *The Origin of Attic Comedy* (London, 1914), give detailed information on the ritual basis of Attic Comedy.

[112] Elizabeth A. Drew, *Discovering Drama* (New York, 1937), p. 170.

[113] James L. Calderwood and Harold E. Toliver, *Perspectives on Drama* (New York, 1968), p. 141.

[114] Henri Bergson, "Laughter" (1900), in *Comedy*, ed. Wylie Sypher (Garden City, 1956), p. 154.

[115] *The Theory of Drama* (London, 1937), p. 196.

[116] "The Argument of Comedy," in *English Institute Essays*, ed. D.A. Robertson, Jr. (New York, 1949), p. 57.

[117] Robert W. Corrigan, ed., *Greek Comedy* (New York, 1965), pp. 6-7. See also, Frye, "The Argument of Comedy," pp. 59-60.

[118] Sylvan Barnet, Morton Berman, and William Burto, *An Introduction to Literature* (New York, 1965), p. 506.

[119] Drew, *Discovering Drama* pp. 144-145.

[120] Frank H. O'Hara and Margueritte H. Bro, *Invitation to the Theater* (New York, 1951), p. 15.

[121] "Laughter," p. 71.

[122] Louis Kronenberger, *The Thread of Laughter* (New York, 1952), p. 3.

[123] It should be noted that this division is not absolute, nor is it accepted by all critics. Some, like Bonamy Dobrée, would make three classifications, altering the title of "non-critical" comedy to "free" comedy, and adding a division for "Great Comedy." See *Restoration Comedy, 1660-1720* (Oxford, 1924), pp. 9-16.

[124] Drew, p. 148.

[125] Nicoll, pp. 188-189.

[126] Dobrée, p. 12.

[127] Robert M. Smith, *Types of Social Comedy* (New York, 1928), p. 5.

[128] Dobrée, p. 10.

[129] Drew, p. 148.

[130] *The Theory of Drama*, p. 180.

[131] "An Essay on Comedy" (1877), in *Comedy*, ed. Wylie Sypher (Garden City, 1956).

[132] *Ibid.*, p. 43.

[133] *The Anatomy of Satire* (Princeton, 1962), pp. 141, 154, 155-156.

[134] *Ibid.*, p. 154.

[135] *Roman Satire* (Hamden, 1964), pp. 6-7.

[136] "The Mythos of Spring: Comedy," in *Comedy*, ed. Robert W. Corrigan (San Francisco, 1965), pp. 154ff.

[137] *Perspectives on Drama* (New York, 1968), p. 168.

[138] Cook, *The Dark Voyage*, p. 48.

[139] Highet has an excellent description of this characteristic of Aristophanes' plays, *Anatomy of Satire* pp. 207-208.

[140] *Greek Comedy* (New York, 1960), p. 7.

[141] *In Praise of Comedy* (London, 1939), pp. 37-38.

[142] J. Wight Duff, *Roman Satire* (1936; rpt. Hamden, 1964), p. 9.

[143] *Ibid.*, pp. 5-6. It is noteworthy that Molière, as I shall show below, was aware of the *castigat*, as is shown by the *Préface* and Placets to *Tartuffe*.

[144] Helena W. Watts, *The Satiric and the Didactic in Ben Jonson's Comedy* (Chapel Hill, 1947), p. 8.

[145]This is the theory of Jacques Grévin, a French dramatist writing in 1562, who described comedy as a "fictitious narrative, not far from the truth, containing in itself the divers concerns of life among citizens of mean estate, from which one may learn what is useful for life, and on the other hand recognize what one must avoid, taught by both the good and evil fate of the characters." *Bref Discours pour l'intelligence de ce Théâtre*, prefixed to *César*, 1562, in *Théâtre Complet et Poésies choisies*, ed. Lucien Pinvert (Paris, 1922), p. 7. See also Giraldi Cinthio, *On the Composition of Comedies and Tragedies*, 1543, in Allan H. Gilbert, ed., *Literary Criticism: Plato to Dryden* (New York, 1940), pp. 252-271.

[146]Giangiorgio Trissino, *Poetica* (1529), in Gilbert, p. 224. Although the didactic purpose of literature was professed by many of the critics of the Renaissance, there was also a justification for the inclusion of aesthetic material as well. This is found in Horace's *Ars Poetica*:

> aut prodesse volunt aut delectare poetae
> aut simul et iucunda et idonea dicere vitae. (333-334)

[147]Highet, *Anatomy of Satire*, pp. 155-156.
[148]Nicoll, *The Theory of Drama*, p. 190.
[149]*Ibid.*, pp. 190-191.
[150]*Ibid.*, pp. 191-192.
[151]Barnet, *Intro. to Lit.*, p. 510. Calderwood, *Perspectives on Drama*, pp. 167-169, also has an excellent discussion of satirical comedy.
[152]Martin Turnell, *The Classical Moment: Studies of Corneille, Molière and Racine* (London, 1963), pp. 61-62.
[153]*Ibid.*, p. 55.
[154]*The Spirit of Molière: An Interpretation*, ed. Jean-Albert Bédé (Princeton, 1940), p. 207.
[155]*Ibid.*, p. 209.
[156]There are noteworthy exceptions to this acceptance of *Tartuffe* as a comedy. Ferdinand Brunetière, *Epoques du théâtre français* (1636-1850), (Paris, 1892), p. 136, would term it a *drame*.
[157]*The Comedy of Intellect* (Berkeley, 1962), p. 105.
[158]"The Argument of Comedy," p. 60.
[159]*Ibid.*, p. 626.
[160]*Ibid.*, p. 96.
[161]*Theory of Drama*, p. 154.
[162]Smith, *Types of Social Comedy*, p. 3.
[163]*The Spirit of Molière*, p. 232.
[164]"Essay on Comedy," p. 108.
[165]"Laughter," p. 121.
[166]*Men and Masks*, pp. 112-113.
[167]Epoques, p. 125.
[168]Calderwood, *Perspectives on Drama*, p. 164.
[169]*Molière* (Paris, 1908), I, 264-265.
[170]*Ibid.*, pp. 263-264.
[171]*Molière: une aventure théâtrale* (Paris, 1963), p. 529.
[172]*The Classical Moment*, p. 62.
[173]Meredith, "Essay on Comedy," p. 77, states: "For exaggeration to be comic, it must not appear as an aim, but rather as a means that the artist is using in order to make manifest to our eyes the distortions which he sees in embryo."
[174]*The Comedy of Intellect*, p. 84.

[175] William Hazlitt, "Introduction to the English Comic Writers" (1818), cited by J. L. Styan, "Types of Comedy," in Corrigan, p. 231.

[176] *Perspectives on Drama*, pp. 163-164.

[177] "Laughter," p. 87.

[178] *Theory of Drama*, p. 202.

[179] "Tartuffe and the Comic Principle in Molière," *MLR*, XLIII (1948), p. 25.

[180] "Laughter," p. 111.

[181] *Ibid.*, pp. 152-153.

[182] *Restoration Comedy*, p. 10. This facet of the play will be considered exactingly in the next chapter in the section on *Sophrosyne*.

[183] *The Classical Moment*, p. 74.

[184] *Molière: une aventure théâtrale*, p. 529.

[185] *Ibid.*, p. 520.

[186] *Ibid.*, p. 521.

[187] *Les Luttes de Molière*, p. 108. He cites 11. 339-344, the importance of which will be considered in the next chapter.

[188] *Molière: une aventure théâtrale*, p. 530.

[189] The opening statement of the first *Placet* to *Tartuffe* is a confirmation, if not of Molière's advocacy, then of his awareness of the didactic and moral nature of comedy: "Le devoir de la comédie étant de corriger les hommes en les divertissant . . . "

[190] Drew, *Discovering Drama*, pp. 155-156.

[191] *Molière: Homme de Théâtre* (Paris, 1954), cited in Robert C. Elliott, *The Power of Satire: Magic, Ritual, Art* (Princeton, 1960), pp. 168-169.

[192] *Molière: une aventure théâtrale*, p. 129.

II

## THE SATIRIC ELEMENT IN *TARTUFFE*

What was Molière's purpose in writing *Tartuffe*? The eminent critic, Gustave Michaut, stated that his end was "de faire rire, tout simplement. Il a montré Orgon dupé par Tartuffe, pour faire rire ..."[1] Yet this same critic candidly admitted that "ce comique de Tartuffe lui-même, le plus souvent, m'échappe."[2] This opinion is echoed in other scholars, such as René Bray, who would agree that "Tartuffe ne fait pas rire ..."[3] Such opinions are in conflict with those of the advocates of *Tartuffe* as a comedy, pure and uncritical, or even a comedy tinged with satire. For it is somewhat doubtful, although not impossible, that a play could be an uncritical comedy with a protagonist who is obviously intended to elicit criticism.

The advocates of *Tartuffe*, the uncritical comedy, generally attempt to show that Molière must have been writing an uncritical comedy in the case of *Tartuffe* because he had written such comedies in the past and because the exigencies of the moment were strongly for a comedy lacking strong satiric elements. They commonly dismiss Molière's own explanations of his purpose.[4] They may, however, be proven wrong in assuming that Molière cannot mean what he says, if his explanations are proven by the work itself. It is possible that through a careful study of these explanations, which are found in the *Préface* of 1669 and the three *Placets au Roi*, an understanding of Molière's intentions in writing *Tartuffe* can be gained. Molière was writing to defend his play, with the hope of gaining the King's authorization of its public performance, but one should not assume that his words are merely apologetic, and therefore to be taken lightly. There is much in Molière's *Préface* and *Placets* which is intended to justify the publication of *Tartuffe*; therein also can be found keys to Molière's purpose in writing *Tartuffe* and his method of composition. Molière asks if the function of comedy is (not) to correct the vices of men.

> Si l'emploi de la comédie est de corriger les vices des hommes
> ... (*Préface*)

Continuing on the assumption that this is so, he points out that the theater is an effective agent for such correction. The next sentence presents an idea which, at first, does not seem to follow: satire is very effective in treating subjects of morality.

> Les plus beaux traits d'une sérieuse morale sont moins puissants le plus souvent que ceux de la satire ...(*Préface*)

Molière had been talking about comedy; suddenly he talks about satire. Why? Does he plan to write satire? Is *Tartuffe*, then, a satirical comedy? This is suggested by Molière's use of the word "satire"; the suggestion is intensified by Molière's statement that he plans to deal with the same moral subjects as satire traditionally had — "une sérieuse morale." This is certainly not the subject matter of farce, nor of uncritical comedy in general, but of critical comedy, which as we have seen, employs satire as one of its primary devices.

Molière goes on to invoke the most famous philosophers to testify on behalf of his comedy. But the terms in which he does so once more suggest that he has also written satire. This is shown to be true when Molière's witnesses turn out to be men "who made a profession of austere wisdom and who decried ... the vices of their age."

> Et si nous voulons ... le témoignage de l'antiquité, elle nous dira que ses plus célèbres philosophes ont donné des louanges à la comédie, eux qui faisoient profession d'une sagesse si austère, et qui crioient sans cesse après les vices de leur siècle ...(*Préface*)

Molière here attempts to justify the presentation of his comedy by showing that it is a respectable literary genre, since such men as Aristotle have given their approval to it. His choice of words, however, shows a deeper intent. Consider again how he describes his witnesses: these men are, as will be shown, especially the Stoic philosophers, whose moral precepts were adopted in many areas of classical literature, the most important of which, for the purpose of this study, was satire. Although they were not Stoics,[5] the satirists Juvenal and Horace, just as the Stoic philosophers Cleanthes, Aristo, and Cato, were considered men of wisdom (if not austerity) who decried the vices of their ages.

Molière has subtly told us what he is going to do. Next he tells how he will do it.

> Et qu'est-ce que dans le monde on ne corrompt point tous les jours? Il n'y a chose si innocente où les hommes ne puissent porter du crime, point d'art si salutaire dont ils ne soient capables de renverser les intentions, rien de si bon en soi qu'ils ne puissent tourner à de mauvais usages.
> (*Préface*)

Molière continues by pointing out medicine and philosophy as particular professions which have been ill-used by corrupt men, with the result that the entire professions have been at times condemned. Comedy is also such a "chose si innocente," Molière notes, continuing his apology. It is the statement above, however, that presents Molière's method in composing *Tartuffe*. Molière depicted objects normally innocent, salutary, and good as turned to bad use by wicked men, who destroy the meanings of these "choses" by reversing their good intentions to criminal ones. Such an object is religion which is perverted (renversé) into hypocrisy. It is hypocrisy that Molière, as he tells us in his *Préface* and *Placets*, is attacking. Moreover, one should note the stress on the idea of corruption in the passage above and throughout the *Préface*. In the term "corruption" it is possible to see the figure of Orgon, just as Tartuffe can be seen in the term "hypocrisy."

Equally wrong is the assumption that the conscious artist, as Molière certainly was, either could not have or would not have "selected a festival at Versailles as a proper occasion for sermonizing,"[6] if he had good reason to do so, as Molière may have thought he did. Another theory that does not give due credit to the skills of the artist states that "the financial fortunes of his company were a constant problem, that therefore the plays had to be written with an eye to popular success, and that to air doctrine or indulge in satire would have been disastrous."[7] All these statements and theories are produced by a limited consideration of Molière's life and times. It is noteworthy that one critic who made such a statement also asserted: "The satire is clear, and abundant, and we cannot assume that its creator was blind to its presence."[8] It is Tartuffe's play. Although Tartuffe does contain incongruities and the play is replete with standard devices of comedy, most critics, as we have seen, have great difficulty in accepting Tartuffe as a comic figure. The problem for these critics arises from the failure to understand the satiric nature of *Tartuffe*.

The intention here is not to deny the comic nature of Molière's *Tartuffe*, but to question the denial of the satiric element in the play or the satiric intent of the author. Certainly there are elements of humor and comedy in *Tartuffe*, although it is doubtful that anyone would go so far as to agree with one scholar who thought that "the play, so far as its earlier acts are concerned, is almost as full of fun as any of Molière's preceding pieces ..."[9]

The scenes of comedy in *Tartuffe* are for the most part those which exclude the figure of the hypocrite from the stage. They are, for instance, the scenes in which Orgon, Dorine, Mariane, and Valère have their interactions. Such a scene is Act II, scene 8, where Orgon prepares to box Dorine's ears the next time she interrupts him — a scene drawn from farce.

Even Will G. Moore, one of the most ardent advocates of *Tartuffe* as a comedy, questions the nature of Tartuffe, saying that he is "comic (if at all) by deep inconsistencies in his character."[10] Elements of Tartuffe's character, however, are drawn from standard comic sources. In Plautus, the main function of the role of the parasite was comedy; but in Plautus the parasite was usually foiled at every turn,[11] adding an element of joyous comedy which is non-existent in Tartuffe. By the time Tartuffe is foiled, there is little opportunity for joy, and laughter is hardly elicited.

It is more in the parasite of Terence that one can see a prototype of Tartuffe. This prototype is the adaptable scoundrel who is forced to live by his wits. He never harms anyone except a fool. The parasite of Terence enjoys luxury and the good life. He takes particular delight in being able to enjoy them without submitting to insult. How very close the parasite of Terence is to Tartuffe, considering especially his relationship with Orgon. Tartuffe has come to the end of his means and is now "forced to live by his wits." Orgon, as a fool, is an "oaf." Tartuffe manages to enjoy his taste for "luxury . . . without submitting to insult," at least from Orgon.

The one Terentian parasite who best serves as a pattern for Tartuffe is Phormio, who controls the course of events in the play from beginning to end with a masterful hand.[12] He "has none of the parasite's usual characteristics, neither the preoccupation with hunger and food nor the desire to win favor by jesting or flattery. Norwood calls him 'far less a parasite than a *sykophantés*, a subtle and elegant blackmailer'."[13] Molière knew the *Phormio*, employing its protagonist as a basis of his *Les Fourberies de Scapin*.[14] It is possible, then, that Phormio formed a germ for Molière's conception of Tartuffe.

Underlying the comedy of Plautus and Terence there is a strong tone of satire, a seriousness of thought which is more obvious in Terence, who satirizes the vices of individuals and the corruption of the times, than it is in Plautus, whose serious ideas are usually obscured by farce and foolery.[15] This satiric strain in comedy must have been obvious to Molière, as it was to Horace, who noted that Lucilius, the first great Roman satirist, had followed the Old Comedy of Greece, as represented by Eupolis, Cratinus, and Aristophanes, by attacking infamous men. (I. 4)

Moore also considers hypocrisy a natural subject for comedy. "The spectacle of a man playing two roles, one natural, the other assumed, illustrates a general principle of comedy, the juxtaposition of contrasting actions or words proceeding from a single character . . . Such a contrast within the same man need not be funny . . . But it is comic, so long as it occurs within a man who claims to be an integral personality."[16] This statement is true, as far as it goes. What Moore fails to consider is the effect which the real nature of Tartuffe has on the family of Orgon. Tartuffe knows his real nature and assumes the false nature merely to satisfy the real. The contrast becomes not merely comic, but ominous and even frightening. One watches the lengths to which evil will go to achieve its ends and shudders at each success. The comedy in *Tartuffe* is almost completely stifled as the satiric effect becomes dominant.

To see *Tartuffe* as a pure or uncritical comedy, one must overlook the effect of the hypocrite on the household of Orgon. "We may admit him to be a sinister figure," says Moore, "but we should at the same time notice that Molière has stressed this aspect far less than other aspects."[17] Molière's *Tartuffe* reveals the disastrous influence of Tartuffe on the family of Orgon. All rational order has been destroyed; the very nature of the family unit is about to be utterly destroyed. Molière may not have said explicitly that Tartuffe was sinister, but he expected his audience to realize it.[18] Tartuffe participates in situations which in many other plays would evoke pure laughter, but which approach tragedy in Molière's play—the mutual kneeling scene, for example. This could easily be a purely comic scene, and many consider it so. If one sees in it, however, the extent to which Tartuffe controls Orgon, who should strive toward a rational and benign rule, but prefers to be ruled, the tragedy of the situation and the threat to Orgon's family prevent a strictly comic interpretation.[19] A scene even more indicative of the tragic situation in the house of Orgon is the second attempt to seduce Elmire. Here the comic element is the presence of Orgon under the table. This is indeed a scene with comic possibilities, but only in another play, with other characters. *Tartuffe* will not allow a purely comic interpretation, for, in the inaction of Orgon and the imminent success of Tartuffe, evil is about to become predominant in the house of Orgon, all order destroyed. If Elmire were not fundamentally moral, it could be funny; but as the scene proceeds from a trap for Tartuffe to the near compromise of a valiant woman, trying to preserve all she holds sacred, while Orgon remains incapable of action, one must be aware of a comedy of a most serious nature. One after another, scenes which should ordinarily be laughable occur, but there is no feeling of delight. If one is aware of the seriousness, the satiric import of Tartuffe, the risible is overwhelmed.

There is really only one time, according to one critic, when Tartuffe could even vaguely be considered comic, when his sting has been removed. "Ce qui rend Tartuffe comique, c'est qu'arrivé au moment où il se croit sûr de son fait, où il pense avoir assez serré le bandeau sur les yeux d'Orgon, il perd toute retenue, et, par son impudence, devient l'artisan de sa propre ruine."[20] The scene certainly contains the essence of comedy. But the meaning of the scene overshadows the humor of the situation. Tartuffe fails in self-restraint, but does not bring about his destruction in the world he knows and understands — the household of Orgon. There he has nothing but success. It is only when he goes outside the house of Orgon that he is destroyed, for then he has ventured into a world in which reason rules. He might have succeeded had he not called the outside law into play. The lesson is clear: a Tartuffe can succeed in situations where corruption has destroyed the desire for order; there he need not exercise restraint; nothing can check him. But should he venture into the world of light, he dooms himself. The scene should be comedy, but somehow it is more.

One of the foremost critics of Molière noted that "considered in its proper chronological order, 'Tartuffe' is seen to reveal an extraordinary advance in Molière's conception of comedy. It has a largeness of theme and a boldness of social satire which nothing in his preceding plays had led us to suspect. from him ... .In this play," he continues, "Molière enlarges the boundaries of comedy and raises it to a more exalted level. He gives us comic plays which are more than mere comic plays. They arouse laughter ... ; but they make us think even more than they make us laugh ... ; they are serious and they are charged with meaning."[21]

*Tartuffe*, then, represents a development in Molière's art. He has made steady progress as an artist, but *Tartuffe* is a leap into comedy of a new kind. Farce, upon which he has relied so heavily in his earlier plays, will not appear here. "Les possibilités de violences physiques, en particulier sont soigneusement étouffées. Les personnages les suggèrent, vont jusqu'au bord de l'acte, mais s'arrêtent ou en sont détournés."[22] This movement away from farce must have some justification. Farce had fit very well into his early plays, and he would employ it again. If farce was well able to evoke the laughter of Molière's audience, why did he reject it in *Tartuffe*? The answer must be that he was trying to do something in which the laughter of farce could have no part — something more meaningful than he had ever attempted.

*Tartuffe* differs from any play Molière had previously written. The play is concerned with evil and vice on a level and at an intensity not previously seen in Molière's plays.[23] Why did such a change occur in the comedy of Molière?

Certain basic facts and factors can be suggested as the causes of this development in Molière's art. An awareness of morality and ethics was provided Molière by his study of Latin literature under the tutelage of the Jesuits. There he encountered a well-worked-out system of characterization on moral principles in the writings of many classical authors, among whom were the satirists Horace and Juvenal and the Stoic philosopher (and satirist) Seneca. Molière's early (pre-1660) plays, however, do not show strong affinities with the "sérieuse morale" and the subject matter of the satirist. It is impossible to say with certainty what caused the development that has been noted in *Tartuffe*. In this author's opinion, however, especially influential upon Molière must have been his association with Boileau. The importance of this relationship with Boileau must be stressed. Boileau, the major satirist of seventeenth-century France, translator and adaptor of Juvenal and Horace, must have recalled to Molière the teachings of his youth. To these, then, the satiric authors, Molière may have turned for a greater understanding of mankind. If he did reread them, as I believe, Molière would possibly have come to that same awareness that Horace had before him, that there was an intimate relationship between comedy and satire. Moreover, seeing the importance of the satiric element in comedy, he would have had time in his years at Auteuil to revitalize his familiarity with the substance of Roman satire. As a man of the theater, he would have looked at the themes of satire with a constant eye to putting them into dramatic form within the structures of his chosen art and profession, comedy.

There are certain criteria[24] which can be applied to *Tartuffe* to aid us in determining the extent of its satiric nature. "There are a number of reliable tests. If some, or most, of them apply to a book," states Gilbert Highet, "it is likely to be a satire."

First, a generic definition by the author. When Juvenal looks at corrupt Rome and cries

> It is difficult not to write satire (I. 30)

we know the pattern he will use ...."[25]

Molière himself in the *Préface* of 1669 implies that his play is a satire. But, at the same time, he is careful to emphasize that *Tartuffe* is a comedy. It must be remembered that it was dangerous to write personal or political satire. The furor aroused by the two versions along with *Tartuffe* shows clearly that there was good reason for Molière to fear that his satire would be taken personally. Furthermore, as will be seen in the next chapter, there is a possibility that Molière's satire was not only personal, but political as well.[26]

Molière also has, perhaps, provided an indirect generic definition of his intentions in *Tartuffe*. This occurs in *La Critique de l'Ecole des Femmes*. In that play, published the year before the original of *Tartuffe*, 1663, Molière has one of his characters, Dorante, ask if Molière was not writing 'satire' in *L'Ecole des Femmes*:

> Dorante: et quant au transport amoureux du cinquième acte, qu'on accuse d'être trop outré et trop comique, je voudrois bien savoir si ce n'est pas faire la satire des amants ...?
>
> Le Marquis: Ma foi, Chevalier, tu ferois mieux de te taire.
>
> (scene vi)

Immediately, Dorant's associates close the damper on the subject. They know that satire can be a dangerous field of endeavor, especially for the author who directs his attack against the rich and powerful. For Molière, however, the field was just opening. That scene, considered in the light of Molière's use of the term "satire" in the *Préface* of 1669, can be understood to signify his announcement that he intended in the near future to enter the lists of satire, but with his standards veiled. His veil would be the panoply of comedy.

The second and third tests merge into one for the purpose of studying *Tartuffe*. There is often a pedigree which proclaims the line of descent from the classical satirists. This pedigree is often disguised as "a choice of some traditionally satiric subject and treatment."[27] Molière, then, if he employs traditional themes found in the Roman satirists, Horace and Juvenal, may be announcing himself as a satirist of the Roman school. This can only be determined by a study of *Tartuffe* in relation to the satires of Horace and Juvenal, which will be the task of the next chapter.

The subject matter of satire is multifarious. The satirist tries to keep his reader "guessing and gasping" by producing the unexpected in plot, in discourse, in emotional tone, and in vocabulary.[28] *Tartuffe* immediately satisfies one category of this test, if one remembers that one of the charges leveled against Molière was that his play was overly complicated in plot.[29]

Most satirists, having read the satiric works of other authors, are aware of the devices which are used to flavor the satiric effect; typical weapons of satire are irony, paradox, antithesis, parody, colloquialism, anticlimax, topicality, obscenity, violence, vividness and exaggeration.[30] If Molière uses these devices to a great extent, then it is likely that he is writing satire.

Nearly all satire employs two special methods, or attitudes: first, a vivid description of a painful or absurd situation, or a foolish or wicked person or group; second, the use of uncompromisingly clear language to describe unpleasant facts and people, in order to shock the reader.[31] It is the first of these methods which is particularly in evidence in *Tartuffe*. There we find vividly described and then presented the "wicked person" in the figure of Tartuffe, and the "fool" in that of Orgon. Moreover, the language used to depict Tartuffe (traitor, usurper) clearly describes him in satiric terms, which are not intended to produce laughter.

Satire is "often improbable ... Of all the improbabilities with which satire deals, the most plausible and the closest to real life is the fraud, the hoax, the swindle."[32] *Tartuffe* is a tale, of a highly improbable nature, about one of the great swindlers (even if he does ultimately fail) of literature. If one stops for a second to consider the action of the play, it becomes even more improbable, but not impossible. Although it is not likely, it could happen that an entire family is led one member after another into "more trials and tribulations than any ordinary man could endure ... [Yet] they survive, apparently untouched, apparently indestructible,"[33] but only because a wisdom greater and more benevolent than any in the play prevails in the universe in which they live. It is precisely in this overstepping, or at least stretching, of the bounds of reality that the satire takes its meaning. For so much evil to be as successful as Tartuffe is, a special world must have been entered. Tartuffe is extraordinary. He is a synthesis of many vices. His most obvious vice is hypocrisy; it is Molière's purpose to depict Tartuffe as representative of this evil. But in the process he makes him a synthesis of many evils — ambition, greed, pride, lust. Such men may exist; but, if they do, they are very rare, for it is improbable that so many vices could exist in any one man. Further evidence of the satiric nature of Tartuffe will be provided if the vices which are exhibited by Tartuffe are those which were traditional subjects of the satirists, especially if they are treated in a satiric manner. This will be examined in the next chapter.

Satire is topical in nature; "it walks the streets with a notebook and draws illustrations from its own time and place."[34] It seeks out the corruptions that manifest themselves in society and describes them in unforgettable terms. The subject matter that one will find in satire is "concrete, usually topical, often personal. It deals with actual cases, mentions real people by name or describes them unmistakably (and often unflatteringly), talks of this moment and this city . . ."[35] In his *Préface* and *Placets*, Molière makes clear the fact that the hypocrites and the corruption he writes about are present and active in his own France. In *Tartuffe*, it is the topicality of his presentation that gave the play its own, special, satiric bite. Everywhere Molière's audience looked, they saw real men and women who could have been to some extent the bases of the plot of *Tartuffe* and of Molière's characters. Dozens of pseudo-religious men have been suggested by the critics as the original of Tartuffe, not the least of whom was Charpy de Sainte-Croix. Doubtlessly, Molière had observed some of the acts of hypocrisy of such men when he wrote *Tartuffe*. But it is impossible to say that any one character of Molière's day was *the* model for Tartuffe, for none of them embraces all the aspects of Tartuffe. Molière's protagonist is a masterful blend of many of the evil and vicious elements exhibited by the characters of Molière's times or recorded in the traditions of the various literatures he read. Tartuffe is typical of so many of the hypocrites of Molière's day because Molière was capable of combining all that he saw, read, or intuited about the characters of men into a valid psychology for all mankind. Men of all times have been led astray by excesses of pride and ambition, lusting for power and wealth, unaware of the wisdom of moderation. This fact was apparent in Rome, in France, and it is still apparent today. "What gives satire its vital importance . . . is . . . its faithful representation of contemporary life and its comments thereupon."[36]

This brief review of the tests for proving a work to be a satire, as applied to *Tartuffe*, reveals that *Tartuffe* readily satisfies two of the categories: Molière has provided us both a direct and indirect "generic definition" of his work, by his use of the word "satire"; although it remains for a later chapter to reveal the extent to which Molière has employed traditionally satiric subjects and treatment, Molière's play fulfills most of the remaining criteria for the subject matter of satire. In particular, it is multifarious, it is topical, and it does present in vivid terms a fool and a wicked person, all in very clear and, as is obvious from the seventeenth-century reaction, shocking terms. One further test, that of the emotion of the satirist, will be applied to *Tartuffe* later in this chapter. However, it is possible to state at this point that, although *Tartuffe* does not fulfill every division of every test (as doubtless few if any satires do), enough of the tests are generally applicable to Molière's play to promote the belief that *Tartuffe* is a satire. Before making any stronger statements on the nature of Tartuffe, it will be profitable to examine it on the basis of other criteria which are not necessarily included among the "tests" we have just considered.

One of the disturbing aspects about Tartuffe is the amazing diversity of his character. Some have faulted Molière for this, while others have come to the defense of the author; one is Félix Hémon, who states: "Il est possible, sans doute, que Molière, désireux, comme on l'a dit, de ne pas limiter le ridicule à une seule catégorie de dévots, ait réuni en ce caractère diverses variétés de l'hypocrisie. . . ."[37] Hémon is right. But, in consideration of the possibility that *Tartuffe* is a satire, although he does not fail as drastically as those who have found in the diversity in plot and characterization in *Tartuffe* subjects for reproval, Hémon's justification can be seen to fail, for he does not understand an important fact about *Tartuffe*. If Molière's play is a satire, the diversity of plot and complexity of character are historically justified. The word *satura* means medley and hodge-podge. Typical of the satirist, Molière may have been "less interested in developing a plot" and a perfected characterization for his protagonist, than he was "in displaying many different aspects of an idea . . ."[38] The idea he wished to present was especially the ideal of *bon sens* exemplified in moderation and the avoidance of excess. This has been shown in the introductory chapter and will be more fully considered in the next chapter. Molière's method of presentation was to show certain exceptions to the ideal, all moulded into as consistent a plot, *Tartuffe*, and characters, Tartuffe and Orgon, as possible. But consistency of plot and character was obviously not his prime consideration. What then was Molière's purpose in writing *Tartuffe*? One can accept Lancaster's statement that "Molière's primary purpose was to write a comedy, not to attack hypocrisy, or, as Brunetière claimed, religion."[39] However, after considering Molière's background, especially his literary relations with such men as Boileau during the 1660's, when *Tartuffe* was being written and rewritten, and in view of the *Préface* of 1669 and the *Placets au Roi*, as well as the play itself, which is replete with Molière's philosophic teachings, it is probable that Molière had a second and equal purpose in writing *Tartuffe* as he did, and that was didactic. If this is accepted, it can be stated that Molière wrote to teach a lesson, and for that reason, Tartuffe is not incoherent; he is complex. The complexity of Tartuffe will be considered exactingly in the next chapter where it will be shown that he exhibits himself not merely as a hypocrite, but as a parasite, a glutton, a wastrel, a lecher, and as numerous other types of moral transgressors. Highet, describing the efforts of the satirist, has provided a perfect answer to the critics of the problems created by any diversities in Tartuffe: "If the results which he offers us are not always smooth with the contours of perfect art, and if their tints are not harmoniously blended, they at least have the urgency and immediacy of actual life."[40]

The satirist is a specialist in looking at society, for he sees through the flaws lying hidden beneath the veneer. These flaws, which remain unseen by the average man, the satirist feels compelled to point out with such unmistakable clarity that even the most insensitive man becomes aware of them. In the process, the vigor of his performance and the importance of his self-imposed mission sometimes cause the satirist to become so involved with his task of revealing the hidden truths to the unseeing that he presents a twisted picture of the truth. He presents a propagandist distortion,[41] in which the flaws of society are magnified out of proportion to normal dimensions. Thus the evil or grossness of a character is likely to be exaggerated. Such is the case with the character of Tartuffe. The elements of his character were carefully selected by Molière to form a possible (although unlikely) whole, and then exaggerated almost to the point of incredibility. This exaggeration is made obvious by a common device of satire: most of the characters, who are engaged in normal human relationships, are set in contrast to some character, who is distorted along one line of stress.[42] Such is the case in Molière's play, where the family represents a norm, against which Tartuffe is set in clear contrast. It is really only the sphere within which Tartuffe functions that lends him any aspect of reality.

> But Tartuffe is not a perfect hypocrite: because his mask is exaggerated, he arouses the suspicions of the more perspicacious members of the household. Without knowing it, he presents not a spectacle of piety but its caricature; as Cléante says, he overdoes it. He is successful only because the world is full of Orgons who, in their hasty search for happiness, never look closely enough.[43]

Any statement such as "Molière has created a living man ..."[44] must be produced by a misunderstanding of Molière's protagonist. It is doubtful that anyone ever has seen or ever will see anyone quite like Tartuffe. Tartuffe is not painted in all his aspects. This was, no doubt, Molière's intention. One should not search for well-rounded characters in satire; two-dimensional figures are the rule. Thus, "in Molière's *Tartuffe* the villain is bigger than life-size, viler than any normal reality; and yet, because such hypocrites are often more intense and convincing than ordinary men, he is real enough."[45] His reality stems not only from the milieu in which he acts, but also from the effect he produces.[46] Accordingly, a critic attempting to justify Tartuffe as a dramatic character adduces arguments "that a type character may ... be devoid of reality, that he may tend to be artificially homogeneous, that he may have little or no life of his own, and that Molière may therefore be guilty of distorting real life, sacrificing the richness of a human personality for the sake of representing one single facet of an admittedly complex being."[47] Such statements may serve to explain the dramatic nature of Tartuffe, but they also further our understanding of him as a satiric figure.

Molière did not allow Tartuffe to proceed beyond the realm of credibility in any of his evil deeds. Molière was much too aware of human psychology and of his art to do that. "Observation and fidelity to what is observed, not only externally, but also psychologically in the deeper realm of character, constitute a realistic check upon unlicensed imagination ..."[48] Satire is a magnified and distorted picture of reality. The distortion in the case of Tartuffe is, accordingly, one of reality. There are people whose constitution contains any number of the elements in Tartuffe's, just as there are men who perform some of the actions of Tartuffe. The distortion of reality that, by comparison, makes *Tartuffe* a satire is the unrestrained and continuous succession of vicious machinations and acts. At first one will say of Tartuffe, "He is an incredibly evil man." Upon reflection, however, one is likely to realize just how incredible he is. He is not really a man at all, but a synthesis of vices. But the immediate dramatic effect does not await reflection — he is a man. He has his human reality in the immediacy of the play, in the effects which he has both onstage and off on the household of Orgon. It is therein that he attains his reality — a reality which temporarily overwhelms the spectators' judgment. Only consideration of the totality of Tartuffe shows his unreality, his distortion, his satiric nature.

The distortion of Tartuffe and, to a lesser extent, of Orgon, appears obvious when one looks at the rest of the characters in the play. They are potentially real and very human individuals. The distortion is in the figure of Tartuffe, "who became a monster dominating everyone, and prepared to crush them utterly ..."[49] and that of Orgon, who is used by Tartuffe.

Distortion in satire has a special division in which there is depicted another world with which the normal world is to be contrasted. Orgon's household functions as such a world in which satire can take effect. There Molière presents a society into which Tartuffe irrupts, with the result that he upsets first the order of the household then of his own intended world. In this world "human vices and weaknesses" can be shown more openly, working more successfully than in the normal world. This is because it is a very special kind of world.

> A satirical picture of our world, which shows only human beings as its inhabitants, must pretend to be a photograph, and in fact be a caricature. It must display their more ridiculous and repellent qualities in full flower, minimize their ability for healthy normal living, mock their virtues and exaggerate their vices, disparage their greatest human gifts, the gift for cooperation and the gift for inventive adaptation, treat their religions as hypocrisy, their art as trash, their literature as opium, their loves as lust, their virtue as hypocrisy, and their happiness as an absurd illusion.[50]

Orgon's household is exactly this kind of world, for only in such a world could a Tartuffe thrive so well, so long.

With rare exceptions the critics, even those who are convinced that *Tartuffe* is an uncritical comedy, have been deeply disturbed by their attempts and subsequent failures to reconcile the effect of Molière's play and his protagonist with that of comedy. One critic candidly states that:

> Cette peinture ne peut pas être comique. On s'est demandé parfois si l'on pouvait rire de Tartuffe. Sans aller jusqu'à dire que le scélérat excite l'horreur ou le dégoût, sentiments mal venus dans l'âme d'un spectateur de comédie, il faut reconnaître qu'il n'est guère plaisant. La situation dans laquelle il se met en essayant de concilier dévotion et libertinage, est fausse et pourrait être une source de ridicule: en fait, on ne rit pas.[51]

This critic is so amazed that *Tartuffe* is not a comedy according to the standards he expects that he cannot quite bring himself to admit that Tartuffe arouses the emotions of horror and disgust; all he will admit is that Tartuffe is not funny.

Along the same lines, Schiller refused to accept a character such as Tartuffe within the realms of comedy, but saw the potential for comedy in the hypocrite if he were kept from being so "repulsive as to arouse our indignation."[52]

Hegel likewise misunderstood Molière's purpose. The German critic finds the character of Tartuffe "harsh and repellent." He could find no comic pleasure (nothing *lustig*) in the unmasking of the religious impostor.[53] The solution to the problem of these critics may be quite simple: the play is, perhaps, not intended to be simply a comedy and, therefore, will not have the ordinary comic effect. Rather, if it is a satire in the form of comedy, a satirical comedy, as I have previously suggested, it will have a satiric effect. It is precisely this effect which the critics have felt and misunderstood.

The emotion which the satiric author desires to evoke in his readers is "a blend of amusement and contempt."[54] These emotions may vary in satire to the extent that one or the other may almost disappear. Such is the case with *Tartuffe*, where whatever amusement exists does so apart from Tartuffe himself, who is an object of unremitting contempt, disgust, and even hatred. "On déteste l'imposteur," says one critic who felt the emotion Molière intended.[55] In order that no one have any doubt that such an emotion is correct, Molière showed (in his play) the proper reaction to Tartuffe. All the members of Orgon's family who represent the norm detest Tartuffe. This is the key to the proper emotion. If the healthy members of Molière's play, represented by the family, detest Tartuffe, so should the healthy members of any society. Highet felt the emotion that Molière desired when he remarked that "we do not laugh at the end of *Tartuffe*, as we do when a comedy closes. We shudder; we want to spit. It is a satire both on the hypocrite and upon the fools who believe him."[56]

"The purpose of satire is, through laughter and invective, to cure folly and to punish evil; but if it does not achieve this purpose, it is content to jeer at folly and to expose evil to bitter contempt."[57] This is the purpose also of *Tartuffe*. The laughter is not the pleasant and joyful laughter of comedy, however, but bitter and derisive laughter; and this is directed at Orgon more than at Tartuffe. The only laughter evoked by Tartuffe is the laugh of one too horrified to express his emotions otherwise or the snarl of one who is relieved at the overthrow of the villain. Molière directs his exposé at two targets: the Tartuffes, the evil men who, under the guise of hypocrisy or any other deceit, attempt to upset the order of the natural universe; and the Orgons, who are the gulls of the Tartuffes.

Molière had a solid training in philosophy in his early education at the Collège de Clermont, where the course of study included philosophy. This subject was taught as an extension and culmination of the moral training given in the earlier years primarily through the study of classical literature. Yet in his early comedies, Molière does not profess strong moral opinions. There he is "l'apôtre d'une moralité commode,"[58] which only rarely takes coherent form. These comedies were probably produced in years when his philosophy of life was still taking form, before he had seen many facets of the world which were to appear in his later comedies (after 1660), before his friendship with Boileau and the resultant incentive toward rereading satire.

*Tartuffe* was among the first of the plays of Molière to reveal a strong tone of morality, found usually in the words of the "raisonneurs." Accordingly, one critic feels that in *Tartuffe* "the moral opposition between hypocrisy and true virtue — Tartuffe and Cléante — was of more importance than the dramatic opposition between guilt and innocence — Tartuffe and the family."[59] The play comes near being a Morality then. But it is not. For even the moral lessons of Tartuffe have a satiric tone, employing many of the conventions of satire.

Satire takes on several shapes, among them the monologue. The satiric monologue may be part of a work not integrally satiric, even part of a dialogue, in which only one of the parts is eminently satire. In it, "the satirist, usually speaking either in his own person or behind a mask which is scarcely intended to hide, addresses us directly. He states his view of a problem, cites examples, pillories opponents and endeavors to impose his view upon the public."[60] Maynard Mack, basing his judgment on classical theories of rhetoric, finds that the satirist often takes on an assumed identity, a *persona*.[61] The weight of authority is directly proportionate to the hearer's estimate of the speaker's *ethos*, his character. Accordingly, if the character who functions as the voice of the satirist is to be an effective teacher, "he must be accepted as a fundamentally virtuous and tolerant man, who challenges the doings of other men not whenever he happens to feel vindictive, but whenever they deserve it."[62] Such a man will be plain living, high thinking, a good friend, a despiser of lies and slanders — a *vir bonus*.[63]

This role in Tartuffe is played by Cléante. Cléante is well-chosen to be Molière's satiric voice. His name and his character are derived from the Stoic sage Cleanthes, a pupil of Zeno, the founder of Stoicism. Cléante's philosophic connections are clearly shown in his speech in Act I, scene v, where he mentions a number of exemplars of virtue, among whom are Aristo and Alcidamas, Greek philosophers of the Stoic and Sophist schools, and Periander, one of the seven sages. There can be no doubt that Molière knew of Cleanthes if he knew of Aristo, Alcidamas and Periander, all of whom are of lesser importance in the history of philosophy than Cleanthes. Molière would also have known of Cleanthes from his study of Seneca, wherein Cleanthes is cited as a model of virtue. Equal proof is provided by his language; his vocabulary is that of philosophy: appearance (336); bounds (341); reason (341); excess (*trop*, 341); knowledge (352); virtue (388). His words announce him as a philosopher as surely as does his name. Orgon himself tells us, in terms carefully chosen by Molière, that Cléante is not just a philosopher, but a member of the Stoic school particularly notable for his continence, a paragon of wisdom and virtue — a Cato:

> Vous êtes le seul sage et le seul éclairé,
> Un oracle, un Caton dans le siècle où nous sommes . . .(348-349)

When he makes this statement, Orgon is being sarcastic and ironic. But, typical of his character, Orgon does not discern between appearance and reality. He does not see that his "joke" is actually the truth.

Cléante himself represents an ideal; this was seen by Michaut, who stated:

> Faudrait-il qu'au lieu de citer Ariston, Périandre et autres, Cléante eût dit: Le vrai dévot, c'est moi? L'idée seule est absurde.

> Mais Cléante, s'il n'est pas sottement pharisien, a toutes les qualités qu'il déclare lui-même admirer dans les dévots véritables; et il en est un, puisque, d'un bout à l'autre, il se montre sage, modéré, dévoué, charitable, qu'à la fin il conseille et pratique le pardon des injures.[64]

It should be obvious, however, that Cléante's character is more that of the philosopher than of the "dévot." His references to God and Heaven are always in the context of his comments on Tartuffe. He does not refer to Heaven repeatedly as an ideal, as one would expect a "dévot" to do.

Why does Cléante perform as he does? One may follow Michaut's suggestion that "il a jugé qu'un 'raisonneur', visible truchement de l'auteur, visible arbitre sans passions, aurait plus d'autorité qu'un personnage plus mêlé à l'action."[65] This is, however, too simple an answer to a question quite complex. Cléante is barely a part of the action in Molière's play.[66] He does not influence the action of the play. He is "le témoin qui généralise, il a une fonction à part qui le situe partiellement en dehors de l'action et en même temps l'oblige à souligner la signification universelle du cas particulier 'raconté' dans la comédie."[67] He may be considered the voice of the satirist, commenting on that special world to which he is an outsider, underlining the meanings of the play which might otherwise go unnoticed or misunderstood. The fact that Cléante's comments serve to point up the satire on both Tartuffe and Orgon suggests "that Molière is out to ridicule excess in any direction."[68] This point cannot be made too strongly, for, as will be shown in the next chapter, the satire is indeed against excess, with hypocrisy, the immediate cause of the satire, being only one facet of Tartuffe's enormity. It remains for us to discover in the next chapter the extent to which Cléante reflects on the philosophic ideals of Roman satire, with its ethical bases, and the extent to which Tartuffe and Orgon represent the excesses depicted in Roman satire.

The most famous character-writer of seventeenth-century France, La Bruyère, in his chapter "De la mode" of the *Caractères*, vehemently criticizes Molière's depiction of the hypocrite Tartuffe:

> S'il se trouve bien d'un homme opulent, à qui il a su imposer, dont il est le parasite, et dont il peut tirer de grands secours, il ne cajole point sa femme, il ne lui fait du moins ni avance ni déclaration; il s'enfuira, il lui laissera son manteau, s'il n'est aussi sûr d'elle que de lui-même. Il est encore plus éloigné d'employer pour la flatter et pour la séduire le jargon de la dévotion; ce n'est point par habitude qu'il le parle, mais avec dessein, et selon qu'il lui est utile, et jamais quand il ne serviroit qu'à la rendre très ridicule . . . . Il ne pense point à profiter de toute sa succession, ni s'attirer une

donation générale de tous ses biens, s'il s'agit surtout de les enlever à un fils, le légitime héritier: un homme dévot n'est ni avare, ni violent, ni injuste, ni même intéressé; Onuphre n'est pas dévot, mais il veut être cru tel, et par une parfaite, quoique fausse imitation de la piété, ménager sourdement ses intérêts: aussi ne se joue-t-il pas à la ligne directe, et il ne s'insinue jamais dans une famille où se trouvent tout à la fois une fille à pourvoir et un fils à établir; il y a là des droits trop forts et trop inviolables: on ne les traverse point sans faire de l'éclat (et il l'appréhende), sans qu'une pareille entreprise vienne aux oreilles du Prince, à qui il dérobe sa marche, par la crainte qu'il a d'être découvert et de paroître ce qu'il est. Il en veut à la ligne collatérale: on l'attaque plus impunément; il est la terreur des cousins et des cousines, du neveu et de la nièce, le flatteur et l'ami déclaré de tous les oncles qui ont fait fortune; il se donne pour l'héritier légitime de tout vieillard qui meurt riche et sans enfants . . . .

If he finds himself on a good footing with a wealthy man, whom he has been able to take in, whose parasite he is, and from whom he can draw great assistance, he does not cajole his wife, at least he does not make advances nor a declaration to her; he will run away, he will leave his cloak in her hands, if he is not as sure of her as of himself. Still less will he employ the jargon of devotion to flatter her and seduce her; he does not speak it from habit, but from design and according as it is useful to him, and never when it would serve only to make him extremely ridiculous . . . . He has no idea of becoming his sole heir, nor of getting him to give him his entire estate, especially if it is a case of taking it away from a son, the legitimate heir: a devout man is neither avaricious nor violent nor unjust nor even interested: Onuphre is not devout, but he wants to be thought so and, by a perfect, though false, imitation of piety, to take care of his interests secretly; hence he never ventures to confront the direct line and he never insinuates himself into a family where there are both a daughter to be provided for and a son to be set up in the world; such rights are too strong and too inviolable: they cannot be infringed without scandal (and he dreads scandal), without such an attempt coming to the ears of the Prince, from whom he hides his course because he fears to be exposed and to appear as what he is. He has designs on the collateral line; it is more safely to be attacked: he is the terror of cousins male and female, of nephew and niece, the flatterer and declared friend of all uncles who have acquired fortunes; he claims to be the legitimate heir of every old man who dies wealthy and childless . . . .[69]

La Bruyère implies that Molière's hypocrite is "so gross that he leaves the real hypocrites unscathed and for La Bruyère the real hypocrites were everywhere."[70] Obviously, La Bruyère makes a mistake in thinking Molière was creating a "character," as he himself did in the figure of Onuphre, the ideal hypocrite. But that is exactly the point: La Bruyère is dealing with real-life hypocrites, whereas Molière's character is a literary creation. Whereas La Bruyère is concerned with a hypocrite whose every action and mannerism is correct for a hypocrite, Molière is not concerned with presenting the one side of a "character"; Molière was building, I believe, a satiric as well as comic figure, and, in so doing, employed a great number of the standard devices of satire along with those of comedy. Although it remains for the next chapter to reveal the extent to which the themes of Roman satire are reflected in *Tartuffe*, it can be pointed out here that several aspects of Tartuffe or Orgon can be found among the *vitia evitanda* in Theophrastus' *Characters*. In the "character" of the Dissembler (Eirōneias), we find a definition which is generally applicable to Tartuffe:

> Now dissembling would seem, to define it generally, to be an affectation of the worse in word and deed; and the Dissembler will be disposed rather to go up to an enemy and talk with them than to show his hatred; he will praise to his face one he has girded at behind his back; he will commiserate even his adversary's ill fortune in losing his care to him. More, he will forgive his vilifiers, and will laugh in approval of what is said against him ....[71]

In Boorishness (Agroikias) one can observe certain traits of Orgon:

> He distrusts his friends and kinsfolk, but confides matters of great importance to his servants....[72]

Tartuffe may fulfill one aspect of Nastiness (Dyschereias) when he is revealed by Dorine to be the sort of man, "when he has drunken with you, to hiccup in your face."[73] He also may be seen to reveal Petty Pride (Mikrophilotimias), "a vulgar appetite for distinction...."[74] In his adoption of the mask of religion, one can see Pretentiousness (Alazoneias), "a laying claim to advantages a man does not possess ...."[75] Although each of these aspects of the different characters must be loosely applied, they do show a strain of character-writing elements in *Tartuffe*. Tartuffe, however, is not a character, partly because he is, in my belief, a satiric figure. Accordingly, Tartuffe is not presented as that perfect characterization one finds in Theophrastus or even in La Bruyère. He is complex, as we have seen; his complexity is partially a product of the fact that Molière embodies in his character so many vices. If these vices are the same as those attacked by the Roman satirists, and if they are presented in a similar manner, then Molière's creation of *Tartuffe* was probably motivated by a desire to achieve the same satiric effect as had Horace and Juvenal before him. In that case Tartuffe, the satiric type, will be varied in his nature, repetitious in order to make the author's point more clear. The play, moreover, will reveal the satiric emotion according to which the satirist would be happy if he heard the subject of his attack "had, in tears and self-abasement, permanently reformed..."[76] This is the purpose of the satirist, and of the writer of satirical comedy: to reform his victim and any others who will profit from his lessons. A conclusive proof of the satirical intent of Molière is provided by Cléante in the closing scene (V. vii) of *Tartuffe,* when he says:

> Souhaitez bien plutôt que son coeur en ce jour
> Au sein de la vertu fasse un heureux retour,
> Qu'il corrige sa vie en détestant son vice ...(1951-53)

Cléante, as the voice of the satirist, states that he wishes Tartuffe would mend his ways and reform his life. This statement at the end of Molière's play reaffirms all the evidences seen throughout the play, in the *Préface* and *Placets*, that Molière's intention in writing *Tartuffe* was to create a satirical comedy.

---

[1]*Les Luttes de Molière* (Paris, 1925), p. 144.

[2]Michaut, *Ibid.* p. 128. Michaut particularly notes the difficulty Molière had in reducing the somber tone by the use of elements from comedy (p. 120).

[3]*Molière: Homme de Théâtre* (Paris, 1954), p. 32.

[4]H.C. Lancaster, *French Dramatic Literature in the Seventeenth Century* (Baltimore, 1936), II, iii, 623.

[5]Horace was an occasional Epicurean and his works are replete with Stoic homilies, but his general attitude (especially in his *Satires*) is one of Stoicism, J. W. Duff, *Roman Satire* (Hamden, Conn., 1964), pp. 72-75. Likewise, although there are many Stoic elements in the works of Juvenal, he does not seem to have been a Stoic. Highet believes that he was converted to Epicureanism in his later life, and actually had an antipathy for Stoicism, "The Philosophy of Juvenal," *TAPA* LXXX (1949), pp. 254-270.

[6]Lancaster, *Fr. Dram. Lit.*, II, iii, p. 623.

[7]Will G. Moore, *French Classical Literature* (London, 1961), p. 82.

[8]*Molière: A New Criticism* (Oxford, 1949), p. 92.

[9]Brander Matthews, *Molière: His Life and Works* (New York, 1916), p. 154.

[10]W. G. Moore, "Tartuffe and the Comic Principle in Molière," *MLR*, XLIII (1948), 48.

[11]George E. Duckworth, *The Nature of Roman Comedy* (Princeton, 1952), p. 91.

[12]*Ibid.* p. 157.

[13]*Ibid.*, p. 267.

[14]*Ibid.*, p. 407.

[15]*Ibid.*, p. 304.

[16]Moore, "Tartuffe and the Comic Principle in Molière," 49.

[17]*Ibid.*, p. 51.

[18]Molière, in the *Préface* of 1669, states: "J'ai mis tout l'art et tous les soins qu'il m'a été possible pour bien distinguer le personnage de l'Hypocrite d'avec celui du vrai Dévot. J'ai employé pour cela deux actes entiers à préparer la venue de mon scélérat. Il ne tient pas un seul moment l'auditeur en balance . . ."

[19]There is no doubt, however, that played by *farceurs*, this scene could become very amusing. Stage presentation allows great latitude in interpretation. Imagine the difference in Tartuffe being played by Basil Rathbone and Peter Ustinov and the difference between the two possibilities can be seen. It should be further noted at this point that an interpretation based on careful reading of *Tartuffe* will differ considerably from one based on a theatrical experience. This interpretation is of the former category and, although Molière was a man of the theater and his plays were not mere closet dramas, but were actually intended for production, a reader's interpretation finds justification in the history of *Tartuffe*. A review of the years between the ban on the original *Tartuffe* in 1664 and the removal of the interdiction in 1669 reveals that the play was privately read and distributed as well as performed. Lancaster, II, iii, 631-632.

[20]Paul Stapfer, *Molière et Shakespeare*, 5th ed. (Paris, 1905), pp. 212-213.

[21]Matthews, *Molière*, pp. 152-153.

[22]Jacques Guicharnaud, "Tartuffe," *Molière: une aventure théâtrale* (Paris, 1963), p. 151.

[23]Lancaster, *Fr. Dram. Lit.*, II, iii, 629.

[24]Gilbert Highet was selected as the basis of this part of the study because his book, *Anatomy of Satire*, (Princeton, 1962), while based in classical satire, is concerned with the traditions of satire. Since he does not analyze *Tartuffe* or any other play, an application of Highet's standards to Molière's play should be indicative of its character.

[25]Gilbert Highet, *Anatomy of Satire*, p. 15.

[26]The quarrel over the presentation of *Tartuffe* and its previous version is discussed in Michaut, *Luttes*, pp. 55ff.

[27]Highet, *Anatomy of Satire*, p. 16.

[28]*Ibid.*, p. 18.

[29]Lancaster, *Fr. Dram. Lit.*, II, iii, 630.

[30]Highet, *Anatomy of Satire*, p. 18.

[31]*Ibid.*, pp. 18-20.

[32]*Ibid.*, pp. 208-210.

[33]*Ibid.*, p. 208.

[34]Highet, *Juvenal the Satirist* (New York, 1954), p. 138; *Anatomy of Satire*, pp. 16-18.

[35]Highet, *Anatomy of Satire*, p. 16.

[36]J. Wight Duff, *Roman Satire* (Hamden, Connecticut, 1964), pp. 6-7.

[37]*Cours de littérature* (Paris, 1893), VI, 22.

[38]Highet, *Anatomy of Satire*, pp. 206-207.

[39]Lancaster, *French Dramatic Lit.*, II, iii, 623.

[40]Highet, *Anatomy of Satire*, p. 3.

[41]Highet, *Anatomy of Satire*, p. 197, notes that "to produce the full effect of satire on the stage, exaggeration is usually needed."

[42]Highet, *Anatomy of Satire*, p. 157.

[43]Jacques Guicharnaud, ed., *Le Tartuffe and Le Médecin malgré lui* (New York, 1962), p. 12.

[44]Arthur Tilley, *Molière* (Cambridge at the University Press, 1921), p. 108.

[45]Highet, *Anatomy of Satire*, pp. 196-197.

[46]This important subject, the effect of satire, will be discussed more fully below.

[47]Eugene H. Falk, "Molière, the Indignant Satirist; 'Le Bourgeois gentilhomme,'" *TDR*, I (1956), 75.

[48]Duff, *Roman Satire*, pp. 7-8.

⁴⁹Highet, *Anatomy of Satire*, p. 157.
⁵⁰Highet, *Anatomy of Satire*, p. 190.
⁵¹Bray, *Molière*, p. 352.
⁵²*Philosophischer Nachlass Tragödie und Komödie*, cited by Burt Edward Young, ed., *Le Tartuffe; ou l'Imposteur*, by Molière (New York, 1918), xxxi.
⁵³*Vorlesungen über die Aesthetik*, 1838 ed., III, ch. iii, 577. Referred to by Young, xxxi.
⁵⁴Highet, *Anatomy of Satire*, p.21.
⁵⁵Stapfer, *Molière et Shakespeare*, p. 214.
⁵⁶*Anatomy of Satire*, p. 197.
⁵⁷*Ibid.*, p. 156.
⁵⁸Jacques Arnavon, *Morale de Molière* (Paris, 1945), p. 14.
⁵⁹Chapman, *The Spirit of Molière*, p. 212.
⁶⁰Highet, *Anatomy of Satire*, p. 13.
⁶¹"The Muse of Satire," *Yale Review*, XLI (1951), 86-90.
⁶²Mack, "The Music of Satire," 86.
⁶³*Ibid.*, pp. 88-90. Mack's article, which deals specifically with the satire of Pope, also presents two other personae, the ingenu, and the hero or public defender.
⁶⁴Michaut, *Luttes*, p. 117.
⁶⁵*Ibid.*, p. 116.
⁶⁶See Bray, *Molière: Homme de Théâtre*, p. 31. Guicharnaud, *Molière: une aventure théâtrale*, p. 92.
⁶⁷Guicharnaud, *Ibid.*, p. 36.
⁶⁸Moore, *Molière*, pp. 85-86.
⁶⁹Erich Auerbach, "The Faux Dévot," in *Mimesis: The Representation of Reality in Western Literature*, tr. Willard Trask (Garden City, New York, 1957), pp. 316-317.
⁷⁰Gossman, *Men and Masks: A Study of Molière* (Baltimore, 1963), p. 123.
⁷¹Theophrastus, *Characters*, ed. and tr. J. M. Edmonds, Loeb Classical Library (New York, 1929), p. 41.
⁷²*Ibid.*, p. 49.
⁷³*Ibid.*, p. 89.
⁷⁴*Ibid.*, p. 93.
⁷⁵*Ibid.*, p. 99.
⁷⁶Highet, *Anatomy of Satire*, p. 155.

III

MOLIÈRE'S *TARTUFFE*: AN INTERPRETATION BASED ON SIGNIFICANT PARALLELS WITH THE TRADITIONS OF ROMAN SATIRIC LITERATURE

It has been shown in the preceding chapters that in his youth Molière was provided an exacting education in the classical Latin authors, and that the thrust of that education was towards a moral knowledge of oneself and one's neighbor. It also has been shown that later in his life Molière was subject to influences toward philosophical considerations, in the persons of Chapelle and Bernier, and toward classical literature and satire in particular, in the person of Boileau. It is further known that Molière possessed volumes of Horace, Juvenal and Seneca at the time of his death, so that the supposition that he actually reread these authors during the time he was writing *Tartuffe* is not unlikely.

This chapter will study the extent to which Molière's *Tartuffe* reflects the classical traditions found especially in satire. This will be achieved primarily by a study of the comic protagonist Tartuffe, his actions and relationships with the other characters of the play, the most important of whom is Orgon. The elements of Tartuffe's character will be considered to see if they were treated by the satirists, who worked within themes traditional to much of classical literature.

My study of *Tartuffe* has shown that there are two satiric aspects of the play: the ethical, as seen in the treatment of the themes of virtue — expressed in terms of *le juste milieu* and *bon sens* — and evil; and the social, as manifested in the comedy of manners, representing certain type characters.[1] The ethical and social satire in *Tartuffe* are blent into an integral whole. It is possible, however, to study them as separate elements, and this will be the method I shall use. The ethical satire, with its emphasis on *bon sens* and *le juste milieu*, will be considered to see to what extent it is a reflection of the classical philosophic ideals of *sophrosyne* and *sapientia*, especially as manifested in the *sapiens* (wise man), who avoids the *vitia* (sins) of *luxury, ambition, avarice, lust*, and *superstition*, which are the main antitheses to moderation as considered in classical literature.[2] The first part of this chapter will study the themes of *sophrosyne* and *sapientia* as reflected in *Tartuffe*, centering on the five classical vices which are in direct opposition to moderation. After an introductory statement on the theme of *sophrosyne* and its employment by classical writers, I shall proceed to analyze *Tartuffe*, chronologically as much as possible, on the basis of the classical traditions, pointing out those elements of Molière's play which are reflections of the themes and traditions of Roman satire especially. The second part of this chapter will consider those social types in Roman satire who are reflected in *Tartuffe*. This consideration will be divided into three subsections: the Hypocrite; Parasite, Client, and Friend; and a study of one of the supreme hypocrites of classical times, Aelius Sejanus, whose career will be examined in relationship to that of Tartuffe in the section entitled "Sejanus and the Corruption of Political Power."

### *Sophrosyne and Sapientia*

The main philosophies of the Roman world, Stoicism, Epicureanism, and Cynicism, all sought to ease "the thousand natural shocks that flesh is heir to . . ." Their adherents believed that this could be achieved by careful discipline of the passions and the realization that wealth, power, and sensual pleasures are unnecessary for the virtuous man. Virtue can be attained through *sophrosyne, mens sana*, that is, soundness of mind.[3] The theme of *sophrosyne* runs throughout Greek and Latin literature. It is found in the earliest poets, for instance in Hesiod, where it takes on one of the aspects which it will have in later times: the ideal of *Mêdèn 'ágan* ("Nothing in excess").[4] It continued from the time of Hesiod, being influenced by the Delphic oracle, who preached restraint, so that it became connected with the religion as well as literature.[5] *Sophrosyne* was closely connected with the ideals of the Cynic-Stoic school of philosophy. Even Socrates was an adherent of *sophrosyne*, for he was proud of his excellence in one of its divisions, consistency, in that his assertions were always the same.[6]

It was only natural that the Romans, several centuries after the inception of the ideal of *sophrosyne* in the Greek world, should adopt it as one of their ideals as well. The *mos maiorum* of the Romans expressed "respect for the characteristics generally considered to be the basis of Rome's rise to greatness: *pudicitia, abstinentia*, and *frugalitas*. All, however, are the result of one ideal — *modestia*, self-restraint, which is a direct equation to *sophrosyne*."[7] Although expressions of *sophrosyne* are found earlier, as in Ennius,[8] the first Roman literature to reveal strong influences of this Greek ideal was the comedy of Plautus and Terence.[9] These two authors set a pattern that would be followed in Roman literature particularly by the satirists: they focused on the "negative aspects of *sophrosyne*, the repression of appetites and desires."[10]

Historians, too, subscribed to the ideal of *sophrosyne*. Livy, in his condemnation of such *vitia* as *amor, cupido, avaritia*, and *superbia*, is attacking those vices which are opposed to *sophrosyne*. His solutions to these vices are traditional: *moderatio* and *temperantia*. Tacitus, too, employs the commonplaces of *sophrosyne* in his histories, attacking especially *superbia* and *libido*,[11] in an attempt to save virtue from oblivion.[12]

The emphasis in Molière's studies of Roman literature was, as has been noted in a preceding chapter, on the moral content. Thus, one should keep the ideals of *Nosce teipsum* and *Vince teipsum* in mind when considering that the classical literature which was influenced by the concept of *sophrosyne* offered many examples especially of the antitheses to self-control and moderation.[13]

Molière had studied the comedies of Plautus and Terence as well as the histories of Livy and Tacitus.[14] He had also studied the satires of Horace and Juvenal and the philosophic works of Seneca. It is impossible to say absolutely what in all this literature particularly caught his attention. Doubtless part of what caught Molière's attention, however, was the concept of *sophrosyne*: a tradition of restraint and respect for the social bond which represses undue independence, and which was part of the classical inheritance received by his fatherland.[15] It may have been this identification process, which would doubtless have been promoted by Molière's relationship with Boileau, which caused Molière to study diligently the theme of *sophrosyne*, turning in his studies once again to satire, as has been suggested on the basis of Molière's possession of copies of Horace and Juvenal at his death.

The philosophic influences on satire will not be studied here in particular, but it is necessary to comment briefly on the relationships of one school of philosophy to satire.[16]

> The Stoicism of the satire was of course the modified Roman Stoicism of Panaetius with its stress on the principle of moderation.[17] *Virtus* was the goal held up by the satirist as by the more legitimate philosopher, but both had a tendency to dwell on the *vitia* (vices) which must be removed or avoided in the attainment of virtue ... As exemplified by Horace, Satire in its philosophic function presented virtue as a general goal and moderation as its greatest element and it held up to scorn the vices which hindered moral progress, stressing particularly *luxury, ambition, avarice, superstition* and *lust*.[18]

According to this statement, the ideal proposed by the satiric poets was the attainment of virtue by the avoidance of vices. Horace and Juvenal normally accomplished their task by showing the negative side, the *vitia*; there is, however, no lack of positive statements through which one may be guided on the road to *virtus* and the attainment of the rank of *sapiens*, philosopher or wise man.

Horace's philosophy of life has *sophrosyne* as its ideal, utilizing the term *aurea mediocritas* to express the Greek words meaning moderation.[19] Horace proposes that life's contentment should be based on very little; that, as death is the common end of all men, there is no reason to indulge one's extravagant desires, especially political ambition and desire for profit.[20] Rather the virtuous man, knowing how to live, will *nil admirari* (be undisturbed in spirit) by all which does not help him to be content. "When a man's conduct misses or exceeds the appropriate mean, he fails to achieve happiness and becomes to that extent *miser*. He may be unaware of this himself; he may not feel unhappy. But the fact that others view him with dislike or contempt is an index of his true condition."[21]

Although he never makes a formal statement or offers a credo which synthesizes it, Molière's philosophy of life is implicit in his works. It has been interpreted as saying: "Reason is a natural guide, and the prime lesson is the error that besets all excesses; safety as well as wisdom lies in the golden mean."[22] This philosophy of life finds its expression throughout *Tartuffe*, most notably in the following words of Cléante, who, it will be remembered, may be considered the voice of the satirist:

> Les hommes la plupart sont étrangement faits!
> Dans la juste nature on ne les voit jamais;
> La raison a pour eux des bornes trop petites;
> En chaque caractère ils passent ses limites;
> Et la plus noble chose, ils la gâtent souvent
> Pour la vouloir outrer et pousser trop avant. (339-344)

It is easy to see in this philosophic statement the influence of the classical traditions, with their emphasis on nature, virtue and *sophrosyne*. It remains for us to see just how strong this influence was, just what elements of the classical tradition are presented in Molière's *Tartuffe* and how Molière's play reflects the classical material.

Molière, establishing his characterization of Tartuffe on themes which are antithetical to the ideal of *sophrosyne*, depicts his protagonist not as a man of virtue, but as a *faux dévot*, not as a man trying to attain virtue by avoiding vice, but as a hypocrite trying to attain vice by pretending virtue. Molière shows this in exactly the way that Horace and Juvenal had before him: by showing the negative side, the *vitia*; and the vices he employs are precisely those the Roman satirists had stressed: *luxury; ambition; avarice; superstition; and lust*.[23]

If Molière based his characterization of Tartuffe on the works of the satirists, the "truths" concerning the characters in Horace or Juvenal should be applicable to Tartuffe as well. So it is with the statement that the man who fails in virtue will be viewed with dislike or contempt by others. Evidence of

Molière's knowledge of this principle is provided by the opening act of *Tartuffe*.

As *Tartuffe* begins, one is projected into the midst of the household of Orgon, and is immediately aware of a mild argument, for Mme. Pernelle is berating the various members of her son's family for failing to do their duties, according to her expectations. A comparative glance at the action and reactions of the members of Orgon's family and at those of Mme. Pernelle makes the spectator aware that it is not Mme. Pernelle, in spite of her criticisms, but the wife and children of Orgon, who, depicted as pleasant, likeable and polite, represent the norm of the play — a standard of behavior which, if not ideal, is at least excellent in relation to the alternative, the world of Tartuffe-Orgon, a world which must be immediately suspect by the very fact that so common a suspicion as that expressed concerning the character of Tartuffe must have some basis.

With this norm, the family, Mme. Pernelle is in conflict, and, thus, in error. When she accuses the members of the family of putting the familial order in danger, it is, on the contrary, she herself who is doing so. When she offers her opinion of Tartuffe, in the first words we hear of him, she says, "C'est un homme de bien." This statement is promptly refuted by the family (including the servant Dorine, who represents one aspect of the family). One after another they name Tartuffe for what he is: arrogant, bigoted, a usurper, a Puritanical zealot, and a lying cheat. Within this initial conflict we have the foreshadowing of the ultimate danger to the family, for, although Mme. Pernelle is a threat to familial order and the reign of "bon sens," she is only a pawn in the ranks of the master — Tartuffe.

The problem of familial order, however, goes much deeper than the threat posed by Tartuffe. It is concerned with the family itself, and particularly the head of the household, Orgon, who, under the influence of Tartuffe, has come to stand against the best interests of the family as a whole. Thus a moral conflict arises when the family, to save itself, must unite to oppose the will of Orgon. But always in the background of this struggle there is the figure of Tartuffe. As the titular hero of the piece, it is he who provides the ultimate drama that grows from his struggle against the representatives of the normal order. We see, moreover, that the function of the quarrel between Mme. Pernelle and the family, the conversations between Cléante and Dorine, between Orgon and Dorine, and between Dorine and Mariane have worked toward one common end: keeping the absent Tartuffe before the audience in spirit while building up the case against him as a constant menace to the family. Tartuffe and Orgon are depicted as opponents against the established order of the family. But the suggestion is stronger, for, being against the family, they are also against "bon sens." Being against "bon sens,"

Tartuffe and Orgon are also fools. To what extent, however, we must ask, do they reflect the fools of classical literature?

Any study of the concept of the "fool" in classical literature must consider especially a theme inextricably connected in classical literature and philosophy with that of *sophrosyne — sapientia*, wisdom. Seneca, one of the great Stoic minds and a writer of Menippean satire, states that human happiness is attainable only through wisdom and virtue. Wisdom is a right understanding, a faculty of discerning good from evil, what is to be chosen and what rejected. It informs us in all the duties of life, piety to our parents, faith to our friends, charity to the miserable, judgment in counsel.[24] This statement provides an immediate understanding of the characters of both Tartuffe and Orgon: they may each be considered as a *demens* (fool) in that they have not attained the level of *sapiens* (wise man or philosopher), and thus virtue. The quotation seems immediately more applicable to Orgon, who does not have the faculty of discerning good from evil, what is to be chosen and what rejected. This is Orgon's problem in the play. It is also Tartuffe's, as will be shown.

The *sapiens* tried to live according to nature and not torment the body, or with exclamations against that which is good and clean, to delight in meanness, or to use an offensive diet. Wisdom preaches temperance, not mortification.[25] Tartuffe is at odds with wisdom. Not only does he openly pretend to mortify his body, but he preaches an asceticism surpassing temperance, which he himself does not follow, but which he tries to impose upon the members of Orgon's family. The fact that Tartuffe establishes a double standard, one for himself and one for the members of the family, is further indication of the status he has as a *demens*, and, thus, of his absence of virtue. The *sapiens* is a man who has gotten the habit of virtue, and whose actions are all equal to one another.[26] There is no room for ambivalence. His counsel and his actions will be congruous.[27]

The *sapiens* is a man who is capable of discerning the good from the bad, and the real from the false. This is one of the important indications of the nature of Orgon, for we find that very early in *Tartuffe* there is presented the theme of values, especially in the juxtaposition of the two values of appearance and reality. From the first scene, wherein Dorine and Cléante in particular try to "rester fidèles à une certaine définition de la vérité et de la réalité,"[28] this theme and its conflicts continue to the end of the play. It is particularly exhibited in Orgon, who continually fails to perceive the reality of those situations in which Tartuffe is involved, accepting the appearances as reality, and proving his *dementia*.

The relationship of Orgon and Tartuffe also reflects the concepts of *sophrosyne* and *sapientia*, for Orgon's "love" for Tartuffe grows out of his *mistaken* appreciation of the *excessive* religious fervor of Tartuffe. The nature of their relationship, however, is very complex, and therefore presents a number of sides that must be considered. One question that immediately arises concerning their relation is: Why does it exist? It seems that Tartuffe has everything to gain by involving himself with Orgon. But what does Orgon gain? Why does he adopt Tartuffe into his household? The answers to these questions, which will be considered more fully later, are provided partially by an understanding of Orgon's character. It has been noted that in the character of Orgon there is a "confusion entre le sublime et l'hyperbole. Il confond la grandiloquence du comportement de Tartuffe avec l'intensité d'un vrai dévot...."[29] To make an equation on the highest level, Orgon is confused as to the nature of God, preferring mistakenly "le grand Dieu" to "le bon Dieu." This attraction to the hyperbolic has also been explained as follows: "Orgon ... est un de ces hommes chez lesquels le défaut de force et d'intelligence se traduit par des exagérations perpétuelles, par un manque complet de mesure; ils sont toujours dans les extrêmes."[30]

The concept of excess, which is antithetical to that of *sophrosyne*, is basic to the character of Orgon. A tendency toward excess is seen in Orgon's description of his first encounter with Tartuffe (I, iv). He mentions a series of devotions all notable for one thing: their spectacular elements. Accordingly, it is interesting to observe that it is the spectacular religious behavior of Tartuffe which entices Orgon. There must have been many men available to Orgon who were deeply religious. Orgon did not want to adopt any of these. He wanted rather someone with a flair for the spectacular. Why so? Because deep within Orgon himself there was a desire to be recognized, to achieve a self-aggrandizement, even if achieved on a secondary level through his sponsorship of one whose works were good, and thus reflected well upon him as sponsor.[31] With this point in mind, we see that Orgon, although he may have been sincerely devout in his own peculiar way, is at his most basic level a selfish man. His actions, even when supposedly directed toward the benefit of others, are self-concerned.

Asceticism on the part of Orgon is the natural result of the teachings of Tartuffe, who has similarly renounced, at least for Orgon's ears, the joys of this world in the most sanctimonious fashion, just as, upon taking the stage, he will say: "Couvrez ce sein que je ne saurois voir ..." (860) Orgon makes a mistake in choosing a life of asceticism. His failing is that he does not see that he does not have the right to make such a choice. He has obligations which require him to act in this world, not contemplate the next. Orgon repeatedly fails to take everything into consideration. He acts on the basis of his religion and the goals which it must be assumed Tartuffe has established for him, so that he may easily say, without giving a thought beyond himself:

> Qui suit bien ses leçons goûte une paix profonde,
> Et comme du fumier regarde tout le monde.
> Oui, je deviens tout autre avec son entretien;
> Il m'enseigne à n'avoir affection pour rien,
> De toutes amitiés il détache mon âme;
> Et je verrois mourir frère, enfants, mère et femme,
> Que je m'en soucierois autant que cela. (273-279)

Assuredly this statement betrays a warped sense of values. But that sense of values is determined by a judgment which fails precisely because it does not take everything into consideration. Orgon continues to act as a *demens*; he is not capable at this time of rising to the level of *sapiens*.

The question of the religiosity of Orgon has often been raised. This aspect of Orgon's character is important, for, besides the immediate comic effect that Molière achieves by having Orgon claim, on the one hand, to be under the influence of a lofty religious ideal (which should include love of his fellowman) and, on the other hand, showing that Orgon's "lofty religious ideal" is carrying him to ridiculous and even frightening measures toward his fellowmen, especially those with whom he is closely tied, Molière has also used Orgon's religion as one of the extremes, indeed the most despicable, which constitute his character. Religion, then, as presented in the figure of Orgon, reveals once more Molière's repeated use of the theme of moderation in all things. It also can be seen as a comment on the importance of *bon sens*, or *sapientia*. This can be revealed by further consideration of the Orgon-Tartuffe relationship.

Orgon was not inspired with his religious fervor by Tartuffe. He did, after all, go daily to church, where he first met Tartuffe. Therefore, the problem is not ultimately one of religion, for, although Tartuffe may have whetted Orgon's passion for religion, he did not initiate that feeling. Tartuffe, then, merely took advantage of a basic flaw which he saw in the character of Orgon — not of his religiosity per se. That Tartuffe saw such a quality in Orgon is emphasized by Dorine's words: "Lui, qui connôit sa dupe ..." (199) The side of Orgon's character which Tartuffe recognized as fallible, especially under the influence of his devices, has been described by Michaut, who remarks that "on n'a pas le droit enfin de voir en Orgon le 'dévot en soi'; il est dévot, mais il est borné, à la fois faible et entêté; c'est comme borné, faible et entêté qu'il est ridicule, non comme dévot."[32] It is through this mental failure that "in Tartuffe [Orgon] sees a choice possession, one that will undoubtedly enhance his prestige in this world and his chances in the next."[33]

Orgon makes a mistake in accepting Tartuffe as an ideal. But he also goes farther, for he puts such faith in the ideal which Tartuffe represents for him that, should Tartuffe's image be proved false, Orgon's whole world will fall into ruin, since that world now rests on a foundation of Tartuffe. Orgon sits at the feet of Tartuffe, as before a great and wise philosopher. But it is of no importance that Tartuffe is a fake, that his words are not the precepts of a wise man dedicated to virtue. Orgon is not ultimately concerned with the attainment of wisdom, and, thus, a good Christian life. Rather, he resembles Seneca's "squatters," who "come to hear and not to learn"; such men do not seek to rid themselves of their vices or "to receive a rule of life . . . ."[34] He has no real desire to become a good Christian, much less a *sapiens*.

Orgon, although he is a fool, is not necessarily evil in himself. It is his misdirection of will, his desire for evil under the aspect of good insofar as he thinks it good,[35] which makes Orgon evil. He is evil indirectly, to the extent that his desires are directed toward evil things — Tartuffe, in particular. Tartuffe brings about destructive effects in Orgon's household.

Another classical concept associated with that of *sophrosyne* and *sapientia* is the Stoic idea of *morbi mentis*, diseases of the mind, which can throw further light on the characters of Orgon and Tartuffe. It has been shown that both men are *dementes* because they are not *sapientes*. But why are they not *sapientes*? Because Molière endows them with "hardened and chronic vices, such as greed and ambition," which are to be viewed, according to classical tradition, as diseases of the mind.[36] Such a disease is a "perversion of judgment"; the result is that one strives after things which are undesirable. Thus Molière has Tartuffe seek those things which have little or no value — position, power, wealth, and sexual love. Similarly, he has Orgon, in his quests for inactivity, for religion with the purpose of self-aggrandizement, act from a perverted sense of judgment. Orgon's attitude toward religion, in fact, in its unquestioning acceptance of Tartuffe as a religious man, approaches superstition, which, according to Horace,[37] as well as to Lucretius before him, is one of the *morbi mentis*.[38]

The concept of the man of diseased mind, of perverted judgment, runs throughout the satires of Horace and Juvenal. One of the best examples is Horace's *corruptus iudex*.[39] The idea of judgment *(iudex)* destroyed or perverted by corruption (corruptus) so that the mind is misled by appearances is a repeated theme in this satire (II. 2). The presentation is different from that in *Tartuffe* in that it is a gourmet who is said to be deceived by meaningless fancies, but the theme is the same: the truly wise man *(sapiens)* sees the truth even through appearances. This is precisely the point that Molière makes: no matter how Tartuffe makes himself up, if Orgon were not a *corruptus iudex*, he would see Tartuffe for what he is.[40] But Orgon is *corruptus*, and his judgment always chooses the unwise path. Such a case of unwise choice is Orgon's decision to put Elmire into the care (hands) of Tartuffe. Horace had made a similar suggestion, but went even farther, proposing that the husband willingly hand over his wife to the lusts of another man. This statement is directed to a fool, whose judgment is so perverted that he will probably consider carrying out the suggestion. This occurs in *Satires* II. 5. 75-76, in which Ulysses is depicted as not only a fool, but of a special category which we shall consider in a moment, the *captator*. A comparison with Ulysses as depicted by Horace intensifies the impression we have of Orgon. Obviously such a suggestion has been planted in the mind of Orgon, who is fool enough to accept it. There is perhaps another interpretation of Orgon's surrendering his wife into Tartuffe's hands. The key is in a statement by Juvenal: *vidua est, locuples quae nupsit avaro* (VI. 141). The implication is that the husband will not care what his wife does as long as his primary desires are fulfilled. Orgon, with Tartuffe in the house, is so free of those responsibilities he finds onerous that he does not even consider the result of any decision to which he may come. His primary desires are being satisfied; let the rest of the world go its way.

It is man's desires which lead him astray. The *demens* is characterized quite easily by that which he does and does not desire. In his Tenth Satire Juvenal says that most men misdirect their wishes (1-53); this mistaken sense of direction is of course one of the symptoms of the Stoic concept of *dementia*.[41] In this state of incorrect reasoning, man usually directs his desires toward foolish things: wealth (X. 12-27) and social distinction (X. 36-46). Again Orgon and Tartuffe fit the pattern exactly. Tartuffe's actions are directed by his desire for the wealth of Orgon, Orgon's by that for the distinction he will gain through association with a spectacularly holy man. Juvenal has provided the solution to the problem of what men should wish for: only health and virtue, leaving the rest to the gods (X. 346-366).

Seneca has also provided an answer to this problem, saying:

> Let us address Jupiter, the pilot of this world-mass, as did our great Cleanthes in these most eloquent lines — lines which I shall allow myself to render in Latin, after the example of the eloquent Cicero. If you like them, make the most of them; if they displease you, you will understand that I have simply been following the practices of Cicero:
>
> Lead me, O Master of the lofty heavens,
> My Father, whithersoever thou shall wish.
> I shall not falter, but obey with speed.
> And though I would not, I shall go, and suffer,
> In sin and sorrow what I might have done
> In noble virtue, Aye, the willing soul
> Fate leads, but the unwilling drags along.[42]

Seneca has provided another, and quite enlightening, view of this question of direction of will. He states that "there are certain goods which reason regards as primary . . . ; these are . . . good children, and the welfare of one's country."[43] Orgon lacks this kind of reason. At no time does he show any interest in the goodness of his children. If one accepts the household of Orgon as a microcosm, it may further be seen that he fails in reason throughout the play, for he puts Tartuffe in a position to disrupt the normal order of the family. The order of the family can be compared to the "welfare of one's country." The household is the country which Orgon should rule. But Orgon does not have a proper sense of values. Nor does Tartuffe. They each repeatedly fail to follow the proper course of action, as prescribed by Stoic doctrine.[44]

We have seen that virtue is the product of *sophrosyne* and *sapientia*. In Horace there is found the idea that evidence of a man's virtue is provided by the greatness of his soul. One important proof of magnanimity is that such a man is happy and indifferent to externals. The following passage from Horace is important to our understanding of Orgon.

> The truly good and wise man will have courage to say: "Pentheus, lord of Thebes, what shame will you compel me to stand and suffer?"
>
> "I will take away your goods."
>
> "You mean my cattle, my substance, couches, plate? You may take them."
>
> "I will keep you in handcuffs and fetters, under a cruel jailer."
>
> "God himself, the moment I choose, will set me free." This, I take it, is his meaning: "I will die." Death is the line that marks the end of all.[45]

Although Tartuffe is motivated in his every action by a concern for externals, the better indication of the validity of the preceding quotation is the case of Orgon. For the first four acts of *Tartuffe*, Orgon has been concerned with the spiritual rather than the ephemeral. Suddenly, when he has been deprived of his worldly goods, it becomes obvious how important these "externals" are to him. Although this aspect of Orgon's character will be discussed more fully below, one fact may be ascertained at this time: if ever he was a brave soldier in the service of the king, those days are past as Orgon shows when he reacts in craven fashion. Orgon proves himself a negative model of magnanimity by his actions in Act V.

Act III provides us unremitting proof of Orgon's *dementia*, as revealed in a succession of scenes wherein he fails to look with due consideration at the words and deeds of Tartuffe. It is thus through Tartuffe that Orgon is revealed. We shall look at scenes iv through vii to appreciate this. Caught in the act of seduction by Damis (III, iv), and denounced to Orgon (III, v),

Tartuffe, true to his character, has recourse to a tried and proven stratagem, self-flagellation (III, vi). Whereas in the past he has supposedly tormented himself with hairshirts and scourges, with self-accusations for having killed a gnat in a moment of passion, now he readily scourges himself with words of rebuke and self-incrimination for a sin of which he is truly guilty. Tartuffe has the utmost confidence in Orgon's blindness to his real nature. This confidence is well-placed. Orgon sees only the true humility of the Christian — a man so pure that he refuses to call another man, even one who lies, a prevaricator or calumniator. Tartuffe is elevated in the eyes of Orgon. He is now a little nearer God himself. This scene is interesting as a further proof of Orgon's inability to tell the true from the false, of his *dementia*. Not only does Tartuffe escape punishment through the trick of telling the truth, but he even tells Orgon one truth which is the key to the whole of his (Tartuffe's) success, and which, if it were accepted as true, would immediately end Orgon's usefulness to Tartuffe: "Non, non: vous vous laissez tromper à l'apparence ..." (1097) Tartuffe, however, has not made a mistake. He knows his man *(connôit sa dupe)*. Almost as proof of Tartuffe's confidence in him, Orgon immediately makes charges against his family which would far better be made against Tartuffe: he calls Damis a "traitor" (1088); and he accuses his family of acting out of "pride" (1126). This is particularly ironic in view not only of what has gone just before, but also of what will immediately follow, for Orgon is doomed to lose possession of his house to Tartuffe just as he has lost (voluntarily) his household.

The status of Orgon as *demens* is further revealed by scene vii, wherein Orgon shows a side of himself which we have long suspected, but without any real evidence to prove the validity of our suspicion. Orgon's mind and emotions are those of a child, with whom the knowing parent easily achieves his end by means of negative psychology. Tartuffe says "I'm leaving" for one reason only: he knows Orgon will beg him to stay. His psychology works. Scene vii is also very interesting in that it is the only scene in which no member of that faction of Orgon's family that represents the normal, rational order is present. It is not a surprise, then, that in this scene Orgon makes one of his most disastrous decisions. This occurs when Orgon, freed from all rational advice, climaxes the banishment of Damis by adopting Tartuffe as his sole heir. The supreme result of the corruption which Tartuffe has effected (perhaps only as a catalyst) is Orgon's gift of all his worldly goods to the hypocrite.

> Et je vais de ce pas, en fort bonne manière
> Vous faire de mon bien donation entière. (117-1178)

Absolute possession of all Orgon's properties now rests with Tartuffe. He reigns supreme as all rightful opposition has been driven into the background. One should note that to this point all that Tartuffe has gained has been freely given, although doubtless time and effort were employed in Tartuffe's applications of his machinations to persuade Orgon of the wisdom and justice of just these or similar acts.

Tartuffe has taken his place in the house of Orgon, where, in the action taking place before the curtain rises, he has successfully thrown the order of the household into confusion by the tyrannical criticism he makes of the way of life which has prevailed before his intrusion. Against an established and effective order he represents a constant threat. This threat is allowed, moreover, to go unchecked by Orgon, who is so demented that he either cannot or will not see Tartuffe for what he is. This continues to be so as Tartuffe brings his threats to bear on one member of the household after another until the condition of Orgon's family has been thrown into disorder. First, Mariane is affected, then Damis, then the rest of the family, as they are ousted from their own home. All that proceeds does so for one reason: Orgon is so great a fool as to allow it to happen (and Tartuffe is clever enough to take advantage of the opportunity).

Molière employed the variations of *sophrosyne*, consistency and self-control, to clarify the image he was presenting to his seventeenth-century French audience. In his *Préface* of 1669, Molière said that the "scélérat" would be identified by certain distinguishable "marcs" that he had given him. Among those "marcs" are certainly Tartuffe's incontinence and inconsistency. These will need to be examined to determine exactly what elements of the classical tradition are reflected in Molière's *Tartuffe*.

In the first two acts of *Tartuffe* one is not only made aware of certain questionable aspects of Tartuffe's behavior and outward appearance, but learns to share the same sense of mistrust and apprehension which affects the family. This is achieved through a series of allusions to Tartuffe's actions and appearance, which are incongruous with his censorious words. It is revealed that Tartuffe had but recently come from the provinces (56ff.), as a shoeless and penniless vagabond (63-64), and, upon entering the house of Orgon, had immediately begun to usurp Orgon's absolute authority over the family (45-46). Among the most revealing statements about the character of Tartuffe is Dorine's insinuation of a possible interest on his part, on a less than heavenly level, in Elmire. Dorine suggests that Tartuffe's actions in prohibiting Elmire from entertaining callers is the product of jealousy (84), which is, of course, a passion antithetical to *sophrosyne*.

Before the entrance onstage of Tartuffe, one is further informed of several significant facts about his appearance and deportment. Dorine informs us that Tartuffe eats as much as six men (192); and that he belches at the table (194). It becomes more and more obvious that he is a highly intemperate man. The fact that this side of his nature is not a recent development is emphasized by his physical appearance. He is "gros et gras" (234); and "il a l'oreille rouge et le teint bien fleuri" (647). These physical aspects of Tartuffe, combined with his deportment, serve a special function, besides the immediate one of the comic: they point out the contradiction which exists in the very nature of Tartuffe between his appearance (the devout ascetic) and his real self (an intemperate parasite and hypocrite). Nor does Tartuffe fail to confirm the image of inconsistency and incontinence which has been established for him. The minute he takes the stage, Tartuffe, continuing to play his pious role, observes the low-cut neckline of Dorine's dress and remarks:

> Couvrez ce sein que je ne saurois voir:
> Par de pareils objets les âmes sont blessées,
> Et cela fait venir de coupables pensées. (860-862)

It is once again obvious that Tartuffe is very much aware of worldly things.

One aspect of Tartuffe's character which is very important to an understanding of his actions is his attitude toward food and drink. The comments of Dorine show that his intemperance is particularly manifest at mealtime. Tartuffe is, in fact, a glutton. He is a glutton for a very good reason: Molière adds this quality to Tartuffe's character in order to reenforce his argument against any form of excess contrary to the ideal of *sophrosyne*. To appreciate Molière's depiction of this aspect of Tartuffe's character, it will be necessary to consider the satiric employment of the theme of gluttony.

Gluttony, excess in food and drink, is naturally treated by many of the classical writers, including the comic as well as the satiric authors. It is most notably present in satiric examples of the *cena*, which will be treated later in this chapter. It is frequently a topic of discussion in Stoic authors, as in the following precept of Seneca, who advises men to "indulge the body only so far as is needful for good health. The body should be treated more rigorously, that it may not be disobedient to the mind. Eat merely to relieve your hunger; drink merely to quench your thirst . . ."[46] Among the satirists it is Horace who most consistently attacks gluttony.[47] Horace's best exposition of the theme is the Second Satire of Book Two. There he applies his doctrine of the mean, a variation on *sophrosyne*, to daily life, particularly eating and drinking. Horace informs the reader that the man who partakes of food to excess finds no real pleasure or lasting satisfaction therein (20-22); that man endangers his health through his variety of dishes,[48] dragging the mind down to a similar state of ill health (71-79).[49]

Inconsistency, a perversion of the ideal of consistency (as a product of self-control) was a traditional theme of Greek literature and philosophy.[50] Horace utilizes this theme in his first three satires. Each of these satires states Horace's view that inconsistency is basic to most men, but each points up slightly different aspects of inconsistency which are fundamental to an understanding of Tartuffe.

The First Satire reveals that no man living is content with the lot which either his choice has given him or chance has thrown in his way, but each praises those who follow different courses (1-4). Tartuffe fits into this statement, which must be understood to exclude the *sapiens*. Tartuffe's reactions stem from this dissatisfaction with his own lot; he tries to alter his lot, as well as that of Orgon's family, according to his misbegotten desires. He fails to see the error of his actions as being in opposition to a providence which controls the universe. Man cannot control his fate. He must exercise *sophrosyne* to live successfully (happily) in this life.

The Second Satire[51] presents a picture of certain actions of Tartuffe, for Horace depicts a number of individuals who, in order to avoid a bad name, go to the opposite extremes. An example is the man who, not wanting to be considered wasteful, begrudges a friend his help (1-28). Such is the case of Tartuffe, who, in preaching certain Christian ideals adaptable to his guise of an ascetic, overlooks much more worthy ideals, such as charity. His words are at odds with the total picture he should present. Not only are his words in contrast to his image, but his actions are as well.

Horace's Third Satire presents a character whose words and actions are constantly in disparity (1-19). This is Tigellius, who one day talks of kings and princes, but the next day talks of the simple life. If his words are inconsistent, leading one to suspect a flaw in his character, his actions are equally so. His gait is unpredictable, and his slaves vary in number. But the proof of his real character is, as with Tartuffe, the complete disparity between words and deeds. Tigellius may preach the frugal life, as Tartuffe does the ascetic, but if either is given the opportunity and resources, he goes far astray from his supposed ideal.[52]

Tartuffe's only consistency is in erroneous judgment. Not only does he constantly pursue the wrong ends — money, power, and sex — but he continues to do so when his better judgment should cry: "Stop!" His problem — a lack of *sophrosyne* in moderating his nefarious designs — was well described by Juvenal, who noted that "never yet could a sinner set a limit to his sins"; or "what wretch have you ever seen who was satisfied with a single crime?"[53] Tartuffe's judgment is so perverted that he not only seeks the wrong things, but he seeks them constantly, with no sense of propriety or timeliness to his actions. He is consistent; consistently a *demens*, and therefore consistently bad.

Molière was quite careful to reveal the various aspects of his protagonist in the order of their importance. Thus we find that Tartuffe is heard of first as a hypocrite, at the same time being seen as a menace to natural order, and then as a parasite. The second is only introduced as an accompanying quality —

one which springs from a personality capable of hypocrisy. Furthermore, just as Tartuffe's hypocrisy forms a threat to the order of the family, so does his parasitism menace the substance of the family, as symbolized by the food that he eats and the money which he spends. The two ideas lead directly to the conclusion, as made earlier by Cléante (369-370), that the religious hypocrisy of Tartuffe has one primary function: to win him a fortune.

Dorine's speech (II, ii), in reaction to Orgon's proposition of marrying Mariane to Tartuffe, reveals another side of Tartuffe's character which is important in our study of *sophrosyne* as reflected in Molière's depiction of his protagonist.

> Oui, c'est lui qui le dit; et cette *vanité*,
> Monsieur, ne sied pas bien avec la piété.
> Qui d'une sainte vie embrasse l'innocence
> Ne doit point *tant prôner son nom et sa naissance*,
> Et l'humble procédé de la dévotion
> Souffre mal les éclats de cette *ambition*.
> A quoi bon cet *orgueil*? (495-501, italics mine)

It is revealed here in no uncertain terms that Tartuffe's actions spring from two motivations which are in opposition to true piety: pride and ambition.

In the following scene (II, iii), Dorine, in trying to dissuade Mariane from her failure to take a stand against her father's decision, provides the following description of Tartuffe:

> Certes Monsieur Tartuffe, à bien prendre la chose,
> N'est pas un homme, non, qui se mouche du pié,
> Et ce n'est pas peu d'heur que d'être sa moitié.
> Tout le monde déjà de gloire le couronne;
> Il est noble chez lui, bien fait de sa personne;
> Il a l'oreille rouge et le teint bien fleuri ...(642-647)

Although the statements made by Dorine are meant to have the effect of irony, there is doubtless some basis of truth in them. It seems obvious that he is not excessively handsome, as the phrase "bien fait de sa personne" is followed immediately by a specific comment on Tartuffe's personal appearance which suggests that he is anything but appealing — his ears are red. From the evidence already given by Dorine, it is possible to conclude that his red complexion is a product of his eating and drinking habits. It is, then, an indication that Tartuffe has been living it up rather than living as an ascetic.[54]

Elmire's entrance onstage brings out clearly several aspects of Tartuffe's character which have been suggested in the earlier acts. First, although it has been indicated that he is a man of great pride, in his first words to Elmire Tartuffe refers to himself as "le plus humble," a statement which, in view of all that has gone before and what is to come, is highly incongruous with his real character. His humility is false, just as his pride is real. Tartuffe's actions in attempting the seduction of his patron's wife are again indicative of the fact that he is a man of pride. The man who is proud and self-confident will believe that he is appealing to any woman and, accordingly, will attempt to fulfill his desires by seduction. The attempted seduction also provides us the opportunity to see that side of Tartuffe which had been suggested in Dorine's discussion of his attitude toward Elmire (79-84). He is interested in her sexually; therefore, sex, or lust, must be counted among his passions. We have already seen that luxury (excess), ambition, avarice, supersitition, and lust were among the vices which classical tradition particularly held up to scorn. It is noteworthy that Molière has endowed his protagonist with four of these vices in the guise of the fifth, superstition or religion.

Why is Elmire, among all the members of the family, best able to check the criminal career of Tartuffe? The answer is fairly simple. For one thing, she brings out his baser nature. Elmire excites the kind of love in Tartuffe that Mariane cannot: a love deeply involved in the sensual; a love for a real woman, not just a girl. Moreover, in this act of "loving" there may be seen an extension of Tartuffe's character into the realm of humanity. Too often he seems the mere spectre of evil brooding over the action, always in the background, ever an influence, but never an actor. Here, in his desire for Elmire, he acts.

Brunetière comments that Tartuffe has "un point faible — c'est sa sensualité."[55] Considering Molière's education and literary relationships, it is likely that Molière chose sensuality as the religious hypocrite's failing, not merely because sensuality has obvious possibilities for comic exploitation, although the latter reason must have strongly influenced his decision, but because Molière was working throughout the play with certain traditions of classical literature in mind. To better understand the classical traditions dealing with these subjects, it will be necessary to look again to the satirists. On the basis of their treatment of the vices particularly of ambition, avarice, and lust, we shall then consider Molière's depiction of Tartuffe.

Both Horace and Juvenal present a strong argument against those desires which run contrary to the attainment of Juvenal's *mens sana in corpore sano*. Thus any subjection to money, power, or the joys of the body must be rejected. This is a large part of the teachings of the satirist, and is inextricably bound to the concept of *sophrosyne*.

Horace opens his first book of satires with an argument against money (I. 1); he next considers sex (I. 2); ultimately he treats power (I. 6). He deals with each as among the most important forces in man's life, and, therefore, among the most destructive to his peace of mind. Horace's views on these subjects are influenced by classical philosophy, in this case especially the

Epicurean, which held that men "are fools when they allow themselves to be led by unlimited desires into unnecessary efforts and dangers."[56]

The treatment of avarice is certainly a commonplace of literature. However, since we are determining the extent to which *Tartuffe* reflects the traditions of classical satire, it will be necessary to look carefully at the presentation of this theme in Horace, Juvenal and Seneca, with the hope that a study of parallel situations or characterizations may clarify our understanding of Molière's depiction of Tartuffe.

Horace's First Satire of Book One is a denunciation of avarice, but it contains near the end of the poem a statement that leaves no doubt as to Horace's meaning: the poem is a plea for moderation, for *sophrosyne*, first of all in the area of money, but in all other areas of life as well. Horace stated:

> est *modus* in rebus, sunt certi denique *fines*,
> quos ultra citraque nequit consistere *rectum*. (Italics mine.)
> 
> There is measure in all things, There are in short, fixed bounds, beyond and short of which right can find no place.[57]

Discontent with one's present lot is a product of greed and envy (108-112). These two are directed at money; therefore money is one basis of man's troubles (108ff.). Discontent with his former lot produced the Tartuffe seen in Molière's play. Tartuffe suffers from greed, which produces a discontent with his lot in life. The fact that Orgon is a man of comparative wealth naturally attracts Tartuffe, and culminates in unhappiness for both men. It is, then, to some extent, money which is to blame for the unhappiness of Orgon and Tartuffe. But the problem is, of course, not money itself. How could an inanimate object cause crimes? No, it is not money. Rather it is a flaw of character, a failure to exercise self-control towards money, which causes unrighteousness and the desertion of virtue's path.[58] This flaw of character prevents Tartuffe from knowing that money is not really desirable.

In the classical viewpoint, any man capable of one crime is capable of another, even though the crimes seem far divergent in motivation. So the man guilty of a crime committed out of avarice is likely to commit other crimes as well. Horace presents this idea in a context particularly relevant to *Tartuffe*. He reveals that an inheritance may produce three distinct forms of madness, along with their resultant crimes: avarice; ambition; and prodigality (II. 3). Tartuffe persuades Orgon to disinherit Damis because of avarice (his desire for Orgon's money) and ambition (his desire for a place of respect in society). The reason which Tartuffe gives for not allowing Damis to inherit the property is a fear that Damis will react with prodigality. Thus wealth has again achieved its effect: a series of madnesses, real or imagined. Horace connects avarice with one crime after another: with deceit (127);

with rashness (150-166); with ambition (250-266); and with stealing and plundering (157). Avarice, which is the primary motivating factor in Tartuffe's character, leads him successively into each of these crimes, just as Horace had predicted avarice would do to any man.

Little information is provided on Tartuffe's background, but what we are told is very significant to our understanding of him and, as will be shown, is consistent with the themes drawn from the classical traditions with which Molière was familiar. The most important information is that provided us by Orgon, who tells that Tartuffe was formerly a man of "biens" (492), and that:

> Ce sont fiefs qu'à bon titre au pays on renomme;
> Et tel que l'on le voit, il est bien gentilhomme. (493-494)

This information may, of course, coming as it doubtless did from the mouth of Tartuffe, be suspect; if true, however, it is a key to Tartuffe's character as well as his past. The information that Tartuffe had come from a well-to-do family and that he enters Orgon's service in a state of virtual poverty, which condition he soon alters, tells a great deal about his nature.

Knowing Tartuffe's tendency toward excess in every aspect of life, one suspects that Tartuffe has lost or wasted away his wealth through his own excesses — a typical "prodigal son." The *Bible*, or course, offers an immediate model; but so does classical tradition, for one of the many types clearly depicted in classical satire is the *prodigus* — the wastrel or spendthrift. Juvenal provides a number of characters who represent the manner in which Tartuffe may have lost his wealth. One possibility is Pollio, who ate and drank away his inheritance, being reduced at last to beggary (XI. 38-43). Another is Rutilus, who spent his entire fortune on luxurious living (XI. 1-23).[59]

Tartuffe's actions are the results of repeated failures to moderate his desires. This problem is compounded by the fact that all the things he wants are wrong. He begins with avarice and covetousness, wanting the money of Orgon. His actions in taking over the household of Orgon are the products of an unrestrained ambition and longing for power. Similarly, his actions toward Elmire (and, to a much lesser extent, Mariane) are the result of a failure to moderate his erotic desires. These actions on the part of Tartuffe further reflect the moral traditions of classical literature, as stated in the satiric poets, Juvenal and Horace, and the Stoic philosopher, Seneca.

Juvenal follows Horace's lead, but for him there is no question of equality between money, sex, and power: it is *money* which is the root of all evils for Juvenal. In his opinion, "wealth = crime, *or* vice, *or* corruption."[60] Money causes greed and extravagance, which Juvenal declares are the special subjects of his satire (I. 88, 92-93, 140). In his famous Tenth Satire, sometimes called "The Vanity of Human Wishes," Juvenal rejects the desire of man for wealth as ignoble and common (23-25). He continues to take account in other satires of the evils of money, *e.g.*, the fact that it causes avarice, which makes men do ridiculous things in order to satisfy their misbegotten desires (XIV. 256-302). But greed is difficult for the satirist to stamp out. The reason is that the Romans taught their children greed as a virtue (XIV. 125). The desire for money and its ill effects were so deeply rooted in the Roman character, in Juvenal's opinion, that it was practically impossible to overcome their influence. The influence of money could be overcome, but only through the attainment of virtue.

By a comparison of Molière's attitudes towards money and avarice in *Tartuffe* with those of Horace and Juvenal, it can be seen that Molière reveals more the tempered viewpoint of Horace than the indignant and vehement attitude of Juvenal. Whereas Juvenal has money as the first and greatest vice of mankind, Horace treats ambition and lust with equal contempt. Accordingly, Tartuffe is presented not as a man motivated only by greed, but also by ambition and lust. Molière incorporates into his creation not just one element of the classical tradition of *sophrosyne*, but every important theme on an equal status (or nearly so). This follows the Stoic teaching that all vices are equally bad and, therefore, equally to be avoided.

Another of the traditional themes of satire is closely connected with that of avarice and is important in the study of Tartuffe — *captatio*, calculated legacy-hunting. This practice became a major vice in the Roman Empire, with the result that it came to the attention of the satirists, who found in it a combination of the vices they had been attacking. Therefore, they attacked *captatio* with a special vehemence. Even Horace, who is rarely vehement about anything, wrote with unusual intensity on this subject.

Juvenal treated legacy-hunting at length in two of his satires, Three and Twelve.[61] Satire Three, as we shall soon see, presents the *graeculus esuriens* (greedy Greekling) as the master hypocrite and parasite (58-125). Satire Twelve studies the *captator* within the context of the traditions of *sophrosyne*, revealing that the legacy-hunter, like so many of the characters of Juvenal, is motivated by greed. He makes friendships and associations only if there is a prospect of some return on his investment (93-120). This poem also provides an example of the man who is fooled by the *captator* into making him his sole heir:

> ... for if the sick man escape the Goddess of Death, he will be caught within the net, he will destroy his will, and after the prodigious services of Pacuvius will maybe by a single word, make him heir to all his possessions, and Pacuvius will strut proudly over his vanquished rivals.[62]

It is in Horace, however, that the best statement is made on the subject of *captatio*. The Fifth Satire of Book Two forms a practical guidebook in the fine art of legacy-hunting. The scene is a continuation of the *Odyssey*, Book XI, where Ulysses goes to the underworld to see the Theban seer, Tiresias, and learn the way home. Horace, playing the scene for its humorous and satiric effects, turns it into a burlesque of the original, having Ulysses greedily ask how he may regain his fortune, since the suitors have eaten away all his substance. Horace has Tiresias inform Ulysses that the best way of making money is by the fine science of *captatio*, whereupon Tiresias lays down the rules which Ulysses must follow.[63]

The successful *captator* must first of all chose his *victim* very carefully. The man should, of course, be wealthy (II. 5. 14), for, after all, the only reason in undertaking the role of *captator* is money; nor should one look for a man of high character (10-17). In fact, it is implied rather strongly that a man of low character is the type most desirable (15-17, 27-30). The man should definitely be old or near death, since the object is to get the inheritance as soon as possible, Also, it is a very good idea to choose a man who is childless or has a sickly heir (27-31, 45-50); that way there will be little or no competition.[64] Once he has set his trap, the *captator* must not give up easily. There are always those clever men who will not take the bait; but, if one persists in his attempts, someone will at last be taken in by the deception (23-26, 39-41). Once a way into the house and favor of the rich, old, childless patron has been found, great care must be taken to maintain, and even improve, one's standing with him. Therefore, it may be necessary to be humble, even to the point of sycophancy (74-75). It may even be necessary to obligingly hand over one's wife to his lusts (75-76). But these actions are unimportant as long as one gets nearer to his ultimate goal — an inheritance. The patron, however, must never be allowed to think that his will is a matter of importance to the *captator*; for, if that should happen, the greedy legacy-hunter is likely to be outwitted by a civil servant (51-69). All the time the *captator* must be on the lookout lest someone rob or cheat his patron out of any of the money he (the *captator*) plans to get (36-37). When the patron finally dies and leaves his estate to him, the *captator* must once more play the role of hypocrite he is so well practiced in, for it is necessary to lament the loss of a friend, although it is hard to keep from showing delight (99-104).[65]

A comparison to the actions of Tartuffe reveals that nearly every one of the rules laid down by Tiresias is followed by Tartuffe. There are exceptions, however, and those exceptions are as important as are the actions of Tartuffe which are consonant with the rules of Tiresias. This can be seen in the fact that Molière completely alters the characters of both his main characters by reversing or altering a number of situations from the usual case represented in Horace's poem. A review of Tartuffe's actions will reveal how a few changes make Tartuffe and Orgon into entirely different men than the typical *captator* and his patron, as depicted by Horace. After scouting the field carefully, Tartuffe, the *captator*,[66] selected his prey on the two bases suggested: Orgon is comparatively wealthy; and Orgon is not a man of high character. Orgon has children, but they are no problem to Tartuffe, who realizes that Mariane can be married off (even to himself), and Damis is a young man of typically volatile temperament, whom it will be easy to have ejected from the house and his birthright. But, if Tartuffe accepted the implication that the children are to be feared more than the wife, as he obviously did, he was led into an error of judgment. It is Elmire who starts him on the way to his fall. He was not, however, mistaken about the character of Orgon. He knew that Orgon was not a man to appreciate subservience. Therefore, Tartuffe sees to it that Orgon arranges for the fulfillment of his (Tartuffe's) every desire, so that Orgon even hands Elmire over to his control, and nearly to his lusts. Further proof that Tartuffe knows his man is provided by the fact that he has managed to insinuate in Orgon's ear the idea of signing over his (Orgon's) property to himself, without incurring the suspicion which is only a natural reaction to such a suggestion. Tartuffe jealously guards the property of Orgon, which he intends to possess. But not just the property is protected from encroachment, but even the person of Elmire, which Tartuffe lustfully covets. When Orgon's estate falls into his hands, Tartuffe reacts with no show of false grief, but with open vindictiveness toward the still living Orgon. It is doubtful that Tartuffe would have reacted differently had Orgon been dead, except that his vindictiveness would have been directed toward the members of Orgon's household who had opposed him rather than Orgon.

A close look at the exceptions to the rules laid down by Tiresias reveals a great deal about Tartuffe and Orgon. Tartuffe makes a mistake in choosing a family in which there are several children and a lively young wife. But, as long as the action is limited to the household of Orgon, this failure to follow the traditional pattern of the *captator* does him no harm. The reason is that he does understand Orgon, who is not concerned with the interests of his family. Every action of Tartuffe which is in contrast to the "rules" is the product of Tartuffe's understanding of Orgon. It is obvious that Orgon is not the typical patron, whether of Roman satire, as we shall see later in this chapter, or of history and story. Tartuffe recognizes this atypicality and acts accordingly, becoming, therefore, an atypical *captator*.

The theme of *captatio* is inseparable from that of avarice in the character of Tartuffe. It is his greed that makes Tartuffe insinuate himself into the favor of Orgon, so that he can eventually make himself not just sole heir, but sole owner of Orgon's properties. Every aspect of Tartuffe's character continues to reflect those themes representative of the antitheses of *sophrosyne* which are presented so vividly in classical satire.

Tartuffe, just as Orgon, brings all his problems on himself. He does so particularly through his failure to achieve wisdom, that knowledge of self which causes one to understand his relationship to the universe and, therefore, temper his actions. Tartuffe suffers from an unbounded egotism which destroys his sense of moderation. Were he not a very proud, vain, and egotistical man, Tartuffe would not have entered the house of Orgon in the belief that it would be possible to delude an entire family and, perhaps, effect a major swindle. The *conman*, by the very nature of his scheme, must have confidence that he will be able to instill a feeling of trust in those he would make gulls.

Egotism is certainly a human trait; but, as noted by Horace (I. 3. 19-24), it is also a fault, for it is the product of a lack of self-restraint. One variation on egotism is conceit. Aristotle established that the "conceited person wrongly thinks himself worthy of great things."[67] Out of Tartuffe's conceit grows the belief that he is worthy of power and riches. He is presumptuous, however, for he is really unworthy. He is but one of the many who do not know what they really want and go from place to place trying to find whatever it may be, never realizing that what they seek is to be sought first of all within themselves. Aristotle noted that "we perform evil actions out of a desire for pleasure, we avoid good or virtuous works because of the sadness we fear in honest labor."[68] This is precisely the problem with Tartuffe. He looks forward to the pleasures of owning and ruling Orgon's house, which he will gain only through evil actions. He could never attain his mistaken desires honestly for the simple reason that he fears, and therefore, avoids "honest labor." He enters on a life of crime as if there were no laws nor supreme power, no justice and no God. In his belief merely in himself and his pleasures, Tartuffe lowers man's dignity to that of the beast, and therein dooms himself.[69]

Another theme developed from the ideal of *sophrosyne* is that of ambition and the desire for power. This theme is closely connected with many of the other antitheses to moderation.[70] Classical tradition established that anyone who was unable to control his passions in respect to one evil would be unable to control them in respect to all the evils. So one finds in practically the same sentence the juxtaposition and interconnection of such *vitia* as envy, anger, sloth, gluttony, and lechery with ambition.[71]

Exactly what is wrong with ambition? First of all, it is another excess. But what is particularly bad about ambition is the fact that it brings men to prominence and arouses the malicious curiosity of many men. Horace provides the example of a commoner who rose to the tribunate, only to be met by cries of "Who is he?" "What was his father?"[72] Horace goes on to say that "he who takes it upon himself to look after his fellow-citizens and the city, the empire and Italy and the temples of the gods, compels all the world to take an interest ..."[73]

There is no doubt that Tartuffe is ambitious. It has already been shown that Tartuffe's ambition grows out of pride, for it is only through such pride in one's self that a man will attempt to rise to greatness. Tartuffe's pride gives rise to an ambition and longing for power which leads him into precisely the situation Horace describes in the preceding paragraph. Tartuffe takes it upon himself, confident in his abilities, to look after: his "fellow-citizens" — the household of Orgon; a microcosmic world — the house of Orgon, equatable to the city of Rome; and the religious affairs of that world.[74] His mistake is not just in how he performs these functions, however. It is equally in the fact that he oversteps his position, as set by the society in which he lives, and thereby brings himself into a position of public view, ultimately even of royal and divine view.

Juvenal, too, condemns the desire for power. In his Tenth Satire, Juvenal considers the misdirected desires of mankind, among which is the desire for power in a prominent position. Violent and humiliating deaths, he writes, were the rewards of Demosthenes and Cicero when they let vain ambition lead them to fame and influence, won by their oratory (X. 114-132). But the most vivid picture of the effects of power is that of Sejanus, who, as minister to the emperor Tiberius, attempted to usurp the reins of power. Eventually Fate threw Sejanus down from the giddy heights to which he had risen. His mistake is proclaimed by Juvenal with axiomatic succinctness:

> omne animi vitium tanto conspectius in se
> crimen habet, quanto maior qui peccat habetur.
>
> The greater the sinner's name, the more signal the guiltiness of the sin.[75]

Although the possible significance of the analogy between Tartuffe and Sejanus will be discussed more fully later in this chapter, it should be noted at this point that, just as Sejanus and the others whom Juvenal depicted as led by a thirst for power or glory were brought to their destruction by their misdirected desires, so is Tartuffe. Had Tartuffe not thrust himself to the fore, he might not have had to fall, at least not from so great a height.

Another of the antitheses to *sophrosyne* which are typical of the enormities of the madman is lust. In Horace's *Satires*, love is considered "a foolish habit,"[76] suitable for the immature and unstable mind of the child rather than the wise man who is prepared for every stroke of Fortune. Concupiscence, that appetite which lusts after the physical pleasures, serves to confuse the reason of the man whose judgment is not properly tempered, leading him to forbidden, or at least dangerous, fruits.[77]

One of the many renderings of *sophrosyne* is *pudicitia*, chastity.[78] This was generally accepted by moral philosophers, working from classical traditions. St. Thomas Aquinas, for instance, commenting on Aristotle's *Ethics*, stated, "We call chastity a form of temperance ...So too one who is not chaste is said to be 'incestuosus' (in-castus)."[79]

Tartuffe's desire to physically possess Elmire is an action representative not just of Tartuffe, not certainly of the religious hypocrite alone, but of all *dementes*, all fools, especially when they have gone from the point of having such wrongful desires as mere passions to having them as habits. Then truly are they *(dementes)* bad men, and bad men desire bodily pleasures.[80] It should not be understood from this, however, that bodily pleasures are bad in themselves.[81] It is rather the failure to use self-restraint and the tendency to excess, both products of bad judgment, which make these wrong.[82]

Virtue is achieved, according to Horace, by the avoidance of vice. "To flee vice is the beginning of virtue, and to have got rid of folly is the beginning of wisdom."[83] But this requires wisdom, which is gained by ridding oneself of folly. In other words, one must understand himself in his relationship to the universe; and, in order to comply with the exigencies of this universe (to live according to nature), he must, through a conscious act of mind, exercise self-control, moderation, in all things. This is a major theme of the works of Horace, who is considered the most *sôphrôn* of Roman authors.[84]

Horace's best known statement on *sophrosyne* is found in his advice to a sailor who would take a voyage:

> Rectius vives, Licini, neque altum
> Semper urgendo neque, dum procellas
> Cautus horrescis, nimium premendo
>     Litus iniquom
>
> Auream quisquis mediocritatem
> Diligit, tutus caret obsoleti
> Sordibus tecti, caret invidenda
>     Sobrius aula.
>
> Live so that you tempt not the sea relentless,
> Neither press too close on the shore forbidding;
> Flee extremes, and choose thou the mean all-golden,
>     Treasure all priceless.
>
> Safe, you dread not poverty's hut repellent;
> Wise, you seek not mansions that men may envy;
> All secure, protected by moderation,
>     Fate cannot harm you.[85]     (*Odes* II. 10. 1-8)

The sailor on the voyage of life can avoid the perils of deficiency by not hugging the shore too closely, of excess by not putting out too far to sea.

Through such actions, a man could avoid many of the difficulties of life which he brings upon himself. He could even raise himeslf from the level of *demens* to *sapiens*, and thus rid himself of whatever vice possesses him — but only through wisdom and virtue.

Tartuffe, as we shall see in the following pages, is the converse of each of the ideals just discussed. Although his position suggests wisdom, Tartuffe lacks totally the wisdom which leads to virtue. This is proven time and again, as has been shown, for Tartuffe has no scene in which he exercises true moderation. He may seem momentarily temperate, but his pose will be proven to be a preparation for the fulfillment of his next vicious desire. Much is made of Tartuffe's inconsistencies, his immoderation in eating, sleeping, and spending. These are all proofs of Tartuffe's real character according to the Stoic system. They are the outer signs of an inner imperfection. The greatest proof of this imperfection in wisdom and virtue, however, is his attempt to gain sexual gratification from Elmire. It is especially the fact that she is a married woman that proves him unvirtuous; equal proof would be provided by consideration of, or participation in, any illicit sexual act. For the Stoics, for Horace, and for many of the Christian faith, "the first honor of virtue is chastity."[86] Any consideration of, or participation in, such an act proves that the character is flawed, not really endowed with true virtue. Such is the case with Tartuffe. He fails on the most basic Stoic level. While the Cynics and Epicureans condemn adultery because of its personal risks, the Stoics looked upon such an act as the product of an unhealthy soul.[87] The virtuous man would not have considered the risks; he would have abstained because his self-knowledge would have enabled him to control his emotions and passions.[88]

Tartuffe's incontinence in attempting the seduction of Elmire can be seen as a reflection of another attitude in the satires of Horace. It has been shown repeatedly that Tartuffe is incapable of moderation and is, therefore, subject to every passion antithetical to moderation. Horace reveals that anytime a man's passions are ungoverned, they become his master and lead him into danger.[89] Tartuffe, cunning and clever though he may be, allows his passions rather than his judgment to govern his actions. The passions in control will naturally seek satisfaction; for, as Horace points out,[90] once the passions are allowed to rule, they can only be stilled by indulgence.

Horace advocates the belief that one category of sexual activity that is always in opposition to *sophrosyne* is adultery. For instance, in the Second Satire of Book One, Horace spends the first thirty-six lines stating his theme, *nil medium est*. The rest of the poem deals with adultery and its disadvantages. Horace leaves no doubt in his readers' minds that the adulterer brings great dangers and penalties on himself.

> It is worth your while, ye who would have disaster wait on adulterers, to hear how on every side they fare ill, and how for them pleasure is marred by much pain, and, rare as it is, comes oft amid cruel perils. One man has thrown himself headlong from the roof; another has been flogged to death; a third, in his flight, has fallen into a savage gang of robbers; another has paid a price to save his life; another been abused by stable-boys; nay, once it so befell that a man mowed down with the sword the testicles and lustful member. "That's the law," cried all, Galba dissenting.[91]

But it is also obvious that adultery is closely connected with other vices which represent failures in self-control. Such a vice is prodigality (61-62). For the man who is intemperate in one area will be intemperate in all areas. It will be this intemperance, the compulsive nature of which[92] he cannot control, which will lead the adulterer into his vice, and thus into his dangers and penalties.

Horace presents another discussion of the resultant dangers and penalties of adultery in Satire Seven of Book Two. There Horace, writing on the Stoic question of the truly free man, exposes himself as a slave to passion. His slave Davus addresses him, saying:

> You, when you have cast aside your badges, the ring of knighthood and your Roman dress, and step forth, no longer a judge, but a low Dama, with a cape hiding your perfumed head, are you not what you pretend to be? Full of fear, you are let into the house, and you tremble with a terror that clashes with your passions. What matters it, whether you go off in bondage, to be scourged and slain with a sword, or whether, shut up in a shameful chest, where the maid, conscious of her mistress's sin, has stowed you away, you touch your crouching head with your knees? Has not the husband of the erring matron a just power over both? Over the seducer a still juster? Yet she does not change either garb or position, and she is not the chief sinner, since she is in dread of you and does not trust her lover. You with eyes open will pass under the yoke, and hand over to a furious master your fortune, your life, your person and repute.[93]

The situation of Tartuffe in the house of Orgon is quite interesting when compared with that of Horace at his mistress's house. They have both had to enter the houses of their prospective lovers (for Tartuffe this is not the primary motivation), Tartuffe in the guise of *dévot*, Horace with all indications of rank and citizenship removed; but there the similarity ceases. Tartuffe holds the regency over Orgon's household and imperiously governs the events therein, maneuvering nearer and nearer his desired end, the seduction of Elmire. Horace, however, has entered the house of his mistress in a state of near terror at the thought of the punishments that could be visited upon him were he caught: he would be carted off to be beaten and killed (58-59); he could be locked up in a trunk to prevent the husband's finding him there (59-61); he could be pilloried (66); and he could even forfeit money, life, person, and good reputation (67). The knowledge that we have of the characters of Orgon and Tartuffe reveals why the situations vary so markedly. Orgon does not represent the awesome figure whose *potestas* (soverign power) Horace knows and fears. Orgon is a man who shuns that very *potestas* which is his right and duty, who eagerly relinquishes it to Tartuffe, who cannot inspire fear or respect. Therefore, by the very nature of their characters, Tartuffe and Orgon reverse places in that exceptional world of Orgon's household. There it is no longer the adulterer who must fear the loss of money, life, and reputation. It is instead the husband, Orgon, whom Tartuffe first robs of his property and then brings to peril by taking the strongbox to the Prince. It would have been impossible for Orgon to have deprived Tartuffe of money or good reputation, for Tartuffe had neither. Ultimately, of course, Tartuffe is handed over to the representatives of the law, with a penalty (possibly of death) awaiting him. But this final victory over Tartuffe is not achieved through the efforts of Orgon.

Molière, altering the traditional comic depiction of the concealed adulterer,[94] utilizes the scene of Orgon hiding under the table, while Tartuffe makes ardent advances to this wife, partly for comic effect, but also to continue his satiric statement and emphasize the extent to which Orgon fails in his duty to wield the *potestas* in his own home; it shows the magnitude of the corruption of Orgon and just how great a fool he truly is. Accordingly, Tartuffe, too, stands in emphasized contrast with what he should be — a cowardly fool, who is met with humiliation, degradation, and legal punishment. Such are the due of the fool who is carried away with his passions. We have seen that Tartuffe fails in one area after another of *sophrosyne*. Tartuffe, an utter slave to his passions, clearly reflects the image of Horace in Satire II, 7, wherein Davus further addresses his master:

> Suppose you have escaped: then, I take it, you will be afraid and cautious after your lesson. No, you will seek occasion so as again to be in terror, again to face ruin, O you slave many times over![95]

Once again it is shown that the man who is a slave to his passions cannot keep from running from one crime to another; he cannot help bringing on his own destruction; he cannot help being a *servus* (slave) to his passions and, therefore, a *demens*. Tartuffe's actions are those of such a *servus*.

The fate that Davus predicts for Horace (II. 7. 67) is precisely that which Tartuffe calls down upon himself in the self-revelation scene (Act III, sc. 6):

> ... traitez-moi de perfide,
> D'*infâme*, de perdu, de voleur, d'*homicide* ...(1101-2; italics mine.)

It is noteworthy that in a parallel situation Molière uses *infâme* and *homicide* as Horace used repute *(famam)* and life *(vitam)*. It can be seen that, just as Horace's poem (II. 7) is a consideration of the Stoic doctrine of moderation, so Molière is utilizing the theme of *bon sens*, his variation of *sophrosyne*, to point up the particular truths he wishes to convey.

Tartuffe's failure to temper his passions toward Elmire precipitates him into all his troubles. He has been guilty of many forms of incontinence. But these have not caused his downfall. It is the repeated, rash act of attempting adultery that crumbles Tartuffe's world. It is adultery which is the beginning of the end of Tartuffe's career.

It has been shown that Horatian satire, directed toward the reform of the reader, tried to persuade the reader against his subjection to money (I. 1), sex (I. 2), and power (I. 6). For Horace these were "the three most magnetic forces in a man's life and the most dangerous to his peace of mind."[96] The same ideas, as we have seen, are present in Juvenal's satires. There is one of Juvenal's satires which has not yet been considered in our study of the themes of ambition, avarice, and lust — this is the Eighth Satire. There Juvenal provides an example of the tenets of *sophrosyne* which is especially relevant to one aspect of Orgon, which will be discussed more fully in the section on Sejanus later in this chapter. This aspect sees Orgon as the corrupted leader of a microcosmic political state, since, as the head of the household, he not only fails to take and hold the reins of power in his home, but does so particularly because he fails to see through to the truth about this own family and Tartuffe (as well as about himself).

In his Eighth Satire, Juvenal offers advice to Ponticus, who is about to depart to a province, on how to be a good governor. The advice, which is applicable to Orgon, the nominal governor of his household, and Tartuffe, the potential governor of himself, as well as Ponticus, is typical of the tradition of *sophrosyne* as found in the satirists. Juvenal pointedly comments that *nobilitas sola est atque unica virtus*.[97] This concept of "virtue," as proposed to Ponticus, entails "his setting a limit to his *ira* (cf. 88), his *avaritia* (cf.89), his *ambitio* (135), and his *libido* (135); it means incorruptibility in himself (142), in his wife (128), in his staff (127); and it means, in general, adherence to the laws (91)."[98]

This advice to Ponticus lists one after another the failings in *sophrosyne* which bring Orgon and Tartuffe to destruction. *Avaritia*, *ambitio*, and *libido* combine so perfectly in the character of Tartuffe that one cannot imagine any one of them being absent. Orgon is easily corruptible. This corruption is a matter of judgment, for herein lie his errors. He mistakenly trusts "his staff," Tartuffe, thereby falling into *ira* against his son, who has suggested to him that his (Orgon's) judgment is, in fact, corrupt, as shown by the choice of Tartuffe as an adherent and advisor.[99] The Ponticus story, with its emphasis on the three main vices emphasized by Horace and Juvenal, will be seen to take on additional relevance later in this chapter, when we treat Sejanus as a possible antecedent of Tartuffe.

The only aspect of the advice to the man who would be a good governor which Tartuffe and Orgon both fail to pervert is the incorruptibility of Orgon's wife. This, however, is through no fault of their own. Tartuffe employs all his deceit and rhetoric to seduce Elmire, whom Orgon has been kind (stupid) enough to put in his care. She is not corrupted, however, for she is representative of good judgment, which one remembers, leads to virtue.

Although both Orgon and Tartuffe are offenders against the ideal of *sophrosyne*, it is Tartuffe who proves the consummate exception to all the advice of Horace. He is "disturbed in spirit" by all the wrong things: he is ambitious, else he would not attempt the accession to power in Orgon's empire; he desires monetary gain, else he would not seek and win the fortune of Orgon. Tartuffe does not achieve happiness, for he does not know what will bring him happiness. He continues to seek the wrong things, plunging himself deeper and deeper into an abyss of misery, from which, although he is not aware of this state, he can escape. Escape, however, is not likely. It would require a progress to wisdom. Tartuffe is not virtuous; therefore, he is unhappy (*miser*). All those in the play who are not fools "view him with dislike or contempt."

One must see that it is through Tartuffe's own words and deeds that he is exposed. The actions of others to unmask him before Orgon serve rather to entrench Tartuffe more deeply in Orgon's heart. It is only when sincerity (and I do not mean purity) of emotion carries him away that Tartuffe is foiled.

It seems obvious that Tartuffe should have known better than to become involved in the second interview with Elmire. This is precisely the point: he should have known better, but he does not. As cunning and clever as he may be, when it comes to matters of the heart (or body is perhaps better here), he is not the rational man he is when the mask is on.

Tartuffe's ultimate blunder is daring to denounce Orgon before the King. Throughout the play it has been obvious that Tartuffe's success can be directly attributed to the failure of Orgon to correctly discern reality and appearance. This was achieved with ease because Orgon is a man of limited intellectual powers. When Molière audaciously extends his game to the world outside Orgon's house, a world ruled by reason in the form of the King, he goes too far. By failing to moderate his desires, he brings himself to the attention of the King. Failing to temper his passions is elemental to Tartuffe's character.

Tartuffe is the more blameworthy because he has the intelligence to see an ideal norm to which he should conform, the ability in self-discipline to conform to the norm when it is to his benefit, and yet an appetite which, with the license of self-indulgence, overrules the mind in its search for the ideal.

Every passion, as an act of failure in self-control, is in opposition to the order of the universe to the extent that each passion "transforme ses rapports avec celui-ci."[100] Tartuffe is a man of passions. The passions which constitute his character are, as we have seen, precisely those attacked in classical satire. There can be little doubt that Molière was aware of this fact, and that he created Tartuffe by employing those vices with which he was most familiar both from his education and from life, and which he thought appropriate to his depiction of a creature of consummate vice.

Ultimately Tartuffe is destroyed by his own character, for he loses all his sense of proportion and, going beyond all reasonable limits, exposes himself to the family and even the King, unmasked. He is over-confident in his abilities to make fortune bend his way. He suffers from a comic variety of "hybris," and this is his downfall. If he had kept his place, instead of being motivated by each success to go one misstep farther, Tartuffe would never have brought down upon himself the judgment of the King.

The character of Orgon has often been misunderstood or oversimplified by those critics who fail to look at his actions in the light of the traditions of classical literature, especially the concept of the *demens*. One critic states that Orgon "is a self-deceived man, a fool, in effect, and when the deception lifts, we have a chastened, middle-aged bourgeois whose eyes are perhaps opened for good to a proper acceptance of reality."[101] A consideration of Orgon's character and actions in the last act will reveal that this statement fails to consider certain important aspects about Orgon which can be interpreted better through an understanding of their significance according to classical tradition.

The fifth act opens with Orgon in a familiar role. Having momentarily taken a stand against Tartuffe at the end of the fourth act, Orgon now slumps back into mental languor, a state of complete indecision at a time when decision is crucial to the welfare of his family.

> Cléante: Où voulez-vous courir?
> Orgon: Las! que sais-je? (1573)

Now Orgon, who put his family into the control of Tartuffe, shares their fate. Orgon, who thought his family would find something to make them laugh when he gave away all his goods, now sees the irony of the fate which he has brought on himself. Yet he finds no blame in himself. It is Tartuffe and men of his kind who have brought him to ruin.

When Orgon does stop to think, however, he does not come up with any creative or corrective solution. Rather he bursts into an angry tirade against "tous les gens de bien." He still cannot see the truth. Because the man in whom he saw a veritable manifestation of piety has been proven false, he assumes that all pious men are false. He is guilty of a primary logical fallacy — the undistributed middle. He is not capable of making a valid decision.

> C'en est fait, je renonce à tous les gens de bien.
> J'en aurai désormais une horreur effroyable
> Et m'en vais devenir pour eux pire qu'un diable. (1604-1606)

Upon hearing this typically rash statement from Orgon, Cléante sums up Orgon's character in these words:

> Hé bien! ne voilà pas de vos emportements!
> Vous ne gardez en rien les doux tempéraments;
> Dans la droite raison jamais n'entre la vôtre,
> Et toujours d'un excès vous vous jetez dans l'autre. (1607-1610)

It is noteworthy that here when Cléante gives the key to Orgon's character, it is tied up in a personality trait already seen — his tendency toward excess. So bound up, in fact, is Orgon in excess, that the minute one excess is taken from him, he immediately plunges into another.[102] Cléante advises Orgon to be moderate; in recommending moderation, he likely expresses the opinion of Molière. At the same time, his stress on the ideal of moderation emphasizes Orgon's lack thereof and underlines again "l'anormalité ou la corruption de la psychologie d'Orgon ..."[103]

The fifth act has presented difficulties to most of the critics attempting an interpretation of the plot and characterizations. The problem centers on two seemingly unnecessary complications of the already adequately complex plot: the theft of Orgon's strongbox by Tartuffe; and the *deus ex machina* intervention of the King through his exempt. The theft of the strongbox has been explained as taking its place within the limits of themes already expressed.

> Orgon fait deux cadeaux à Tartuffe: sa fille et sa fortune. Tartuffe tente de voler deux des propriétés d'Orgon: sa femme et la cassette. Dans les deux cas, Tartuffe renchérit sur les dons d'Orgon: non content de sa fille, il tente de lui dérober sa sécurité.[104]

There is much validity in this analysis, for it continues a line of development in the characterizations of Orgon and Tartuffe. Orgon is seen again as always having used the worst of judgment, for the very evils he wished to avoid by entrusting his wife and strongbox to Tartuffe are visited upon him as a result of his choice. Tartuffe continues to drop his mask and show his real character, *immoderate* to the point of rapacity.

Juvenal provides a meaningful parallel to the "strongbox episode" in *Tartuffe*. This is the story of Calvinus, who, just as Orgon, has been defrauded of a trust by a friend.[105] Juvenal's version points up clearly two aspects that Molière must have wanted to demonstrate in his version. First, the actions of the "friend" are obviously those of a false friend. Therefore, the concept of the education to be a good neighbor, offered by the Jesuits, is revealed here as another of the failures of Tartuffe in wisdom and virtue.[106] The second point is made even more clearly: Orgon is a fool. This is shown by his similarity to Calvinus, who, upon losing his treasure chest, becomes quite disturbed over the matter, behaving like a child (5-173). Juvenal asks if Calvinus has not profited at all from the teachings of Philosophy, who can conquer the adversities of fortune (18-20). The point is clearly made that Calvinus' actions are those of a *demens*. This applies equally to Orgon. Like Calvinus, Orgon becomes very disturbed when a trust, involving property in each case, is betrayed by a "friend." Neither man accepts the loss of the property, which is inconsequential to the philosopher, for whom the only important possessions are wisdom and virtue. Rather they both rave like madmen, paying no attention to the wisdom of philosophy as offered by Juvenal to Calvinus and by Cléante to Orgon. Once again the *dementia* of Orgon is emphasized when seen as a reflection of the traditions of Roman satire.

In Act V, near the end of the play, a part of Tartuffe's background is revealed to us. Molière points out that Tartuffe is a veritable criminal with a record, who has committed "actions toutes noires" and has taken an alias to throw the law off his track, just as he has taken on a false character to further his career of crime.

Although one sees and knows that Tartuffe is utterly bad, one retains a hope for Orgon to recover his senses so that he may redirect his loyalties and serve once more as the worthy head of his household. This hope is shattered almost beyond recovery by the opening scenes of the final act. There it appears that Orgon, like Tartuffe, is so far gone from the path of right that he must be counted one of those for whom "there is no longer any room for a cure, now that those things which once were vices have become habits."[107] Orgon's tendency towards excess of loyalty based upon improper reasoning seems to have become a habit. He is lost; there seems to be no doubt. But so is Tartuffe. For when the hypocrite has been unmasked for all to see, he still must employ the language of his guise. Having so long misdirected his life, Tartuffe now is so in the habit that he cannot accept the truth. Falsity and deceit are his way of life; they have become his truth. Just as Orgon's world rests on the false figure of Tartuffe, so does Tartuffe's rest on the false world — the illusion of piety — he has created.

Orgon makes a mistake in accepting Tartuffe's pretense as reality. This, however, is a very common mistake, for few men are wise. Orgon's initial mistake, then, is not grounds for condemning him utterly. It is only when he does not see through Tartuffe after ample opportunity for examination of Tartuffe's character has been given that it becomes obvious how great a fool Orgon is. It is the ever-increasing reliance which Orgon places on the character of Tartuffe which doubly dooms him. *"Miserum est aliorum incumbere famae,/ ne conlapsa ruant subductis tecta columnis."*[108] By placing his entire world in Tartuffe, making him his "tout," Orgon has made Tartuffe's fall from power not a happy event, but a personal tragedy. As a man now aware of his mistake, does Orgon now temper his judgment or try to exercise self-control? No. He assumes that if Tartuffe is a charlatan, so must be all religious men, and he promises his undying hatred for all Tartuffe's kind, meaning not just hypocrites, but anyone professing to be religious, for Orgon now equates the two. Orgon has made the classic mistake: in trying to avoid one vice, he has run in the opposite direction, falling into a vice equally as bad as the first. His problem is still that he does not have the wisdom to know the difference between good and bad, true and false.

Ideally, Orgon should come to his senses and begin to direct himself towards virtue and wisdom after Tartuffe has been exposed. But he does not show any immediate improvement. Molière may have been building his characterization of Orgon on his own awareness of human character; or he may have based this element in the characterization of Orgon on doctrines of Stoic philosophy, which state: "If you have rid a man of insanity, he becomes sane again, but if we have removed false opinions, insight into practical conduct does not follow at once."[109] Accordingly, Orgon can also be seen as representative of the man chained down by "vicious dogmas," whose natural disposition has been crushed.[110] If so, even the sound advice of Cléante (the training that comes from philosophy) cannot help him. The latter of the two choices seems better to describe Orgon. This can be seen by his actions in the last act of the play. He does not try to improve his understanding of reality, once his false reality has been destroyed. Instead, he ventures immediately in the opposite direction, one that is equally foolish. There is very little hope for Orgon. He is not one of Juvenal's few who see good or evil in its correct perspective, who know what to wish for and direct their lives accordingly.[111]

Tartuffe is a mass of contradictions; he is consistently one thing: inconsistent. But what of Orgon? If he were consistent, would he not be commendable? Yes, to the extent that consistency even in misdirection is better than inconsistency now towards the right, now towards the wrong things. But Orgon is not consistent, as is seen in the fifth act. There he reverses his ideals and heads in a completely opposite direction. Whereas he had formerly been devoted to religion, he has now been so alienated by Tartuffe that he rejects "tous les gens de bien." He has done an about-face, acting exactly as Horace had said a *demens* would. In fact, Cléante's description of Orgon's actions:

> Et toujours d'un excès vous vous jetez dans l'autre (1610)

closely parallels Horace's comment on the tendency of man to run from one extreme to another:

> dum vitant stulti vitia, in contraria currunt.[112]

Even as they are leading Tartuffe away to prison, Orgon is exhibiting himself, "a devil of a man," as he rages at Tartuffe:

> Hé bien, te voilà, traître ....(1947)

It seems that he has learned nothing, that he is still the Orgon he was. But Orgon is not the same throughout the play, for his last speech shows that he has undergone a change of heart and that he has, within the scope of the play, returned to normalcy and *bon sens*:

> Oui c'est bien dit: allons à ses pieds avec joie
> Nous louer des bontés que son coeur nous déploie.
> Puis, acquittés un peu de ce premier devoir,
> Aux justes soins d'un autre il nous faudra pourvoir,
> Et par un doux hymen couronner en Valère
> La flamme d'un amant généreux et sincère. (1957-1962)

Here Orgon has at last become aware of true goodness and wisdom, in the person of the King, and of sincerity, in the person of Valère. There remains, however, the shadow of his past excesses and inconsistencies, and one wonders how long it will be before Orgon runs from his position of moderation and *bon sens* into another excess, and another, and another. As one looks at Molière's characters, an awareness that most of his great comic figures do not go through any sudden reformation or repentance reenforces this presentiment. One recalls, in particular, Don Juan, Alceste, Harpagon, M. Jourdain, Arnolphe, and Argan, as well as Tartuffe. Each is essentially the same man he was at the beginning of the play, and no amount of revelation has destroyed his tendency toward excess.[113] Accordingly, Orgon stands in clear contrast to Cléante, who is also the same man he has been throughout the play. Cléante, if not the ideal, represents an ideal. Thus, when Orgon is on the point of physically attacking Tartuffe, it is Cléante who restrains him and at the same time pronounces his hopes for a moral recovery on the part of Tartuffe.

Throughout the play an idealized norm has been suggested, particularly by the words of Cléante. Now, in the closing scene of the play, we are allowed to know that this ideal does exist. In the Prince, who stands offstage, we see the leader that Orgon should have been. The contrast between the corrupt and the ideal leader is seen particularly in the fact that Orgon, who is pardoned for his treason by the Prince, cannot also pardon Tartuffe, his personal traitor.

### The Hypocrite

Although numerous critics have said that the figure of Tartuffe, the hypocrite,[114] has no basis in antiquity, the hypocrite was, nonetheless, just as he was in the literatures of many nations and of many times, an actual and vital type in classical literature, who elicited his share of moral and character-writing. The hypocrite was notably in evidence in the satires of Horace and Juvenal, as well as the Stoic teachings of Seneca. The difference of opinion that arises is caused by the failure of those same scholars to see that a classical borrowing is not always presented in the same light. This must be the nature of the effective artists in a changing world. Therefore, if critics have dismissed the possibility of finding sources for Tartuffe's hypocrisy in classical literature, they have failed to appreciate the genius of the artist. True, there are few religious hypocrites per se in Greek and Roman literature. But the hypocrites in the classical repertory provide a number of parallels for the actions and character of Tartuffe, especially when seen in the light of the classical traditions within which they are presented.

A hypocrite is by definition "an actor on the stage . . . : one who pretends to be what he is not or to have principles or beliefs that he does not have; esp.: one who falsely assumes an appearance of virtue or religion . . ."[115]

Classical literature is full of hypocrites. Their desires are typical of all the fools of the world, as of Tartuffe; they seek those antitheses to *sophrosyne*, the ill effects of which have just been considered. But, not having the wisdom to temper their judgments, the hypocrites head in the wrong direction, toward truly undesirable ends, although they recognize that those ends are evil in that good men find them bad. Therefore, they must find a way to conceal their true desires; and that is why, as Seneca noted, "ambition, luxury, and incontinence need a stage to act upon."[116] It is noteworthy that Seneca makes such a comment about precisely those vices which we have seen to be exhibited in Tartuffe.

There are many explanations available for the tendency toward hypocrisy. One proposed by Aristotle is that certain men, *blato-panurgi*, find pleasure in a "certain cunning pretense."[117] This must apply to some extent to Tartuffe. There can be little doubt that he enjoys his little game. Fooling Orgon serves as a form of self-aggrandizement for Tartuffe. But Tartuffe is interested in far more profitable and delightful experiences than any momentary feeling of superiority to a fool like Orgon. What Tartuffe seeks are the pleasures of power and wealth — especially the immediate delights of food, wine, and love. His only problem is how to gratify his desires.

In the second seduction scene we see an answer to a problem which has troubled many critics: why has Tartuffe taken on the mask of religion, rather than any other? The answer now becomes clear. The illusion of piety serves as a means to Tartuffe's ends by masking his true intent.[118] It is with the language of religion, as well as the appearance, that Tartuffe achieves what success he has. Tartuffe's motivation for donning the mask of religion can be found in the character of Orgon. Since Orgon was obviously a fool, and since he was becoming more and more deeply, if not intelligently, involved in religion, Tartuffe would naturally adapt himself to the passion of his intended gull. Although the religious interests of Orgon must have been a primary motivating factor for Tartuffe's religious mask, it is possible that other factors influenced his choice of method. Consider, for instance, the following statement by Seneca about virtue as a reason for the veil of hypocrisy:

> There is so wonderful a grace and authority in it, that even the worst of men approve it, and set up for the reputation of being accounted virtuous themselves. They covet the fruit, indeed, and the profit of wickedness, but they hate, and are ashamed of the importation of it. It is by an impression of nature, that all men have a reverence for virtue: they know it and they have a respect for it, though they do not practice it; nay for the countenance of their very wickedness, they miscall it virtue. Their injuries they call benefits, and expect a man should thank them for doing him a mischief; they cover their most notorious iniquities with a pretext of justice.[119]

Tartuffe, according to this statement, would have found religion, the Christian equivalent of virtue, a likely method even had his intended gull not been the religiously-inclined Orgon. For, in fact, like all evil men, Tartuffe approves of virtue and even desires it. It is, however, in conflict with his temporal desires, and Tartuffe must choose between his desires and virtue. He chooses his desires, but keeps the pretense of virtue because he basically reveres it.

Classical tradition, then, has provided motivations for hypocrisy. It is necessary to look next at the variety of hypocrites presented therein, again looking particularly to the satirists.

Horace provides but a brief comment on hypocrisy, but that is of great importance in that it is very appropriate for Tartuffe; the poet addresses the hypocrite, saying:

> But you, since you are just the same and maybe worse, would you presume to assail me, as though you were a better man, and would you throw over your vices a cloak of seemly words?[120]

This is precisely the hypocrisy of Tartuffe — a pretense to be what he is not through a proof of "seemly words" and deeds. And does Tartuffe not literally "assail" the members of Orgon's household on the matter of their behavior, as if he were a better man, not only than they, but also than he himself is?

Precisely this sort of hypocrite must have paraded through the streets of every great city in history; they certainly were common in Rome in the days of Juvenal as well, for that satiric poet depicted numerous examples of the type. His Satire II is a virtual procession of hypocrites. First comes the philosopher who attacks men's lusts, but turns out to be a homosexual (8-10). There follows another, who speaks loudly in praise of virtue, but turns out to be equally perverted (19-21). Next there follows a series of potential examples of hypocrisy, each the perpetrator of a heinous crime, and each prospectively denouncing his own crime, as Verres theft, Clodius adultery, and Catiline treason. Then there parades by an entire category of hypocrites who function as censors, but are themselves worthy of censure (34-35). There follows then the pretender to greatness, who would have the world believe him the scion of a noble family rather than the peasant he is (39-43).[121] Tartuffe is a hypocrite and he is certainly related generically to the hypocrites I have been discussing. He is, however, of a more specialized class; it is this specialization to which we must now turn our attention.

Tartuffe is a master of words and illusions, of logical fallacies. This is only natural. The successful seducer must be the supreme "con-man." He must not only have his standard "line," but he must be prepared to rationalize against every defense and excuse. Such is the case with Tartuffe. Exercising the "direction d'intention," Tartuffe tries to free Elmire of any religious scruple, saying:

> Le Ciel défend, de vrai, certains contentements;
> Mais on trouve avec lui des accommodements;
> Selon divers besoins, il est une science
> D'étendre les liens de notre conscience,
> Avec la pureté de notre intention. (1487-1492)

For an age in which casuistry was a commonplace, the logic of Tartuffe must have seemed quite natural to many — especially to those who wished to accept it. Molière, however, intended his audience to regard the use of religion to achieve one's personal (as opposed to altruistic) ends as an odious maneuver. Accordingly, Elmire is not one of those easily persuaded. Tartuffe's attempt to give her freedom of conscience does not reckon that her conscience is far too deeply involved with someone else to adapt to his ends. Her conscience is inextricably involved in the welfare of her family.

Tartuffe's attempt at seduction (III, iii) utilizes the language of gallantry, which is little more than a seventeenth-century version of the language of Courtly Love. This is quite fitting when one remembers that for the courtly lover, Courtly Love was a religion. But equally important is the fact that for the men involved the practice of Courtly Love was doubtless many times an act of hypocrisy, merely a means to an end — the seduction of a lady.

When Tartuffe refers to women as "folles" because of their infatuation with "aristocratic gallants" (989), whose language he uses to court Elmire, we can see a veiled jealousy, grown out of his pride, of these men who represent something Tartuffe can only aspire to but never achieve.[122] Jealousy is an important element in the character of Tartuffe. Dorine, in the first act, suggested it as a motivating factor for Tartuffe's actions. Now again we find jealousy as a source of motivation, although it is kept always a little in the background by Tartuffe. We know that jealousy is not an emotion of a true man of God, but is more characteristic of a man aware of his own inferiorities. A jealous man cannot be an "homme de bien," in the Christian sense of the words.

Hypocrisy is Tartuffe's main device, and consequently it becomes his primary vice. Tartuffe as hypocrite, however, is inseparable from Tartuffe the proud, ambitious, gluttonous, and lustful. Molière keeps intensifying the idea that we have seen before: that a man subject to one vice is subject to all vices. The vices Molière employs as interwoven in the character of Tartuffe are those depicted so vividly in Roman Satire.

The special method of hypocrisy is not so much gesture and deed, then, as it is rhetoric, that fine art of persuasion. So it was in the Graeco-Roman culture,[123] just as in the medieval[124] and seventeenth-century French cultures, that words were the method of the clever man to achieve his desires. Whether through out-and-out lies or the more subtle and clever methods of casuistry and the direction of intention, the primary device is the same — words.

Horace, like Juvenal, was aware of the hypocrisy of the world around him. And, just as much as Juvenal, Horace saw the hypocrite as the dealer in meaningless words as well as vain gestures. Consider, for instance, the importance of words in this comment on the baseness of hypocrisy:

The man who backbites an absent friend; who fails to defend him when another finds fault; the man who courts the loud laughter of others, and the reputation of a wit; who can invent what he never saw; who cannot keep a secret — that man is black of heart; of him beware, good Roman.[125]

But gestures and deeds are considered equally worthy of censure by Horace,[126] who tells the reader that, following the course set by Lucilius, his intention is "to strip off the skin with which each strutted all bedecked before the eyes of men, though foul within . . ."[127] What Horace says, then, is that one of the purposes of satire is the revelation of hypocrisy, especially that brand which covers an evil heart with a veil of virtue.

Hypocrisy had its many forms in Rome as in every city that has ever grown to greatness. But those hypocrites who particularly caught the attention of the satiric poets were of a breed directly related to Tartuffe — religious and philosophic hypocrites. Although one might think they are much the same, there is a large difference between the religious and the philosophic hypocrite. As will be shown, however, they both provide traditional views of hypocrisy which were available to Molière for his depiction of Tartuffe.

Religion was a subject for satire from its generic inception in Rome. Lucilius, for instance, attempted to censure, among other forms of what he considered moral weakness, that division of religion which is called superstitition. This tradition continued in Horace, who took *superstitio* and *timor deorum* as two of his main topics in Satire II. 3. Juvenal also considers religion.[128] Both are concerned with the decline in the morality of the good old days to that of their own times when men are no longer humble before the gods.[129] Rather it was commonplace for men to flaunt their wanton desires in the very faces of the gods. Typical of such men is Juvenal's fat Lateranus, who is of a respectable family and holds high governmental office, but prefers to spend his time foolishly racing horses. Lateranus is expected, by virtue of his office, to offer sacrifices and prayers to Jupiter. He does perform the sacrifices, but the silent prayers he says are not to Jupiter but to Epona, the goddess of horseraces.[130]

It is interesting to note that many of the elements in Molière's characterization of Tartuffe are found in Juvenal's discussions of religious topics. Following his belief that there had been a decline in the traditional faith, Juvenal shows that the temples of the gods had become gathering-places for men without virtue and honor. He especially attacks the pervert Naevolus whose custom it was to make his pick-ups at the temple of Isis, the statue of Ganymede in the temple of Peace, the *secreta Palatia* of Magna Mater, and the temple of Ceres (IX. 22-24). Juvenal's comment at the end of this passage is also interesting in its relationship to Tartuffe:

> nam quo non prostat femina templo (24)?

It can be seen that Tartuffe's actions in placing himself at a church and awaiting a likely taker for his services have a parallel in classical satire.

Tartuffe's spectacular devotions at the church also find a parallel in Juvenal, where it is shown that the Romans were often quite vocal in addressing their gods:

> We summon Gods and men to our aid with cries as loud as that which the vocal dole applauds Faesidius when he pleads.[131]

These elements in both Molière's play and Juvenal's satire come into the proper perspective when one recalls that, in Juvenal's opinion, the real god of the Romans was wealth (I. 109-116). Accordingly, we can see that Molière's characterization of Tartuffe continues to reflect the concept of *sophrosyne*, with Tartuffe endowed again with antitheses to that ideal. The antitheses here are the same ones previously considered in the section on *sophrosyne*: wealth (avarice) and excess.

Juvenal makes several further comments about religion which continue the pattern we have seen, and which are again relevant to *Tartuffe*. In Satire XIII, Juvenal shows that it is easy for a man to scorn the gods, if no one knows about it — *si mortalis idem nemo sciat* (76). It is obvious that Tartuffe is a despiser of God, since his every action is a travesty of Christian charity. He completely neglects that very important ethical teaching of Christ, the Golden Rule. His activities are not designed to benefit his neighbor, but himself. The fact that Tartuffe is one of Juvenal's despisers of the gods is suggested by the fact that his statement:

> Le scandale du monde est ce qui fait l'offense,
> Et ce n'est pas pécher que pécher en silence (1505-1506)

is a variation on Juvenal's (76). The same despiser of the gods, in his self-concern, does not care what he has to do, as long as he can keep the profit of his crime:

> if he be a father, "May I eat," he tearfully declares, "my own son's head boiled, and dripping with Egyptian vinegar."

This is, of course, the same attitude as Tartuffe is seen to exhibit in Act V, scene vii, where he states:

> Et je sacrifierois à de si puissants nœuds
> Ami, femme, parents, et moi-même avec eux. (1883-1884)

This statement, with the exception of the "moi-même," which is doubtless inserted by Tartuffe as further proof of his supposed subservience and sense of duty, is a variation on the early words of Orgon: "Et je verrois mourir frère, enfants, mère et femme ..." (278) Both of these statements show clearly the lack of humanity and the extreme self-concern of the speakers, Tartuffe and Orgon. This self-concern on the part of Tartuffe was also seen in Dorine's description of his actions in Act I, scene v, where we saw his lack of Christian charity emphasized by his unconcern for the sick Elmire. Tartuffe is all self-concern. But, it will be recalled, his primary motivation is not toward mere food and wine. He wants money. Satire XIII reveals that this is a prime concern of the man who scorns the gods:

> Let Isis deal with my body as she wills, and blast my sight with her avenging rattle, provided only that even when blind I may keep the money which I disavow.[132]

Again we see the theme of avarice, so often repeated in Juvenal, and an antithesis to *sophrosyne*, connected with a character of the nature of Tartuffe.

Horace also provides an excellent example of the hypocrite who employs religion for his own benefit.

> This "good man," for forum and tribunal the cynosure of every eye, whenever with swine or ox he makes atonement to the gods, cries with loud voice "Father Janus," with loud voice "Apollo," then moves his lips, fearing to be heard: "Fair Laverna, grant me to escape detection; grant me to pass as just and upright, shroud my sins in night, my lies in clouds."[133]

Tartuffe follows closely in the steps of these two religious hypocrites. We know from the evidence of the play that Tartuffe is more concerned with his worldly desires than with his spiritual salvation. Accordingly, and on the basis of the depiction of Lateranus and Horace's "good man," one can question Tartuffe's motives. What was going through the mind of Molière's "homme de bien" as he knelt in prayer before the church, as he waited for Orgon to pass? Was he in reality saying a secret prayer that Orgon would come up to his expectations and provide him with an opportunity to fulfill his every desire? It is impossible to know. However, the earliest picture we have of Tartuffe and the evidence throughout the play suggest that he is not a good Christian, but a hypocrite. Yet his hypocrisy is not necessarily that of the atheist. Tartuffe at no time gives any evidence of such unbelief. For many people, however, the very fact that he could employ religion selfishly suggests or even proves that he must be an atheist. That is hardly so. Tartuffe is confused; his judgment is unbalanced. But it does not follow necessarily that he denies God. Rather he is probably one of those hypocrites who does have religious convictions, but think:

> Great though it is, yet the anger of the gods is slow: so if they take the time to punish all the guilty when will they ever reach me? Yet perhaps I'll find that God is merciful, *c'est son métier*. Many commit the same crimes and meet different fates: one is rewarded by the gallows, one by a crown.[134]

Tartuffe simply believes that he will not get caught. This belief is typically a product of his faulty judgment, which here fails to understand the inevitability of divine justice and the omniscience of God.

Another type, unique to the classical world, but probably coming closer to the Tartuffian religious hypocrite than does the one who merely veils his true desires while practicing his religious ceremonies, is the philosopher-hypocrite. Classical times saw many philosophies come into existence; most of them were dedicated to the attainment of virtue. One such philosophy was Stoicism, and there were many who followed its beliefs in the hope of attaining the good life. There were those, too, who saw in Stoicism the opportunity to fulfill their vicious desires. Seneca, one of the great Stoic thinkers of the classical world, commented on this phenomenon that there were "those who masquerade under the guise of the Stoic school and at the same time urge us on into vice."[135] Seneca noted also that there were those who "studied philosophy as if it were some marketable trade," and who failed to live in the manner which they themselves advised.[136] He found also philosophers who accepted doles, kept mistresses, and indulged their appetites in various other ways.[137] Seneca, a man deeply committed to the Stoic philosophy, saw these hypocrites and found them disgusting.

The higher a man aspires, the greater his fall. Such was the case with the Stoics. They proposed incredibly difficult ideals of virtue for themselves, and people naturally equated the Stoics with virtue. Therefore, when any member of their sect proved unvirtuous the magnitude of his failure was proportionate to the distance between him and his ideal. So the Stoics met with much criticism. One of the foremost of these critics was Juvenal, who attacked the Stoics for the same sort of hypocrisy as Seneca had before him — preaching virtue, but acting immorally.[138] Juvenal's attack on these pretended Stoics is given early in the poems, where he notes that these men are unlearned (*indocti*, II.4). The suggestion is again that they are not men of judgment, they have not educated themselves to the point of wisdom so that they can see and desire virtue alone.

The hypocrisy of Tartuffe is precisely of the type attacked by Horace, Juvenal, and Seneca. A similar action was described by Juvenal a millennium and a half before Molière wrote his play:

> For that vice has a deceptive appearance and semblance of virtue, being gloomy of mien, severe in face and garb.[139]

He puts on the appearance of virtue to hide his real nature, his *vitium*.

The concept of the deceptiveness of appearances is a commonplace in the Stoic philosophy.[140] The problem is that which confronted Orgon: how does one tell when appearances are deceiving? The answer, which Orgon obviously did not know, is that in many instances one can only tell through the test of time. Orgon could not have been absolutely sure of Tartuffe's character at their first meeting. Had he not been a *demens*, he could have realized this. But it had become Orgon's nature to leap into things without proper consideration. If, however, he had been trained in the Stoic philosophy, especially if he had read Seneca, Orgon could have known the kind of man Tartuffe was, for time and again Tartuffe fails to live up to his virtuous pose in precisely the same way which Seneca had described. His very first meeting with Tartuffe should have been a clue to Orgon, for Tartuffe's behavior at the church is immodest, not to say flamboyant. Such actions are entirely out of place and unnecessary for a man who understands the true nature of virtue and God. This would have been understood by Orgon if he had studied, as Molière did, the classical teachings on the subject of *sophrosyne*, as found in the satirists and Seneca.[141]

For the populace of seventeenth-century France, religion held a similar place of importance as a guide to life and a support against the buffets of fate to that played by the Stoic philosophy for the peoples of antiquity. Had Orgon made this equation, he could once again have recognized a flaw in the image Tartuffe presented on the basis of this further advice from Seneca:

> But this very philosophy must never be vaunted by you; for philosophy when employed with insolence and arrogance has been perilous to many. Let her strip off your faults, rather than assist you to decry the faults of others. Let her not hold aloof from the customs of mankind, nor make it her business to condemn whatever she herself does not do. A man may be wise without parade and without arousing enmity.[142]

The actions which Seneca tried to dissuade men from performing are precisely those which Tartuffe practices. He wears his religion (philosophy) as a headband so that everyone can see at first glance that he is a *dévot*. And, once in a position of respect, he insolently points out the faults of all the family of Orgon. He tries to keep Orgon's family separate from the customs of mankind, while he himself makes a false show of being aloof therefrom. Such obvious actions on the part of a hypocrite could not but arouse the enmity of any who were not fools.

The only time that Tartuffe will follow any of Seneca's advice is when he uses it as a ploy. Such is the case with Seneca's advice to strip off one's faults.[143] Tartuffe does so when accused of treachery in his attempt to seduce Elmire; but the effect Molière obtains from Tartuffe's speech is that of irony.[144] Tartuffe would never have made such a confession, had he expected Orgon to believe it. Such a self-denunciation was typical of the true ascetic who wished to castigate himself, not of Tartuffe. For the hypocrite it was an ingenious device produced by a complete understanding of Orgon and a basic knowledge of the actions of some ascetics.

The one proof of Tartuffe's actual character, which even Orgon should have recognized, was the obvious inconsistency between the words and deeds of the hypocrite. Had Tartuffe been a truly devout man, he would have achieved a consistency in his life. But not being truly devout, Tartuffe has not attempted to attain the wisdom which would temper his judgment so that he could see everything in its proper perspective. Such a wisdom is derived from philosophy, which "teaches us to act, not to speak; it exacts of every man that he should live according to his own standards, that his life should be of one hue and not out of harmony with all his activities. This, I say, is the highest duty and highest proof of wisdom, — that deed and word should be in accord, that a man should be equal to himself under all conditions, and always the same."[145]

This failure in wisdom is not only part of Tartuffe's character, but also of Orgon's. Orgon should have recognized the inequalities of precepts and activities in the life of Tartuffe, but he did not. The reason that Orgon did not recognize the flaws in Tartuffe's character is that he is a *demens*, just as is Tartuffe. Both are pursuing ends which, although different for each man, are equally wrong. A healthy mind in a healthy body would know that and direct a man toward legitimate desires. But this is impossible for Tartuffe. He is so corrupt that he no longer has the capability of self-rectification.

Tartuffe's covert sensuality, which was in evidence in the second scene of Act III, wherein Tartuffe chides Dorine for showing excessive cleavage (of which he is very much aware), is obviously opposed to the preachments he is continually making to the family, and to Orgon especially. This discrepancy, however, although it should make his real nature possible to assess, does not prevent Tartuffe from knowing the correct things to say on most occasions. In fact, although the earlier evidence of the play suggests, and the later evidence proves, that Tartuffe's actions are those of a religious hypocrite, his words at the beginning of Act III, scene iii, are precisely what they should be:

> Que le ciel à jamais par sa toute bonté
> Et de l'âme et du corps vous donne la santé ...

This prayer, hypocritical though it may be, recalls the ideal prayer of Juvenal:

> orandum est ut sit *mens sana in corpore sano* ...(X. 356)

Tartuffe, of course, wishes for no such thing. If the family were healthy in body and soul, there would be no chance of Tartuffe's gaining his ends. What these lines by Tartuffe do reveal is an awareness of a greater truth and good, which, in his state of *dementia*, Tartuffe can only misuse. Tartuffe's employment of Juvenal's concept of *mens sana in corpore sano*, then, serves merely to prove further that Tartuffe is truly a *demens* of the most corrupt nature.

### *Parasite, Client, and Friend*

Molière, the writer and actor of comedies, was concerned with the sociability of mankind. This is evident from his plays. Such a concern was doubtless in part due to the education he received at the hands of the Jesuits. At the Collège de Clermont stress was placed, as we have seen in the Introduction, on human relations, on the concept that all men are neighbors, and that one should be educated in the good and right in order to be of benefit to his neighbors. Such an education, utilizing among other means the literature of ancient Rome, must have influenced Molière's production of comedies, making him, perhaps unconsciously, particularly aware of many varieties of human relationships.

There is a special relationship, common to literary and artistic men of many ages, which is important to our understanding of *Tartuffe*. This relationship is patronage. It will be remembered that Molière knew the patronage of Louis XIV, as well as other patrons of the arts such as the Prince de Condé. Under such patrons the rewards to the protégé were money, particularly, but also, and of equal importance to men without powerful families, influence.[146] Many of the protégés must have been little more than parasites. But, for the actual creative genius such as Molière, the relative credits and debits of subservience to Louis's patronage must have caused him some anguish. This relationship has been delineated by Palmer, who states that Molière "was obliged to spend largely of the years of his prime in organizing entertainments for the Court which he should have been free to employ in other ways. The King overworked and misused his genius ..."[147] There can be little doubt that Molière gave considerable thought to human relationships, patronage among them. It is this relationship, wherein one man offers his substance in return for another man's services, that we see in *Tartuffe*. The question that remains is: to what extent is Tartuffe-Orgon a reflection of the relationships depicted in Roman satire, among which we must consider especially parasitism, clientage, and friendship?

The parasite is a frequent character in classical literature. He was not known, however, until after the days of Athenian greatness. The parasite emerged as a common type only after the conquests of Alexander had brought the wealth of the East to Greece. Then, when luxury and extravagance stood in vivid contrast to the sordid life of the poor, this social phenomenon sprang into existence.

The parasite is to be found especially in the comedies and satires. Although in each comedy his presentation may vary slightly, there is one characteristic which typifies him — "love of good food and a desire for free meals."[148] Tartuffe certainly is in accord with this aspect of the classical concept of the parasite. One has but to recall the words of Dorine in Act I, scene v, to see how important food is to Tartuffe. Dorine's lengthy speech in Act I, scene ii, describing the relationship between Orgon and Tartuffe, as she has seen it, is more indicative of the character of Orgon than it is of Tartuffe's. Only indirectly can one draw conclusions about Tartuffe, except for the one fact that comes out explicitly at this point — Tartuffe is a parasite.

Molière's Tartuffe is a parasite. That is well established by the evidence of the play. It has been noted that his actions resemble those of the traditional parasite.[149] Tartuffe is not, however, the typical parasite of comedy or satire, for he enjoys a position of power and prominence that most parasites would hardly have thought possible. To understand this contrast it will be necessary to consider the parasite as depicted in Roman satire.

The parasite of Roman satire was the product, for the most part, of an institution called *clientela*, or clientage.[150] According to this system, a patron, usually a member of the upstart rich, accepted as dependents a number of clients to insure himself a prominent position in the gaze of society. These clients were nearly always men who had no definite way of earning a living. They tried, therefore, by flattery and sycophancy to win the favor of the rich and great. The one requisite duty of the client was his attendance on his patron. This usually consisted of a call to pay his respects in the early morning, in return for which the client expected a meal a day as his due.[151] But he was often lucky to get even that. This was the system which was attacked by the satiric poets, and which can, perhaps, provide a better understanding of the Orgon-Tartuffe relationship.

The clients generally had to endure humiliating treatment at the hands of their patrons. Seneca rebuked them for doing so.[152] But they were not such men as could endure poverty when mere debasement stood in the way of a crust of bread. Therefore, the clients were treated much as they deserved. When they came to call, the patron often made no salutation and sometimes refused them entrance. But their greatest humiliations came at the dinner table. There the client was made painfully aware of his lower standing by being served table scraps and vinegar while the patron and his guests ate and drank luxuriously. The dinner party occurs as a satiric theme in both Horace and Juvenal.[153] Such a party, which reveals the satiric sides of host and guests, is sometimes called the Painful Dinner.[154]

The Painful Dinner itself is not employed by Molière. What Molière does employ is the concept of the importance of food to the parasite, as seen in Tartuffe's actions as described above by Dorine. Molière did not need to employ elaborately the motif of the Painful Dinner to reveal the satiric side of Tartuffe and Orgon. He managed to achieve the same result through a combination of several devices, one of which is closely related to the theme of the Painful Dinner. This device is seen in the "le pauvre homme" scene, wherein the self-concern of Tartuffe and the Tartuffe-concern of Orgon are presented to the view of the audience. What is revealed in this scene is the comical and satirical aspect of the relationship between Tartuffe and Orgon. A better understanding of this relationship may be achieved through a comparison with the "friendship" of one of the noteworthy patrons of Roman satire — Virro.

In Juvenal's Fifth Satire, the cruelty and inhumanity of the host, Virro, are stressed. At every opportunity he shows his contempt for the clients who "share" his dinner. "Juvenal makes it clear that Virro's behavior is due solely to malice. His object is to degrade his dependents while enjoying his own sense of power."[155] Virro is guilty of *sordes*, stinginess, towards his clients. This action, another of the enormities exceptional to *sophrosyne*, marks him clearly as a *demens*. This condemnation is intensified by the fact that his *sordes* is displayed intentionally to torment the clients; it is an act of unrestrained cruelty. By considering the similarities and dissimilarities in Virro and Orgon, we may be able to come to a better understanding of the character of Orgon, and so of Tartuffe.

Orgon is the nominal ruler of his household. He has accepted Tartuffe into that household as a guest in return for certain duties. The duties are, of course, those of a spiritual adviser. It has been proposed, however, that Orgon benefits from Tartuffe in two other ways: first, his real desire to exhibit the "sadism of a family tyrant" can be satisfied through the person of Tartuffe;[156] also, Orgon attains the self-aggrandizement which can be achieved through association with a truly "religious" man.[157] Orgon, however, is the head of the household, and, as the patron, should clearly stand on a level superior to that of Tartuffe. This is not the case at all. A complete reversal of position has taken place.[158] Tartuffe stands now in the patron's position, grudgingly receiving Orgon for his morning call, treating the family as well as Orgon with utter disrespect. Tartuffe eats, drinks, and sleeps as he pleases. He is the lord and master, the parton, now. But, although he may be wicked, it is only indirectly (by getting Orgon to treat his family so harshly) that Tartuffe takes on the aspect of cruelty which was seen in Virro's character. Direct cruelty is left for Orgon. Nor does Orgon, patron in name only, direct this cruelty toward his new client-patron, but rather toward his own family, whom he seems to enjoy tormenting. Orgon's actions speak for themselves: he acts rudely with Cléante; he plays the tyrant over his daughter; he is cold and insolent to Elmire; he drives his son away; and finally he disinherits his entire family. Each of these actions, including the last, is typical of the treatment a client could have expected from a patron such as Virro.[159] But never would a man treat his family in such a way, while some stranger played the tyrant in his household, unless that man were mad.[160]

In Juvenal's Satire IX there occurs another parton named Virro, who is very likely the same man as encountered in Satire V. In IX there is a further similarity between that poem and Molière's *Tartuffe*. Act IV, scene v of *Tartuffe* illustrates an important subspecies of satire. There Molière causes Tartuffe to reveal himself completely. Up to this point there may have been some doubt (in the minds of a few) that Tartuffe was a hypocrite. But Tartuffe's statements that Heaven is no obstacle to his wishes (1481-1483), and that sinning in private is not sinning at all (1506) leave no doubt in anyone's mind. Tartuffe has displayed his hypocrisy for all to see: but even more despicable is that he should, as Gilbert Highet says, "glory in his outrageous vices."[161] This technique of self-revelation is an important trick whereby the satirist or comedian allows his subject to incriminate or reveal himself. It is employed as the primary device in Horace's Satire II, 4, and in Juvenal's Satire IX. The latter poem is particularly relevant here, for, along with Satire Five, it is one of the keys to the understanding of the Tartuffe-Orgon relationship. Naevolus, the aging pervert, concerned with his future, reveals himself utterly. Since Molière's depiction of the Tartuffe-Orgon relationship presents a comic inversion of Juvenal's version of the patron-client relationship, it is interesting that he allowed Tartuffe to expose himself in the same manner as Naevolus.

The self-exposure scene is typical of the art of the satirist. It presents one more scene in the series that has continued from the opening curtain, all designed to present as vividly as possible the effects of a foolish and wicked person, Tartuffe, on a normal world. It presents, to be added to those that have preceded it, one more painful and absurd situation. The destructiveness of Tartuffe should be self-evident. But the satirist does not have the confidence in people to believe that they can see his true nature. Therefore, the enormity of Tartuffe's character is stressed time and time again, until the people cannot help but see him as he really is. This is part of the satirist's art.

The clients often became highly skilled in the devices and deceits of sycophancy. They knew how to hold their tongues in order to insure themselves a meal, since, as Martial remarked, "You can't be both outspoken and a glutton."[162] That is, you cannot, unless you have a patron such as Orgon — a man who can be led by the nose, a man who wants to be mastered. But most patrons were cut from a different cloth and made of stouter material than Orgon. To get a meal from such men as these took a client of cunning and craft; it took — a Greek.

No character of ancient Rome is a closer antecedent to the parasite-hypocrite Tartuffe than the *Graeculus esuriens* (the hungry Greekling), at least as he was depicted by Juvenal in his Third Satire. Juvenal saw foreigners, especially the Greeks, as a threat to Roman society and morals. The satirist "distrusted Greek versatility, elusiveness, lack of principle."[163] He saw that these "outsiders" managed to wheedle their way into households where they replaced in the favor of the patron those who were more deserving of the position (such as Juvenal himself). But what was most disgusting were the ways in which the Greeks achieved their ends. First of all, they are the most highly skilled of sycophants; they know all the tricks of the trade. They are all "quick of wit," "of unbound impudence," and "ready of speech."[164] They are "experts of flattery," who can win their patrons' affection by lies that would be unbelievable if told by any other (83-96). But their skills are not limited to lying words. They are actors from a nation of actors (100). The Greek can play any role (93-97). But he is best at putting on the precise face which his patron has on, whether it shows joy or sorrow, ready at a moment's notice to change faces (105-106). And if his patron happens to belch or perform some other insignificant act, the Greek stands ever ready with praise for a job well done (106-107). But this is only one side of the character of the Greek, for, besides being a parasite, he is a hypocrite.

The Greek enters the house of his patron as a client, but his intention is not to stay one. His plan is to become the master (72). If he cannot become master in name, he at least will live like one, so he seduces the master's wife (109-110). His progress is a direct result of his ability to deceive, to "turn black into white" (30). A typical deception of a Greek is the poisoning of his patron's mind toward a member of the household so that that man is expelled and the Greek gains a firm standing in his master's estimation (122-125). And, when caught in the act of a deception, it is hardly surprising that the Greek, almost as if emboldened by the circumstances, vaunts his crime with a confidence in the position he has built up.[165]

The points of comparison and contrast between Tartuffe and the *Graeculus* are very important to this study; therefore, they will be commented on in some detail. Tartuffe enters the household of his patron, but he does not have to wheedle to do so. He does so rather by knowing, like the Greek, the "tricks of the trade," and especially by knowing his man: he "connôit sa dupe" (199). That Tartuffe is "quick of wit" and ready of speech is ably demonstrated by his casuistry in the seduction scenes. Were he not "of unbounded impudence," he would not have attempted any of his schemes, especially the seduction of his patron's wife. Tartuffe does not reveal himself an "expert in flattery," but there can be no doubt that had there been need of flattery, he would have been more than able to produce the most believable of lies. Although Tartuffe does not tell an out-and-out lie in the play, his whole career in the life of Orgon is a lie, for it is an act, just as Tartuffe is an actor. What is Tartuffe's act but an imposture of the "precise face which his patron has on," namely religion or virtue. Moreover, as we have seen, at the end of the play Tartuffe proves that he is "ready at a moment's notice to change faces," as he proceeds from his posture of religion to one of politics. Tartuffe does not stand ready with praise for his patron or his family; rather, it is he whose belch receives a blessing, and that from his patron Orgon (194). Like the *Graeculus*, Tartuffe enters the household of his patron as a client, but he has no intention of staying one. Tartuffe is even more successful in his attempt to become master of the household than the *Graeculus*, for he actually succeeds in having all the properties put into his name. But, before that happens, Tartuffe lives as if he were the master of the household, imposing his will on the members, eating and spending of its substance, and even attempting the seduction of the patron's wife. His success is achieved through the same device as the Greek's: he is able to "turn black into white"; to make himself, a criminal and fool, appear what he is not, virtuous and wise. His success in obtaining the properties of Orgon is achieved largely through that very clever device typical of the Greek, "the poisoning of his patron's mind toward a member of the household," in his case, the turning of Orgon against his son, Damis, with the result that he is projected into an even higher position in his patron's estimation.

The points of comparison between Tartuffe and the *Graeculus esuriens* reveal a certain affinity between Molière and Juvenal and suggest a knowledge, or at least an awareness on the part of Molière, of the traditional treatments of the theme of patronage. The points of contrast, however, are equally important, for there can be seen in them a significant difference in the character of Orgon from that of the Greek's patron. It has been noted that Tartuffe did not have to play the sycophant to obtain his position in Orgon's household; and, in the fourth act, Tartuffe is completely successful in becoming master of Orgon's house. These points of variation show that there is a basic difference between the Graeculus-patron and Tartuffe-Orgon relationships. This difference is to be found in the character of Orgon, however, more than in that of Tartuffe.

It has been suggested that Orgon must *of his own nature* "serve."[166] He is not happy unless he has someone in whose service he may function. His mistake is in going from the service of a good king to a wicked imposter. For his servitude takes on part of the nature of whomsoever he serves.[167] By serving, furthermore, Orgon is able to avoid a certain aspect of a normal life which he finds himself incapable of accepting — the requirement to make decisions. Thus, by foregoing his power as head of the household in favor of Tartuffe, he effectually removes these obligations from his shoulders. The motivating impulses are: "une attitude générale de fuite devant ses responsibilités fonctionelles, un refus de s'assimiler complètement à sa fonction de paterfamilias."[168] Anyone can flatter and fawn, for there are many who are pleased by such actions. Orgon is not strictly one of that category of men who can be pleased by flattery, and this is part of the mastery of Molière's characterization of Tartuffe. Tartuffe thoroughly scouted his man before beginning his game. He knew that Orgon was a man who would rather be governed than be governor, mastered than master.[169] For Orgon would find the same pleasure the masters of the sycophants found, but in precisely the opposite relationship. The key to Tartuffe's actions is always the character of Orgon.

The *Graeculus esuriens* certainly parallels the career of Tartuffe in a number of ways. But he is not Tartuffe, for Tartuffe is a combination of many causes and effects. Among the causes, Orgon must rank high, for it is the interaction of the two characters which produces the Tartuffe of the play. One has no doubt that Tartuffe, had he been injected into a different situation, under a masterful patron, would have been a cringing sycophant rather than an imperious lieutenant for Orgon. The desire to be mastered which is central to the character of Orgon causes a complete reversal of roles so that, as we have seen, it is not the patron (Orgon) who says his "God bless you" to the client (Tartuffe).[170]

This modification of the situation established in Juvenal creates a particularly significant difference directed at the man familiar with satire. The variation is great, but it has not really been seen before. In the past it has been looked upon as merely a comic show of Orgon's stupidity and the command of Tartuffe's feigned personality over him. This is, of course, a valid view — as far as it goes. What it fails to consider, in relation to the traditions of satire, are the immense humiliations and cruelties normally directed toward the client by the patron. It is this difference between the actions of Orgon and a Virro which gives the role of Orgon a satiric, dramatic irony.

Juvenal's Third and Fifth Satires, like Molière's *Tartuffe*, satirize both the individuals, patron and dependent, lay-director and paterfamilias, who are involved in normally salutary human relationships. They present perversions of relationships originally intended as benefits to both parties. Molière, in his concern for human sociability, provides in the figures of Tartuffe and Orgon negative models from whose flaws one can hopefully profit. This is, of course, the same method employed by Horace and Juvenal in their continuous struggle against vice. Molière, however, does not limit himself to negative examples, for there are a number of figures who represent an ideal in his plays. These are especially the *raisonneurs*, among whose number is Cléante of *Tartuffe*. Although he may not be the complete model for all that is good in a human relationship, Cléante's character comprises a number of elements which are traditionally desirable in a friend, companion, or adviser. It will be profitable to consider the patron-dependent relationship of that of the friend and adviser as they are depicted in Roman satire and the philosophic works of Seneca in order to see which elements, both good and bad, are reflected in Molière's depiction of Orgon, Tartuffe and Cléante. Emphasis should again be made of the fact that contrasts and variations are as meaningful (if not more so) as resemblances or parallels within similar traditions.

The ideal patron-dependent relationship is described at considerable length by Horace in Satire I. 6. There he employs the relationship he knows best and understands — that which he had with his patron Maecenas — as a model. Maecenas was a truly great man, who was never patron to the unworthy. Rather, he was always careful to accept only dependents who were proven worthy, keeping at a distance those who were motivated by base ambition (51-52). Maecenas was not the sort of man who was impressed with appearances.[171] Rather, he sought men who wanted not merely the wealth or fame of an association with him, but the opportunity to perform some beneficial or creative function. Nor was he the "sort of patron who would demand unreasonable sacrifices on the part of his clients ..."[172] In return for his kind treatment from Maecenas, Horace "realized that he owed some respect to Maecenas in virtue of his superior position, and that in winning his patronage he had contracted certain obligations in return."[173]

At first glance it would appear that there is no basis for consideration of Horace's depiction of his relationship with Maecenas as a meaningful statement on human relationships, which finds a reflection in *Tartuffe*. The two relationships are not really at all similar, but that is exactly the point. The contrast between the relationship of Horace-Maecenas and that of Tartuffe-Orgon is important. Each positive point Horace makes is negated in Molière's play. Orgon is an insignificant man compared to Maecenas. Orgon's every action is a fool's move; at no time does he properly consider his actions or their consequences. Therefore, no respect is due to him. Nor does he receive any from Tartuffe. Rather, Tartuffe shows him scorn at this earliest opportunity; the character of Tartuffe allows no feeling of obligation.

There is, however, in *Tartuffe* an implied relationship which closely compares to the ideal established by Horace. The patron in this relationship is the Prince, Louis XIV, who was, in fact, Molière's patron, and who is established as the ideal leader, as seen in Act V, scene vii, where the Exempt states:

> Nous vivons sous un prince ennemi de la fraude,
> Un prince dont les yeux se font jour dans les cœurs,
> Et que ne peut tromper tout l'art des imposteurs.
> D'un fin discernement sa grande âme pourvue
> Sur les choses toujours jette une droite vue;
> Chez elle jamais rien ne surprend trop d'accès,
> Et sa ferme raison ne tombe en nul excès.
> Il donne aux gens de bien une gloire immortelle;
> Mais sans aveuglement il fait briller ce zèle,
> Et l'amour pour les vrais ne ferme point son coeur
> A tout ce que les faux doivent donner d'horreur.
> Celui-ci n'étoit pas pour le pouvoir surprendre,
> Et de pièges plus fins on le voit se défendre.
> D'abord il a percé, par de vives clartés,
> Des replis de son cœur toutes les lâchetés. (1906-1920)

Both Maecenas and Louis are concerned with true worth, particularly as proven by good works. Neither is impressed by appearance or tricks, but each searches through to the heart of the man, and rewards him according to his true merits. It becomes obvious that the same traits (especially perspicacity and wisdom) which constitute a good patron are found in a good leader. This is doubtless partly what Molière is saying in *Tartuffe*, for, throughout the play, we have seen reiterated the concept of the destructiveness of any and all forms of *dementia*, and the necessity of the attainment of wisdom and virtue. Thus, in the closing act of *Tartuffe*, Molière provides a picture not merely of a good leader, but of one who embodies precisely those traits which have been idealized and whose antitheses have been attacked throughout the play.

An example of a bad dependent is provided by Horace in his depiction of the "bore" in Satire I. 9. This man tells Horace that he is willing to go to any lengths to get into Maecenas' good graces. He will bribe Maecenas' servants (57), keep trying to get in (57-58), look for the opportunities to meet him in the street (58-59), and join his escort (59).

The comparison with the way in which Tartuffe and Orgon met is quite striking. Tartuffe does not have to look for corruption in Orgon's household to gain entrance; Orgon is already a fool given to extremes. It is not difficult for Tartuffe to lead him into corruption. Therefore, Tartuffe does not bother to bribe Orgon's servants. He does persist in his attempts; knowing the times Orgon goes to church, Tartuffe awaits him there, only to be himself escorted to Orgon's home. The reversal of situation is typical of the approach Molière applies to traditional material: he repeatedly reverses the normal, expected or ideal circumstances, so as to emphasize, as here, the enormity of Orgon's folly, the influence of Tartuffe's evil, or the extent of Tartuffe's immoderation. It is further noteworthy that the "bore," although he never attains the status of client to Maecenas, is ultimately arrested and dragged off to court just as is his counterpart Tartuffe. Therefore, the outcome of the potentially bad client is the same as that of the really bad client.

Two other poems of Horace, each concerned with the proper behavior of a dependent toward a patron, reveal further contrasts between Tartuffe and the ideal client. Horace advises the prospective protégé first of all to use tact in making requests.[174] Tartuffe has, in contrast, made known his every desire, except Elmire, to Orgon, who has promptly granted all Tartuffe's needs: wealth; food and drink; power; even an opportunity to vent his lust on either Mariane (in marriage) or Elmire (in adultery), the one with Orgon's hearty approval, the other with unwitting encouragement. The extent and object of these requests should have revealed Tartuffe for what he was, and would have to anyone but an utter fool.

Horace continues his advice, resuming his lectures on *sophrosyne* and the "mean." He advises the dependent to seek the virtuous mean between the two vices, equally wrong, of excessive servility and excessive independence.[175] Tartuffe suffers from the latter of the two vices. But this is a direct result of Orgon's character. Orgon would not have reacted favorably to fawning flattery. He needed the masterful independence of Tartuffe, even if that independence was a vice exceptional to the ideal of the "mean."

Another admonition offered by Horace to the dependent is: "Respect the confidences of your patron."[176] But Tartuffe does not respect Orgon; therefore, why should he respect his confidences? He does not; he reveals them when it appears that such actions will remove Orgon, who can only be a source of distress to him, from his now legally-possessed home. Respect and honor are virtues; they have no place in the character of Tartuffe.

The only time Tartuffe complies with Horace's advice is when that advice works to his benefit. Therefore, Tartuffe manages to gain entrance to Orgon's house by following Horace's admonition to take an active interest in the interests of the patron.[177] This is exactly the means by which Tartuffe wangles his way into the household of Orgon: by becoming a seeming proponent of Orgon's major interest of the moment — religion.

Critics who regard Orgon as the central caracter of the drama treat the first meeting of Orgon and Tartuffe in this light, and make such claims as: "Tout s'est passé comme si Orgon, prêt à rencontrer exactement Tartuffe, s'était contenté jusqu'ici de pis'aller."[178] Such claims, presuming that Orgon is the primary agent in the choosing of Tartuffe, seem to miss the most important point because they insist on underestimating Tartuffe. This point is simply that it was Tartuffe who chose Orgon, and not the reverse. This most important aspect of Tartuffe comes out in Dorine's speech in Act I, scene ii. We find that Tartuffe has not merely presented himself and been loved for his own natural self, but rather has intentionally formed himself into the image of a man who could fulfill Orgon's needs and desires:

> Lui qui connoît sa dupe et qui veut en jouir,
> Par cent dehors farda l'art de l'éblouir ...(199-200)

Tartuffe's intent is the cause of all that happens.[179] Orgon is only a tool whereby Tartuffe can work his end.

Once Tartuffe has attained his initial goal by complying with Horace's advice to take an active interest in the interests of his patron (prospective), he immediately begins to go against it. The dependent should not criticize the interests of others.[180] But that is exactly what Tartuffe does once he is installed as a member of Orgon's household; he criticizes the activities of everyone in the family, much to the displeasure of everyone except Madame Pernelle and Orgon, who takes pleasure in seeing his family tormented. Nor does Tartuffe comply with Horace's suggestion that a dependent should avoid "improper conduct" with members of his patron's household,[181] a suggestion also made in Juvenal's reference to the activities of the Greek.[182] He merely awaits his opportunity to attempt the seduction of Elmire without the least fear of reprisal from Orgon. He knows his man too well.

The education which Molière was provided, it will be remembered, stressed the relationships of men, in the belief that men of virtue and wisdom could help their neighbors in the progress toward *Christianas costumbres*.[183] This concept of the neighbor-function of mankind was drawn from the Bible and from the precepts and examples provided by classical literature on the recurrent theme of friendship. Moreover, in his period of retirement at Auteuil, Molière must have given much consideration to friendship and other human relationships.[184] It is possible that, under the influence of Boileau, Molière reread the classical literature on friendship during this period. We have seen that Molière has presented the ideals found in classical satire in their perversions by depicting in Tartuffe or Orgon the antitheses particularly of *sophrosyne* and *sapientia*. One would expect Molière to continue to pervert *(renverser)* the other ideals which constitute his two main characters, Tartuffe and Orgon. It remains for us, then, to see if the relationship of Orgon-Tartuffe is a perversion of yet another ideal — the institution of friendship.

It is made obvious to us that the relationship of Orgon and Tartuffe is much closer than that we should expect from an ordinary patron-client business arrangement. It certainly approaches, through the guile of Tartuffe, a friendship. In fact, in Act III, scene vii, we find Tartuffe speaking to Orgon of their "friendship" (1169), in terms which Orgon readily accepts. Moreover, in Act IV, scene i, we find Tartuffe expressing a concern for "the good of his neighbor" (*le bien du prochain*, 1248). This concept of the neighbor-function of mankind combines with that of friendship, when used by Tartuffe, to form not Christian or classical ideals, but successful devices for the religious hypocrite who is aware of the traditional values, and uses them not for the betterment of mankind, but for his own enrichment. As used in the two scenes discussed above, and as seen implicitly throughout the play, friendship and neighborliness are turned into perversions by Tartuffe, just as he perverted every ideal he should represent throughout the play. The extent to which this is true of friendship can be seen by a consideration of Tartuffe in relation to the presentation of friendship in classical literature.

Friendship was an ideal for the men of classical times, but that ideal was as often tarnished then by the nature of man as it is now. Therefore, much discussion of friendship and the choice of a friend took place. Although opinions varied, some rules for choosing a friend were generally accepted. First, he should be virtuous, and he ought to be a wise man.[185] The choice of a friend should be made on the basis of that man's personal character.[186] Once a friend has been selected, the friendship can only be maintained by mutual tolerance, for a friend must be willing to overlook his friend's faults in consideration of those virtues for which he was chosen.[187] Nor should a friend be rejected just because he does not fall readily into the standard categories. He must be judged on his own merits, especially his true inner character.[188] If these rules are followed, one can make and maintain a lasting friendship. But the great difficulty lies in the choice of a friend who is truly virtuous.

A good example of a bad friend is provided in this story from Seneca.

> A soldier who had proven his worth to Philip of Macedon was shipwrecked. Discovered half-dead by a charitable man, the soldier was taken in and provided for by the man until his recovery was complete. Then the man provided the soldier a viaticum on his parting, and was told by the soldier that Philip would be told of his

kindness. The soldier, however, did not tell of the good man's many services, but instead asked the king for that man's estates as a reward for his services. The good man, ejected from his property, sent a letter to Philip telling the true story. Philip, incensed at the abuse, ordered the estate to be returned to the rightful owner, and the thankless friend to be chastized as an example for others.[189]

This story provides an occasion of divine intervention somewhat similar to that in *Tartuffe* in that bad friends are punished by kings, in each case unexpectedly. The major difference is in the character of the good man as compared with Orgon. Whereas Orgon was trying to fulfill his needs by taking in Tartuffe, the good man is merely performing an act of charity.

One can find out if a man is truly worthy of friendship only by considering "his soul, its quality and stature," thus learning "whether its greatness is borrowed, or its own."[190] There is always the hypocrite, who has "decked himself out or painted himself up," who arrives only "after being announced," who attempts to deceive men by the "mask that is easily drawn over the face."[191] But he is easily recognized, if you examine him with care. One particular type to avoid is the voluptuous man, for he "can neither be a good man, a good patriot, nor a good friend," since he is "transported with his appetites . . ."[192]

Had Orgon been the sort of man to examine carefully according to the tenets set forth by Seneca the life of the man he was about to choose as a friend, he would have known that Tartuffe, being a voluptuous person, could not be a good friend. And, accordingly, Orgon would not have trusted his secrets and the cassette full of incriminating evidence to Tartuffe, had he known the real Tartuffe. But he did not, for Molière depicted Orgon as a man lacking precisely the kind of wisdom that Seneca and the satirists presented as an ideal toward which the good man constantly strives.

Juvenal, as we saw in the section of this chapter on *sophrosyne*, in the account of Calvinus' troubles, provides an instance of a false friend who accepts a deposit on trust from a friend, but intends to use the contents for his own benefit.[193] This seems to have been a common occurrence in Juvenal's day;[194] it could have been a lesson for Orgon. But Orgon never did learn his lessons very well.

This general category of friendship also includes a classical parallel for the position of Tartuffe as lay director of conscience to Orgon. This is Seneca's guardian *(custos)*. The Stoic philosopher and satirist states that men of weaker character need someone to precede them, saying, "Avoid this," or "Do that."[195] Such a guardian is necessary, but one should be very careful that he is truly a man deserving of respect.[196] Therefore, it is necessary to look not for a man of great glibness, who makes a display of his philosophy or religion, but a man whose very life is a model from which one can learn virtue, who lives exactly as he tells others to live.[197] Seneca provides an extended description of the relationship between the guardian and the man seeking true wisdom and virtue. It is worth quoting *in toto* since it presents the ideal against which Tartuffe-Orgon stand as a travesty.

> "Cherish some man of high character, and keep him ever before your eyes, living as if he were watching you, and ordering all your actions as if he beheld them." Such, my dear Lucilius, is the counsel of Epicurus: he has quite properly given us a guardian and an attendant. We can get rid of most sins, if we have a witness who stands near us when we are likely to go wrong. The soul should have someone whom it can respect, — one by whose authority it may make even its inner shrine more hallowed. Happy is the man who can make others better, not merely when he is in their company, but even when he is in their thoughts! And happy also is he who can so revere a man as to calm and regulate himself by calling him to mind! One who can so revere another, will soon be himself worthy of reverence. Choose therefore a Cato; or, if Cato seems too severe a model, choose some Laelius, a gentler spirit. Choose a master whose life, conversation, and soul-expressing face have satisfied you; picture him always to yourself as your protector or your pattern. For we must indeed have someone according to whom we may regulate our characters; you can never straighten that which is crooked unless you use a ruler.[198]

Seneca goes on to provide examples of men who have attained wisdom by following a philosopher-guardian. Such a man was Cleanthes, the Stoic sage and proponent of *sophrosyne*,[199] who took as his guardian Zeno, the founder of the Stoic school. Cleanthes is, of course, the Greek name from which Cléante is derived. It will be remembered that Cléante in Molière's play is compared by Orgon directly to Cato, a Roman Stoic noted for his continence. Molière knew of the Stoic sages at least by name. Seneca, who took his teacher Attalus as his model of virtue,[200] can also be numbered among the Stoic sages who profited from a *custos*.

It is, however, Horace who provides us the most immediate and striking example of such a *custos*: his own father, who performed exactly the tasks which Tartuffe, as director of conscience, should have.

> He himself, a guardian true and tried, went with me among all my teachers. Need I say more? He kept me chaste — and that is virtue's first grace — free not only from every deed of shame, but from all scandal.[201]

Horace's father was absolutely incorruptible; he honored virtue, especially chastity. He was, if not a Stoic, at least a sage, as Horace represents him, for he had the faculty of discerning between the good and the bad so that he was able to keep his charge from wrongdoing and the resultant criticism. Horace's guardian was his own father. What he is doing in this passage is two things: first, he is extolling his father; second, he is presenting an ideal which is obviously within the same tradition as Seneca's concept of the *custos*. The fact that Horace's father is his *custos* is exceptional; the actions of his father are not — they are typical of a wise and virtuous guardian.[202]

We have seen in the previous sections of this chapter that Molière has successfully carried out his plan of inverting *(renverser)* normally beneficial and salutary human relationships and ideals. It is obvious that in respect to the concept of friendship, Tartuffe is once again depicted as the reverse, a perversion, of the ideal. Tartuffe has a complete misunderstanding of the basic problem of what is good and what bad, what should be sought and what avoided. He shows this particularly by failing in the very virtue which was so honored by Horace's father — chastity.

In another of his autobiographical passages, Horace further presents this image of his father:

> Your philosopher will give you theories for shunning or seeking this or that: enough for me, if I can uphold the rule our fathers have handed down, and if, so long as you need a guardian, I can keep your health and name from harm. When years have brought strength to body and mind, you will swim without the cork.[203]

Here Horace's father sets himself up as a *custos* of his young son's morals and life, pointing out to him what is to be avoided and sought. It is such an exemplar of wisdom and morality that Orgon should have sought, but did not.

The character of Orgon has brought forth much critical debate. One authority finds the key to Orgon in the idea that "Orgon's real desire is . . . to have himself recognized by all around him as divinely absolute and self-sufficient."[204] This theory follows the line of thought put forth by Erich Auerbach, whose proposition is important enough to be stated at length:

> Orgon's most deeply instinctive and secret craving, which he can indulge precisely by selling himself and his soul to Tartuffe, is the sadism of a family tyrant. What he would never dare to do without piety making it legitimate, for he is as sentimental and uncertain of himself as he is choleric, he can now give himself up to with a clear conscience: *faire enrager le monde est ma plus grand joie!* (3, 7; cf. also 4, 3: *je porte en ce contrat de quoi vous faire rire*). He loves

Tartuffe and lets himself be duped by him because Tartuffe makes it possible for him to satisfy his instinctive urge to tyrannize over and torment his family. This further weakens his power of judgment, which in itself is not too highly developed.[205]

Orgon did, perhaps, have an incipient urge for spiritual health and a desire for wisdom and virtue. The possibility of obtaining these, however, was effectually checked by the nature of his character and rational powers. It has been shown in this chapter that Orgon incorporates a number of the aspects of the *demens* which are found in Roman satire. His *dementia* is nowhere better revealed than in his acceptance of Tartuffe as a spiritual guardian. Orgon did not obtain a guardian who was truly a man of wisdom and virtue; therefore, he could not himself expect to attain these goals. He failed, then, at the most basic level. But the desires for spiritual health, wisdom and virtue were not his only urges; more potent than those were his desires for self-aggrandizement through association with a truly devout man, for freedom from the burdens of responsibility, and for the opportunity to play the tyrant over his family indirectly, as he would never have dared to do so directly. For Orgon the choice was made according to a list of priorities, which had been made by an already defective mind. When it came to making a choice, we see how really unimportant such goods as wisdom and virtue were to Orgon. That incipient urge for virtue was readily replaced by the secret cravings of Orgon. Tartuffe, brought into the household as a spiritual guardian, but, in fact, a hypocrite and fool, signifies that appetency on the part of Orgon toward virtue which merely conceals the tendency toward vice. What Orgon really wanted was the means to flaunt his religiosity, and, freed of responsibilities, to tyrannize and torment his family. Tartuffe served as a means to these ends. What more could Orgon have asked? A true friend?

### *Sejanus and the Corruption of Political Power*

It has been shown that every important aspect of the characters of Tartuffe and Orgon is a reflection of the traditions of classical literature, represented for the purposes of this study by satire. There remain a number of issues which have not been resolved by the relationships between *Tartuffe* and classical literature which we have examined. These are especially the political setting and the plot of the play. The answer to these cruxes can again be found in classical satire. But before looking for solutions, the problems must be examined in detail. The political setting of *Tartuffe* can best be seen in the figure of Orgon. However, since Orgon's political significance depends on an understanding of the "comic microcosm," we must consider that term before looking at Orgon.

"*Microcosm* means 'small world'; its corollary, always implied if not always stated, is the *macrocosm*, the 'great world,'" state the authors of one study of this convention.[206] Writers have always, intentionally or not, created microcosms which, while they are self-contained worlds, at the same time are reflections of the greater world. Within such microcosms one sees depicted particularly "relationships of human beings to each other, to themselves, and to the universe."[207] Since this author considers the household of Orgon a microcosm, it will be helpful to look more exactingly at this convention as it is used in comedy. L.J. Potts, in his book on comedy, states that certain writers "have discovered an excellent convention which is sometimes called the Comic Microcosm. They take for the setting of their comedy a 'little world,' a strictly limited society with fairly homogeneous traditions, standards, and habits." Potts continues, stating: "In such a world, where the rules of the game of life are the same for everybody, where all know the rules and accept them in theory at least, it is easy to measure men and women against each other fairly, and to pick out the good and the bad mixers, at the same time depicting even in the good mixers those faults of temperament and foibles of the intellect that cause both the graver irritations and the pleasant smaller frictions provocative of nothing worse than a smile."[208] There are, of course, many types of microcosm, but one of the most important is the private household, since "the domestic world offers an obvious microcosm to the comic writer."[209]

Orgon is much more than a character in a play; he is also a symbol: he represents a power, that of the head over a household, and his corruption presages the potential corruption of that or any power.[210] For Orgon, as for many a paterfamilias of Molière's France, the nature of this power, in its microcosmic view, could easily be compared to the royal — to that of the king himself, Louis XIV.

Orgon's corruption as head of the household, beginning in his desire to be relieved of the rule which he finds onerous, reaches a high point when he relinquishes his power over the welfare of the family to Tartuffe, who has no right nor even claim to it. The reaction of Damis at this point is only natural from one who is aware of the basic order in the nature of things, and sees that order begin to be disturbed:

> Quoi? je souffrirai, moi, qu'un cagot de critique
> Vienne usurper céans un pouvoir tyrannique ...(45-46)

The words "usurper" and "tyrannique" are precise and to the point, designating Tartuffe as one who will take that to which he has no claim. Although Tartuffe as yet has not usurped Orgon's power, for all practical purposes, he has it in his possession. The words of Damis serve to foreshadow the future actions of Tartuffe.

The "le pauvre homme" scene (I, iv) is indicative again of Orgon's displacement as paterfamilias, for we see that he is so completely involved in Tartuffe that he has no concern for the physical, not to mention the spiritual, welfare of his family. A further aspect of Orgon's character is revealed by this scene: he is unfeeling, inhuman, the kind of man who could ignore the distress of his entire family. This same theme of inhumanity is repeated in Orgon's attempt to marry his daughter to Tartuffe.

As Act II opens, it is obvious that Orgon's desire to have Tartuffe as his son-in-law develops quite naturally out of his misguided respect and love for what he thinks Tartuffe represents — true religion. His action is an attempt to bring his daughter, Mariane, into the realm of piety. When Orgon decides to go against his daughter's choice, made on the grounds of true love and presumably good sense, he confirms what we already know — that he has been corrupted to the point that he no longer belongs to the normal order of his family. Orgon now is living under the regimen of Tartuffe.

What we observe at the beginning of Act II is, then, a continuation of the idea of the potential for disaster which the absolute power of any leader, whether of a household or a kingdom, can lead to when that power is misunderstood, misused, or misplaced. For, when a leader is corrupted, the corruption does not end there. He is not a man alone; all that with which he is connected suffers with him and from him.

The second encounter between Elmire and Tartuffe is one of utmost importance to further understanding of the political nature of the setting and action of *Tartuffe*. Elmire attempts to show Tartuffe as he really is, a "man of flesh," and thus destroy once and for all the passion which clouds the reasoning of her husband. For Orgon, it is an opportunity to reassert himself as paterfamilias. He must first of all grasp the reality of Tartuffe. Then he must, if the play is to remain in the ranks of comedy, assert himself to a point of personal decision and, embarking upon a course of his own choosing for the first time in days, displace, or attempt to, the intruder in his world. If Orgon fails to come out of his hiding place, he will very likely be cuckolded, largely through his own fault. If this happens, it will be clear that Orgon has been corrupted beyond recovery. But this does not quite happen. Although it takes a long time for Orgon to wake from his stupor (symbolic of the depths to which he has sunk in self-deception), he can and does recover to take his place for the moment as protector of his family. Guicharnaud analyzes the significance of the scene as follows: "Orgon, sous la table, est acculé à assumer sa fonction. Jamais, au cours de la pièce, il n'a été aussi puissant et aussi seul — puisqu'on lui abandonne la décision, qu'on le rend responsable en dernier ressort de la ruine définitive de l'ordre familial et du même coup, de sa propre ruine."[211]

It is obvious from this brief sketch that Orgon's household can be interpreted as a microcosmic world in which the power of the rightful leader is corrupted and usurped by a tyrant. The political nature of Molière's play is further revealed by the action of the fifth act. There we see the actions of an ideal political leader. In *Tartuffe*, Molière presents the view that the king alone, in the whole universe, is capable of saving the kingdom or any constituent part of it from any corruption therein. At the height of Tartuffe's success (V, vii), when all his plans are going perfectly and he is about to see Orgon arrested, by a marvelous reversal of fortune, a virtual *deus ex machina* in the form of the agent of the king, he is plummeted from his position of power to the place he had planned for Orgon, that of a prisoner of the Prince. He expected to hear news that would confirm his hold on the house of Orgon; instead, he becomes the occupant of a prison cell.

There are three problems involving the plot of *Tartuffe* which have plagued scholars for years: what is the source of the plot line; why is the plot further complicated by Tartuffe's theft of the cassette and his informing on Orgon; and why does Molière find it necessary to end the play with a *deus ex machina*? An examination of the main actions of Tartuffe in the light of the political atmosphere which has been observed in Molière's play will provide us a point from which to begin to examine these problems.

Driven by pride and greed, Tartuffe has entered the realm in which Orgon is ruler and has attempted to displace him. He has set himself in opposition to the interests of the rightful heirs of his host. He has threatened to possess sexually one, and possibly two, of the women of his host's household. He has, in the role of informer, betrayed the trust of his host. He has ultimately been hurled from the heights of success to the depths of failure through the actions of the leader of the nation, who remains unseen.

The critics have been deeply disturbed by the fifth act of *Tartuffe*. They find in the miraculous intervention of the king's agent the poet's way of solving "le nœud, qu'il n'a su dénouer."[212] To them Molière seems to be taking the easy way out of a problem (his plot) that he did not know how to resolve. It is possible that this is not so, however, for Molière may have had a basis for the denouement of the fifth act. This basis can be found in the career of Aelius Sejanus, which as will be seen, closely parallels that of Tartuffe.

It is, of course, possible to find other examples in classical literature, or elsewhere, which can provide bases for the intervention of the king. One possibility is the story of Philip of Macedon as told by Seneca, which was employed in the preceding section on friendship, page 123. Another is the following passage from Plutarch, who, it will be remembered, was read in the Jesuit schools.

> Then when will our life be that of a beast, savage and without fellowship? When the laws are swept away, but the arguments that

summon us to a life of pleasure are left standing, when the providence of heaven is not believed in, and when men take for sages those who 'spit on excellence, unless pleasure attends it' and who scoff and jeer at such words as these:

            An eye there is of Justice, that sees all

and

            For God looks closely, ever standing near

and

     God, even as the ancient account relates, holding the beginning, middle, and end of the universe, proceeds directly, as is his nature, in his round; upon him follows Justice, who visits with punishments all who fall short of the divine law.

For it is men who look with contempt on all these things as old wives' tales and think that our good is to be found in the belly and the other passages by which pleasure makes her entry — it is these who stand in need of law, fear, blows and some king or magistrate with justice in his strong right arm to deter them from proceeding to devour their neighbours when their ravening appetite, prompted by their godlessness, casts off restraint.[213]

There is found in classical literature a figure whom Tartuffe resembles in many ways. This is Aelius Sejanus, the minister of the Emperor Tiberius Caesar. In order to determine whether there is any possibility that Tartuffe was based partly on the figure and career of Sejanus, it will be necessary to examine his character and career in detail, comparing them with those of Tartuffe. Before beginning our consideration of the classical Sejanus, we must examine the literature of the seventeenth century to see if the figure of Sejanus was available to Molière in the work of recent or contemporary authors.

Although Molière read the works of Tacitus and Juvenal in which accounts of Sejanus' career are given, further reason to believe that he was aware of the career of Sejanus, the supreme political hypocrite, is provided by Molière's acquaintance with the works of two of the more important minor authors of his time — Jean Magnon and Cyrano de Bergerac.[21]

Jean Magnon (1620-62) wrote eight plays, most of them on classical subjects. Two of these, the *Artaxerce* and the *Séjanus*, are particularly interesting for the purposes of our study. *Artaxerce*, Magnon's first play (1644) was acted by Molière's troupe.[215] In it one finds the presentation of a monarch who is easily influenced by those around him. Equally interesting, however, is the series of alterations Magnon makes in his classical material, Plutarch's *Life of Artaxerxes*. Magnon adds the facts that Artaxerxes is weary of ruling, keeps only two of the king's sons, making one of them not only a rival but a slanderer of his brother. Aspazie he elevates in rank, making her the daughter of the King of Lydia, while he makes Amestris, daughter and wife of Artaxerxes in Plutarch, only his daughter. Magnon worked to simplify the overly complex family background and to eliminate relationships that would have shocked his audience.[216] This he obviously felt was within the powers of the creative artist working from one genre to another.

It is, however, in Magnon's second tragedy, *Séjanus*, that one can find a possible influence on Molière's *Tartuffe*. There, as in the case of *Artaxerce*, one finds a monarch influenced by a powerful favorite, who seeks a union with a princess and forms a conspiracy against his protector which results in his own destruction. The plot, as developed by Magnon, is based on the accounts of Tacitus and Suetonius, which had been collated by such seventeenth-century authors as Pierre Matthieu in his *Aelius Sejanus*, published at Rouen in 1635, and Coeffeteau in his *Histoire Romaine*, Paris, 1621, I, 192-202.[217] Magnon's play follows the account of Tacitus in the main; he does, however, make one change which is worth consideration in our study — he changes the character of Livia (whom I would equate with Elmire), by having her, instead of participating in infidelity and conspiracy with Séjanus, no longer guilty of adultery with Séjanus nor of helping to murder her husband. Instead, Livia, in her desire to avenge her murdered husband, pretends to love Séjanus, facing the loss of her honor, in order to thwart Séjanus' schemes and bring about his downfall. Lancaster describes her (in terms equally applicable to Elmire) as "a proud, virtuous, patriotic, and clever woman . . ."[218] Séjanus, following the tradition of Tacitus' *Annales*, is depicted as a cunning and hypocritical villain. Tiberius, although he is duped at first by Séjanus, is represented as a "just and thoughtful ruler,"[219] who rises to the moment when danger threatens. It is, moreover, interesting that Magnon is very careful to reveal Livia's true and honorable character to the audience before false charges are brought against her, much as Molière was careful to reveal the vicious nature of Tartuffe so that he could not be mistaken for a true *dévot*.[220]

Magnon's plays, especially *Séjanus*, could have influenced Molière directly, since he came into contact with Molière several times in the course of his career, and is even thought to have been a friend of Molière.[221] It is possible, however, that his influence was indirect, for *Séjanus* has been suggested as one of the sources of Cyrano de Bergerac's play *La Mort d'Agrippine*, which, if one accepts the basis of the character of Tartuffe on that of Sejanus, is another important link between Molière and the classical Latin authors.

Molière was acquainted with Cyrano, and, in fact, borrowed from him material for at least one of his plays — *Les Fourberies de Scapin* from *Le Pédant Joué*.[222] It is, however, not a comedy, but in a tragedy by Cyrano that characters and plot resembling those in *Tartuffe* can be found — *La Mort d'Agrippine*. This play suggests a development from Magnon's *Séjanus* to *Tartuffe* particularly in the role of Agrippine, who follows Livia and precedes Elmire in pretending to love a villain in order to achieve his destruction.[223] The connection between *Agrippine* and *Tartuffe* is not limited to the character and actions of their heroines nor to any similarities in plot.[224] It extends to another facet of their characters in that both Séjanus (Cyrano's) and Tartuffe are represented as despisers of the gods.[225] Séjanus was considered both a *méchant* and an *athée* by the audiences observing the play.[226] Séjanus' attitude toward the gods is evident in in the following dialogue:

> Terentius: Respecte et crains des Dieux l'effroyable tonnerre!
>
> Sejanus: Il ne tombe jamais en Hyver sur la terre:
> J'ay six mois pour le moins à me moquer des Dieux,
> En suitte je feray ma paix avec les Cieux. (V, 6)

Furthermore, in the same dialogue, Séjanus says:

> Ces Dieux que l'homme a faicts, et qui n'ont point faict l'homme,
> Des plus fermes Estats ce fantasque soustien,
> Va, Va, Terentius, qui les craint, ne craint rien.

Certainly here Séjanus, as depicted by Cyrano, has ceased to be merely a political hypocrite, having become associated with strong (anti-) religious views. It is not difficult to conceive a creative mind like Molière's adapting the whole plot line and all the characters of the play so that his one facet of Séjanus' character — his irreligiosity — becomes his principal trait and his hypocrisy becomes religious rather than political.

One other occurrence in the *Agrippine* is further reminiscent of *Tartuffe*. In Act Two, scenes ii-iii, Agrippine, plotting against Séjanus and Tiberius, is overheard by Tiberius. She quickly invents an explanation for her words, which, overheard by Séjanus, makes him think he is betrayed. Accordingly, Séjanus begins a confession, so that Agrippine must reinterpret her words and then Séjanus his. This self-revelation scene although functioning in a somewhat different way is one more link between the characters of Séjanus and Tartuffe. It is, however, the role of Agrippine, and Livia before her, which, when compared to that of Elmire, most strongly suggests Séjanus as a basis for Tartuffe.

If Molière did know and use Magnon's and Cyrano's plays for his creation of *Tartuffe*, it is not unlikely that he went to the sources of these plays as well. Certainly the collations of Matthieu and Coeffeteau were available to him as were the works of Juvenal and Tacitus, as well as those of Suetonius and Dio Cassius, all of whom treated Sejanus. We shall limit our examination of the classical Sejanus to Tacitus and, to a lesser extent, Juvenal. If Molière knew and based his play on the character and career of Tacitus' Sejanus, there should be frequent parallels between the two works.

Sejanus is utilized by Juvenal in Satire X as one of his examples of what human beings should not pray for. Sejanus is depicted as typical of those whom the desire for excessive power hurls from the envied heights (56ff.). But Juvenal's brief statement gives hardly any information on the career of the man who, Juvenal thinks, best represents the destructiveness of a desire for power. The satirist says that Sejanus was "but recently second in the whole world ..." (63); he had a notable face, and especially lips (67-68); he was condemned by a "great and wordy letter from Capri ..." (71-72); he had been the "guardian of a Prince seated on the narrow ledge of Capri with his herd of Chaldean astrologers ..." (93-95); and finally that "Sejanus did not know what things were to be desired; for in coveting excessive wealth," he brought upon himself a greater fall (104-107).

One is immediately aware of the similarities between Sejanus and Tartuffe. As we have shown in this chapter, it is Tartuffe's greed and ambition that lead him to his perilous pinnacle of success, from which he is ultimately hurled. Within the microcosm of Orgon's household, Tartuffe was "second in the whole world," until he became first; but it is soon revealed that, in the greater scheme of things, there is still one greater, so that, within the play, Tartuffe really never occupies a position higher than "second in the world." Louis XIV is always first. Tartuffe is condemned by the actions of the unseen king. Tartuffe is the "guardian" of Orgon, the ruler of his household, who was as separated from his own world as if he had been at Capri. Orgon is under the influence of a "faux dévot," just as Juvenal's Prince, Tiberius, was influenced by the despicable foreign astrologers. Tartuffe, as we have shown in this chapter, is proven a *demens* by the very fact that he does not know what things are to be desired, and it is specifically his greed which leads him to enter the household of Orgon in the first place. Also noteworthy is one statement which has an analogue in *Tartuffe*: Sejanus had a remarkable face, especially his lips. Much the same comment is made of Tartuffe, whose "teint frais et la bouche vermeille" and "l'oreille rouge et le teint bien fleuri" recall Juvenal's lines in Molière's only description of any part of Tartuffe's body. All of these similarities could, of course, be fortuitous. But, if more elements in the characterization of Tartuffe and the plot of Molière's play can be shown to have parallels in the figure and career of Sejanus, it is likely that the resemblances are more than fortuitous, and are, in fact, purposeful.

The modest morsel of information which Juvenal provides in Satire X merely whets the appetite, and one desires to know more about his prime example of a *demens*, whose failure in *sophrosyne* brought him to destruction. The best account of the career of Sejanus is found in Tacitus' *Annales*.[227] It is to this work that we will turn. There, in the words and implications of Tacitus, it is possible to see the basic framework of Tartuffe's character in the figure of Sejanus and the plot of Molière's play in Sejanus' career.

Tartuffe came to Paris from the provinces. Although he was of a good family and was well-educated, Tartuffe was not accepted in the family of Orgon. They had their suspicions about an "outsider." Sejanus had a similar problem. Coming from a borough town, he had no ancestral claims to respect since his family name had never been inscribed on the calendar of consuls *(Fasti)*. Even though he came of an old Etruscan house, to the Roman nobility he was just another upstart seeking fame and fortune — most likely at their expense.[228] Sejanus entered the service of the Emperor Tiberius. There, by a series of ingratiating maneuvers, he insinuated himself so deeply in the favor of the Emperor that he became his chief minister and adviser. Tartuffe's goal and the results are the same as those of Sejanus. Both Sejanus and Tartuffe put themselves in positions from which they plan to take control of the universe into which they have thrust themselves: the one the macrocosm of the Roman Empire; the other the microcosm of Orgon's household.

Tiberius, as depicted by Tacitus, is very similar to Orgon. Both were men of commendable character in their earlier years; both served their rulers honorably in a time of revolt: Tiberius against the legions in Pannonia; Orgon against the Fronde. But with the passing of time each began to reveal a different character, either throwing off the mask of hypocrisy, as suggested in the example of Tiberius by Tacitus, and allowing his real character to show through, or, possibly, going through a development of character until that which was most natural and comfortable for him was settled upon.[229] The role which was most natural for Tiberius was also important for Orgon — that of a tyrant. Each man found a peculiar pleasure in lording it over others, or in encouraging and ordering someone else to perform tyrannical acts.

Tacitus attributes this change of character in Tiberius to Sejanus. Similarly, Orgon's tendency to play the tyrant is encouraged by Tartuffe, as Auerbach has shown. It is only through Tartuffe that Orgon can let out his vindictive and cruel tendencies. Tartuffe serves as a catalyst to the character of Orgon, and then participates in the action, exactly as Sejanus did. Orgon's tyranny is generally effected only through Tartuffe, so that it is seen indirectly.

Juvenal tells very little about Sejanus' character. After reading the Tenth Satire, one knows little more than that Sejanus desired the wrong things, seeking honors and wealth. This does not immediately suggest any close connection between Sejanus and Tartuffe. It is only after one encounters the character analysis of Sejanus by Tacitus that we realize how similar the two figures are.

> Soon afterwards *he won the heart* of Tiberius so effectually *by various artifices* that the *emperor*, ever dark and mysterious towards others, *was with Sejanus* alone *careless and freespoken* He was one who *screened himself*, while he was *attacking others*; he was as cringing as he was *imperious; before the world* he affected humility; *in his heart he lusted after supremacy,* for the sake of which he was *sometimes lavish* and *luxurious*, but oftener energetic and *watchful* . . .[230] (Italics mine.)

A direct comparison between Sejanus and Tartuffe can now be proposed, based on the analysis above by Tacitus.

| Tacitus | Molière |
| --- | --- |
| Sejanus won the heart of Tiberius. | Tartuffe won the heart of Orgon. |
| Sejanus employed various devices. | Tartuffe employed the devices of religious imposture. |
| The Emperor Tiberius was careless and freespoken with Sejanus. | Orgon, ruler of his household, carelessly entrusted Tartuffe with his secret papers. |
| Sejanus screened himself, while attacking others. | Tartuffe covered his true desires with the guise of a *faux dévot*, while he criticized the family for their manner of life. |
| Sejanus was imperious. | Tartuffe literally ruled the household of Orgon. |
| Sejanus affected humility. | Tartuffe affected humility, as in his asceticism. |
| Sejanus lusted after supremacy. | Tartuffe lusted after supremacy in the world of Orgon's household. |
| Sejanus was sometimes lavish and luxurious. | Tartuffe was lavish with the wealth and property of Orgon; his character tended toward luxury. |
| Sejanus was watchful. | Tartuffe was watchful, except when his emotions ran away with him. |

The resemblance to Tartuffe is remarkable. He has won the heart of Orgon so completely that he is Orgon's "everything." He has achieved this goal by various devices, beginning with his show of faith, continuing with his asceticism and preachments, so that Orgon, who would never have dreamt of telling another soul, tells Tartuffe freely, and without thought or concern for the possible consequences, all the details of his treason, even putting the proof in Tartuffe's own hands. Only the fool Orgon failed to see that Tartuffe's guise was merely a screen to cover his real desires; but then Tartuffe, by attacking the family, was performing as Orgon would have, had he been able. Orgon is quite satisfied with Tartuffe until Tartuffe decides to act against him. He has no reason to see that Tartuffe's imperiousness is in contrast to his affected humility, or that Tartuffe's own lavish spending and luxurious living are in contrast with the life he so watchfully imposes on the members of Orgon's household. Orgon has no reason to look into Tartuffe's character to see the desires for power and money which are his primary motivations. He is satisfied with Tartuffe the way he is, because Tartuffe fulfills his (Orgon's) own needs. Orgon is self-centered, blind to all but his own problems.

One is struck immediately by this similarity in the characters of Sejanus and Tartuffe. There are questions that must be asked, however: does the total picture of Sejanus, as presented by Tacitus, offer as striking a parallel as this one passage or are there notable differences? These questions can be answered through a comparison of Tacitus' comments on Sejanus and Tiberius with the information on Tartuffe and Orgon, which can be obtained from Molière's play.

| Sejanus - Tiberius | Tartuffe - Orgon |
|---|---|
| Tiberius had a family background notable for treachery and intrigue. (*Ann.* I. 3) | Orgon's family background is not given. |
| Tiberius, as a young man, showed his bad side. (I. 4) | No such detail is provided for Orgon. If anything, Orgon showed promise in his young manhood. |
| Tiberius was motivated by fear that Germanicus would take possession of the empire. (I. 7) | No such detail is provided for Orgon. |

| Sejanus - Tiberius | Tartuffe - Orgon |
|---|---|
| The first mention of Sejanus emphasizes the fact that he had great influence with the emperor, and that he had been given the duties of advising and directing the young prince, and holding out punishment and rewards to the soldiers. (I. 24) | Tartuffe had great influence with Orgon. Tartuffe advised and directed not just the young heir, but the entire family. Tartuffe did *not* reward or punish soldiers. |
| Tiberius is connected with religion, but it is made obvious that he does not value sharing in the popular religion. (I. 54) | Orgon has a passion for religion, and he particularly values the popularity of Tartuffe's religion. |
| Sejanus had saved the city from a conflagration and had been voted a statue therefor. (III. 73) | There is no account of such an occurrence for Tartuffe. |
| Tiberius suddenly became a cruel tyrant as well as an abettor of cruelty in others. The cause of this was Sejanus. (IV. 1) | It was through Tartuffe that Orgon was allowed to express his latent urge to exercise the role of family tyrant. Orgon is not only cruel himself, but an abettor of Tartuffe's cruelties. |
| There were obstacles to Sejanus' ambitions in the royal house with its many princes, a son in youthful manhood, and grown-up grandsons. (IV. 3) | Tartuffe had only a son and the immediate family to fear. |
| Sejanus seduced Livia, the wife of Drusus, son of Tiberius. (IV. 3) | Tartuffe attempted the seduction of Elmire, the wife of Orgon. |
| Sejanus was married, but divorced his wife, by whom he had three children. (IV. 3) | Tartuffe is never revealed to have either a wife or children. |
| Within the royal family, only Drusus, the heir apparent, complained openly of Sejanus. Drusus particularly lamented the fact that a stranger helped rule the empire while the emperor's son was alive. (Iv. 7) | All of Orgon's family (except Mme. Pernelle, but including Dorine and Cléante) complain of Tartuffe's actions, but Damis is the most vociferous. |

# MOLIÈRE'S TARTUFFE: AN INTERPRETATION 139

| Sejanus - Tiberius | Tartuffe - Orgon |
|---|---|
| Drusus also commented on Sejanus' ambition and lack of self-control. (Iv. 7) | Dorine notes Tartuffe's ambition, and she and Cléante underline his lack of self-control. |
| Sejanus had Drusus poisoned in order to remove him as a competitor for the empire. (IV. 8) | Tartuffe had Damis ejected from Orgon's home and disinherited from his patrimony. |
| Tiberius stated that he wished someone else would take over the reins of government. (IV. 9) | For all practical purposes, Orgon puts the control of his household into the hands of Tartuffe. |
| Sejanus contrived every sort of wickedness. (IV. 11) | Tartuffe was "un fourbe renommé," who had a history of "actions toutes noires." |
| Sejanus was the emperor's special favorite. (IV. 11) | Tartuffe was Orgon's "tout." |
| Both were hated by the rest of the world. (IV. 11) | Tartuffe was hated by the rest of the household, who did not hate Orgon, but did complain of his actions. |
| After the removal of Drusus, Sejanus grew bold in wickedness, speculating on the possibility of destroying the remaining heirs. (IV. 2 and IV. 54) | There were *no* remaining male heirs to be destroyed once Damis was removed. |
| To get rid of his enemies, Sejanus used *delatores*, paid informers. (IV. 34) | Tartuffe, himself, informed on Orgon. |
| Sejanus requested the hand of Livia in marriage. (IV. 39) | Within the play, Tartuffe made no such request. |
| Tiberius hesitated, but said he would not oppose Sejanus' marriage to Livia. (IV. 40) | Orgon suggested the marriage. |
| Sejanus tried to influence Tiberius to leave the seat of Empire. (IV. 41) | Tartuffe forcibly attempts to evict Orgon from his home. |

| Sejanus - Tiberius | Tartuffe - Orgon |
|---|---|
| Sejanus saved the life of Tiberius, and thereafter was listened to with greater confidence.<br>(IV. 59) | Tartuffe did not save Orgon's life. He was, however, given greater trust and reward after he was accused by Damis. |
| Tiberius retired voluntarily to Capri.<br>(IV. 67) | Orgon was to be evicted forcibly by Tartuffe. |
| At Capri, Tiberius began to reveal his machinations against his relatives.<br>(IV. 67) | Orgon began to reveal his machinations toward his family after Tartuffe had, to Orgon's way of thinking, disproved Damis's accusations. (*Je porte en ce contrat de quoi de faire vous rire* ...) |
| Tiberius, in retirement, lived a profligate life.<br>(IV. 67) | Orgon never enters his forced retirement. |
| Tiberius censured his daughter-in-law for her insolent tongue and defiant spirit.<br>(V. 3) | Mme. Pernelle, Orgon's mother, censures her daughter-in-law for her insolence and extravagance. |
| Criticisms of Sejanus were published anonymously, eliciting the wrath of Sejanus.<br>(V. 4) | All the family of Orgon criticizes Tartuffe behind his back. Damis' open accusation elicits Tartuffe's ill will. |
| After Sejanus was toppled from power, Tiberius excused his error. The rest of the people, who had formerly encouraged him, now reviled Sejanus. | After Tartuffe revealed himself, Orgon admitted his error, reviling all men of Tartuffe's "type": "Je renonce à tous les gens de bien ..." |
| The children of Sejanus were punished for their father's crime.<br>(V. 9) | Tartuffe had no children, as far as we know. |
| Sejanus was a political hypocrite. | Tartuffe was a religious hypocrite. |

The suggestion has been made that Molière may actually have used the figure of Sejanus as a partial model for Tartuffe. We cannot know that this is true, but the comparative study of both will clarify the possibility if any variations or differences between the two can be explained. This comparison of Sejanus-Tiberius with Tartuffe-Orgon reveals far more similarities than differences. The differences that do exist may partially be explained by the necessities of Molière's art. Certainly it is difficult to be all-inclusive in so succinct a work as a comedy. The fact that Molière includes so much detail is attributable, perhaps, to the time he had to ruminate before the final version of *Tartuffe* was published. The first three differences apply to Orgon's family background and character. Molière obviously did not want to paint Orgon as black as Tacitus did Tiberius. Therefore, such items as family treachery would naturally have been omitted. Tartuffe does not punish and reward soldiers because there are no soldiers in Orgon's household, which is a far more modest world than was Tiberius' Roman Empire. However, Tartuffe does seem to hold out reward and even punishment for the family of Orgon. Tartuffe, of course, neither saved a city from conflagration nor did he save the life of Orgon. Molière depicts a man who has no saving graces. He is "all black." It is possible to suggest why Molière would not have depicted Tartuffe as a married man with children. If he were already married, and Orgon knew it, Tartuffe could not function in the play as he does. Moreover, being married, with children, would lend Tartuffe an air of humanity, which would not be in accord with the "all black" character Molière created in Tartuffe. The elimination of a wife and children, moreover, would simplify an already overly complex plot and highly complicated protagonist. Certainly the mention of a wife and children for Tartuffe would have technically required a denouement that would resolve their problems as well as those of Orgon's family and Tartuffe. Many slight variations occur as the words or actions of one character are transferred not to that character's counterpart, but to another member of Orgon's family. This is merely the product of a tendency toward dramatic variation. Certainly, for it to be drama, any character cannot be the only actor. The limitations of drama similarly would require that a household of princes be modified to one or two. Tartuffe does not request the hand of Mariane, as far as we know. In fact, such an action is in opposition to his real desire for Elmire. The contrast between the request of Sejanus and the offer of Orgon are appropriate to Molière's total plan in *Tartuffe*, wherein every effort is made to show that Orgon is "all kinds of a fool." Whereas Orgon, the fool, loses control of the action in his household, Tiberius, even in retirement, retains his lordship, so that he himself can destroy the usurper. But, whereas Tiberius reveals himself a profligate at Capri, Orgon makes a partial recovery from his status of fool. The reason for this variation may be seen in Molière's attitude toward the family, which he considered a sacrosanct unit. The father, as head of the household, had obligations which required him to be sane, rational, and devoted to his family's welfare. Profligacy had no place in this picture; it would have merely made Orgon a worse fool. In Molière's play we are actually given hope of Orgon's recovery from his *dementia*, with the possibility of his taking his place as leader of the family.

Ultimately we come to the fact that Sejanus is a political hypocrite and Tartuffe is a religious hypocrite. Why, if Molière did employ Sejanus as a model, would he have altered the kind of hypocrisy which is elemental in the character of his protagonist? This question can be answered by recalling the difficulties that Molière had suffered at the hands of the Compagnie du Saint-Sacrement. This body of "dévots" had hindered and harassed Molière with what he must have considered hypocritical sanctimoniousness. Therefore, on the basis of his knowledge of this group, as well as the countless other religious hypocrites with whose histories he may have been familiar, it is likely that Molière altered the type of hypocrisy from the political, with which he was probably less well acquainted, to the religious, which he had encountered personally. Furthermore, a look at the underlying structures of the plot and setting of *Tartuffe* reveals that Molière has put his religious hypocrite into a house, where the action, although on a limited scale, is of a more political than a religious nature. The opening scenes clarify this point, for Tartuffe is criticized not just for his religious hypocrisy, but for his tyrannical and usurpative actions. The terms "tyrant" and "usurper" are certainly indicative of a political play, and the plot of *Tartuffe* justifies this conclusion. Futhermore, as we have seen, Sejanus was presented by Cyrano de Bergerac as a despiser of the gods — an atheist. It is a quick step from atheist to religious hypocrite.

Sejanus can also provide an answer to the problem of Molière's introduction of Tartuffe. One wonders why Tartuffe does not appear until the third act, but stands only in the background of all the action in the first two acts. It is certainly an effective dramatic device, but Molière himself felt the need to justify or at least explain his method. Molière offered an answer, saying he wanted to have time to prepare the audience for the introduction of an utter scoundrel and villain. The idea, however, may well have been drawn from Tacitus' introduction of Sejanus. Sejanus is referred to twice in Book I of the *Annales*, five times in Book III. Each mention notes his evil influence in increasingly alarming terms.[231] In Book IV he is brought directly into the action. There the idea of his pervasive evil, which was stated in vague terms earlier becomes an active and destructive reality.

Sejanus knew his man, Tiberius. He knew that he must give the Emperor no reason for fear or suspicion of him. Therefore, Sejanus constantly affected humility and modesty to cover his desires for power and wealth. He deprecated the desire for the "fulgor honorum." His way to the top had to be different — especially, it had to be stealthy. It would have done him no good to overthrow Tiberius, for he did not have sufficient power and influence to take control of the government, if the opportunity were given. Rather, his method was to put Tiberius under his control, and thus gain control of the government.

Sejanus did exert an extraordinary influence over Tiberius. This is shown from the time of his first introduction in the *Annales*, where emphasis is put on the *auctoritas* which Sejanus has with Tiberius.[232] This influence is shown steadily increasing throughout Book IV, as Tiberius resigns the control of government more and more to Sejanus.

Why Tiberius surrendered power to Sejanus is a somewhat difficult question. The answer lies to some extent in Sejanus' background. He came from the second estate, the *equites*; he was apparently not self-seeking, but loyal to Tiberius. He was just the man Tiberius needed at the time. There can be little doubt that Sejanus studied his man well, so that he could put on just the mask that would find special favor with Tiberius. Tiberius cherished dissimulation;[233] he also cherished Sejanus.[234] It seems quite likely that he saw in Sejanus the quality he appreciated, but did not stop to analyze its nature. He accepted the emotion without really asking its cause. Tiberius' affection for dissimulation and Sejanus is interesting since the verb employed to denote that affection is used only once elsewhere in the *Annales*, and there it designates a man's feeling for his wife.[235] The feeling of Tiberius toward Sejanus may be seen as one which is part of a relationship much closer and in which the participants are much more interdependent than in mere friendship. This is a love in which each fulfills the needs and desires of the other.

The way into favor for Tartuffe had to be somewhat different from that of Sejanus because each of them was directing his course towards empires and rulers of somewhat similar, but at the same time quite variant, natures. Tartuffe found his means in religion; Sejanus, his in politics. Each attained his position by a show of modesty which covered vicious desires. The path to power for each was stealthy, for there was no other way for a man who had not been born to power and influence, and who was basically unworthy, to scale the heights. One might reach a modest level, but never the apogee. For men of ambition and pride, only the summit is sufficient. Both Tartuffe and Sejanus attained control of their governments by exercise of *auctoritas* on the nominal rulers, because the rulers see in them a means of achieving their own desires, without any fear that the powers put into the hands of those they trust and love may be turned against them. Neither of the rulers takes the time to adequately consider what he is doing. Each acts for his own selfish interests.

Molière's play is a study in the development of power. In the background of the first two acts, one can see the evil influence of Tartuffe at work. As the play develops, Tartuffe becomes more and more influential and powerful as he achieves one of his ends after another. He has Mariane betrothed (for all practical purposes) to himself, Damis ejected, Elmire in his control, and the house of Orgon surrendered to him. Ultimately, he seizes control completely. He has at that moment attained the supreme power; he has reached his goal.

The reasons for Orgon's surrender of control of his household to Tartuffe parallel the situation in Tacitus. Orgon, like Tiberius, finds in his replacement a solution to the rigors of government which are onerous to him. He would rather be ruled than rule. Tartuffe fulfills this need. But Tartuffe also fills another need for Orgon. This is the need for an affection which will not call his manhood into play. Orgon seeks a love in which he can play the woman's role; if not physically, at least emotionally.

The road to ultimate power has further parallels in the careers of Sejanus and Tartuffe. Tacitus provides the following information about Sejanus:

> There were, however, obstacles to his ambition in the imperial house with its many princes, a son in youthful manhood and grown-up grandsons. As it would be unsafe to sweep off such a number at once by violence, whil craft would necessitate successive intervals in crime, he chose, on the whole, the stealthier way, and to begin with Drusus, who could not brook a rival and was somewhat irascible, had, in a casual dispute, raised his fist at Sejanus, and, when he defended himself, had struck him in the face.[236]

Sejanus' immediate problem, then, is precisely the same as Tartuffe's. The rulers of their respective universes do not oppose them; if anything, Tiberius and Orgon further the careers of Sejanus and Tartuffe. It is the families, especially the sons of Tiberius and Orgon, who are the primary obstacles. They must therefore be done away with.

Sejanus had met strong opposition from Drusus, Tiberius' son, from the inception of his career. They had actually come to blows, causing deep resentment in Sejanus. Therefore, he conspired to have Drusus murdered. This conspiracy was furthered by his seduction of Livilla, wife of Drusus and granddaughter of Augustus. Having removed his primary obstacle, Sejanus continued his mad career by working for the destruction of those elements of the imperial family who yet stood between him and his goal. In these maneuvers he made frequent use of the *delatores* to discredit and undermine the influence of Tiberius' family, Agrippina and her eldest son Nero (not to be confused with the Emperor Nero). Sejanus can thus be seen to present another parallel to the career of Tartuffe, who informed on Orgon. Sejanus was guilty of *delatio*, a common practice in the early empire and the subject of numerous literary attacks. The practice of making false accusations was usually performed by paid informers, but the crime could be of any nature. All the *delator* was concerned with was his reward, not the penalty some innocent man might have to pay. Therefore, these informers "specialized in ferreting out prominent men who had voiced, or hinted, or thought opposition to the emperor, prosecuting them for high treason, and collecting a large proportion of their property as a reward."[237]

Sejanus' plans were working. Things were going well, although more slowly, perhaps, than he wanted. He was even finding help of sorts in his operations, and that from a most unexpected source — the aged widow of Augustus, Livia. Not only was he not hindered by Tiberius' mother, but she almost seemed to take a positive pleasure in furthering his attempts to the discomfort of her stepchildren.

It appeared that nothing could stop Sejanus from gaining his ends. He reached the heights of rule as consul, the Emperor being his colleague, and received the pro-consular *imperium*, authority over all the members of his designated province. Desiring a permanent and visible connection with the royal family, Sejanus had himself betrothed to a princess of the royal house, Julia. He was virtually the equal of the Emperor himself. All that remained for him was to consolidate the government under his sole control.

Tartuffe's progress follows the pattern established by Sejanus. Having been taken into the household by Orgon, Tartuffe gains greater and greater *auctoritas* with him, until he is awarded virtual *imperium* over the whole household. He manages to have himself affianced to Mariane, a member of the house of Orgon. Tartuffe does not find it necessary to murder Damis; he merely has him disinherited and banished. He effectually has rid himself of the first challenge from the family of Orgon. There remains one more — Elmire. He attempts to counter this challenge, just as Sejanus had done with Livilla, by the seduction of Elmire. Since he desires her physically, Tartuffe's successful seduction of Elmire would accomplish two ends for him: it would immediately satisfy his sexual passion for her; and it would potentially satisfy his ambition for power by facilitating his rise to absolute control of the household. The attempt, however, fails, and he is not allowed to proceed absolutely unchallenged. His first major encounter, following the career of Sejanus, is with the son of Orgon. It is noteworthy here that Molière, eschewing the conventions of farce, allows only the intent of violence on the part of Damis instead of the actual blow as struck by Drusus. Although Tartuffe's actions vary somewhat from Sejanus' owing to Elmire's character and the fact that Molière is writing his satire within the conventions of comedy, Tartuffe continues to function according to Sejanus' career.

Furthermore, although Tartuffe will function as a *delator* (informer) directly against Orgon, his self-chastisement in Act III, scene vi, has the immediate effect of an accusation against Damis, who, accordingly, is banished, just as were Agrippina and Nero. Moreover, Mme. Pernelle, in her actions at the beginning of the play, reflects much the same pleasure in the discomfort of her son's family as was seen in the actions of Livia. At the conclusion of Act III, all that remains for Tartuffe to do, just as for Sejanus before him, is to consolidate under himself the control of the government of Orgon's universe, his house and properties.

Tartuffe is repeatedly referred to as a "tyrant" and a "usurper." In this connection he and Sejanus are closely related — each is a tyrant in the classical tradition in that he attains the supreme power by overthrowing the lawful government (or attempting to overthrow it). They both usurp powers to which they have no right by law. Even the legalization of Tartuffe's position by means of Orgon's signing over his properties does not make Tartuffe any less a tyrant. In the modern sense they are tyrants because they exercise their powers oppressively and cruelly.

Sejanus stood now near the pinnacle of success — or the edge of catastrophe. One obstacle remained in his path — the Emperor Tiberius. With him out of the way, Sejanus would have the Empire firmly in his hands. Therefore, he employed his devices to persuade Tiberius to retire from active politics.[238] The wiles of Sejanus were successful, and the Emperor left the capital, never to return, going to the island of Capri, where, accompanied by his herd of Chaldaean astrologers, he was to spend his remaining years.

The reins of government were now in the hands of Sejanus. But always behind him there loomed the awful might of an Emperor who at any time could regain his supremacy. Therefore, Sejanus worked to the end that Tiberius would actually hand over the total control of government to him. Sejanus failed in this, however. Tacitus tells us that he became rash as his plans worked out perfectly, one after another.[239] Tiberius somehow became aware of the threat which Sejanus posed to him. "Tiberius began to waver. He had raised up Sejanus, and now he resolved to destroy him. A lengthy despatch came from Capreae, 'verbosa et grandis epistula.' The consul, privy to the Emperor's design, proceeded to read it out, while Sejanus, without suspicion, expected to hear further honours and a full partnership with Tiberius in the imperial power. The artful convolutions ended in a sharp and sudden denunciation. Sejanus, deceived and dazed, could offer no resistance."[240]

Tartuffe, too, stood on the very brink of complete success. He had only to take complete possession of the universe in which he functions to achieve it. Orgon, doubtlessly persuaded by the rhetoric of Tartuffe, surrenders the legal control of the universe to Tartuffe when he signs over his properties to the interloper. Immediately, Orgon is thrust into exile; not the voluntary exile of Tiberius, but an exile imposed by a tyrant. Orgon differs from Tiberius in his complete surrender of power; Tiberius had relinquished the reins, but kept the possession and rights of leadership. Tiberius still had the power and faculties to recover his position; Orgon did not.

The denouement of the fifth act of *Tartuffe* is a mirror image of the description of the fall of Sejanus. Tartuffe is waiting for the news of one further success — the arrest of Orgon for treason. He triumphantly leads the messenger of the King onto the stage. But appearances are deceiving, as, for the first time, the trick is played against Tartuffe. He, not Orgon, is arrested. The Exempt, as if reading a "lengthy despatch," tells of Tartuffe's crimes and the benevolent omniscience of the King. Tartuffe, completely shattered, cannot say a word. He has been deceived by a master, who happens to be the King, just as Sejanus had been before him.

A review of the parallels between the careers of Sejanus and Tartuffe will reveal how many of the important elements in the plot of *Tartuffe* can be found in the combined versions of Sejanus' history as told by Juvenal and Tacitus. It is not necessary to reiterate every item we have just covered; we shall here consider only the most striking similarities.

1. The characters and relationship of Orgon and Tartuffe closely parallel those of Tiberius and Sejanus.
2. Tartuffe's entrance into Orgon's household parallels Sejanus' entrance into Tiberius' service.
3. Tartuffe's hypocrisy, covering selfish goals, parallels that of Sejanus.
4. Mme. Pernelle's character and actions toward the family of Orgon parallel the figure of Livia and her actions.
5. The growth of Tartuffe's influence over Orgon follows the development of Sejanus' *auctoritas* over Tiberius.
6. Tartuffe, like Sejanus, is given (proconsular) *imperium*.
7. Tartuffe is betrothed to Mariane as Sejanus is to Julia.
8. Tartuffe attempts to seduce Elmire; Sejanus did seduce Drusus' wife, Livilla.
9. Tartuffe is confronted by Damis; Sejanus was accosted by Drusus.
10. Damis is expelled by his father; Drusus is killed by Sejanus' agent and Agrippina and Nero (heir to throne) are banished.
11. Orgon is ousted from his home; Tiberius goes in self-imposed exile to Capri.
12. Tartuffe informs on Orgon; Sejanus' agent had informed against Agrippina and Nero.

13. Tartuffe falls when the just eye of the King beholds him; Sejanus falls when Tiberius finds out the truth about him.

There is one major point of variance between the falls of Tartuffe and Sejanus — it is not Orgon, who raised Tartuffe to the heights, that throws him down. It is the unseen King, Louis XIV. This employment of the King seems, on an immediate level, to be the product of Molière's concept of religion, the universe, and France, wherein true religion is embodied in the King, who rules by divine right as God's agent on earth. Accordingly, it is seen as a tribute to Louis, as no doubt it is. However, on the basis of the comparison of the careers of Sejanus and Tartuffe, one finds it necessary to ask if Molière's denouement is merely a sycophantic tribute to the King, or whether it has a greater significance. The latter case seems likely, especially in light of the similarities of Orgon-Tartuffe to Tiberius-Sejanus.

Before it will be possible to consider the significance of the fact that Orgon and Tartuffe are drawn along the same lines as Tiberius and Sejanus, and that the employment of Louis XIV in the final act parallels the role formerly played by Tiberius, certain problems involving Molière and his artistic concept must be considered once again.

Why did Molière write *Tartuffe*, his first great invective against religious hypocrisy and other odious vices of humanity, as a satirical comedy? He had already raised many aspects of his comic artistry to a level of near-perfection. What caused him to charge his play with such significant and (for him) novel subject matter, writing in mid-career? The answers to these questions require a brief look at the literary theory of the seventeenth century.

Boileau, representative of other proponents of the literary theories of the classical critics, Aristotle and Horace, charged literature with the obligation of blending the *utile* with the *dulce*, the useful with the enjoyable. It was generally agreed that art should please. But to this a second and more important function was added — art should instruct and elevate. This second function fell particularly to the lot of poets, who, "in [Molière's] day, felt themselves to be members of a small group who were privileged to inhabit the kingdom of the spirit, and whose relations with their public were rather those of seer or prophet than of entertainer."[241] Under the influence of such men as Boileau, Molière must have, accordingly, ceased to see himself only as an entertainer, and come to see himself as a teacher, whose field of specialization was morality, whose method was satirical comedy; for his comedies do employ satire as a device for attacking those who deviated from the accepted norms or offended the ideals of order and restraint.

Molière was familiar with the current theories of literature. This is proven by his invocation of the *castigat ridendo mores* in the first *Placet*: "Le devoir de la comédie étant de corriger les hommes en les divertissant . . ." In the second *Placet* he shows again his knowledge of the theory of the *utile*, when he states that "les plus scrupuleux en ont trouvé la représentation *profitable*." (Italics mine.)

Molière himself, then, has told us that he had didactic purposes in writing *Tartuffe*. But he has not told us explicitly toward whom his satirical comedy is directed. Of course, it is against all those who are or could become Orgons of Tartuffes. There is a possibility, however, that Molière did not direct his didacticism merely at the general audience, but at someone in particular. This author believes that the particular someone was no less than Louis XIV, the King himself. In order to justify such a belief one must consider not just the play, but the events surrounding the play, and Molière's attitude toward the King and his court. Molière, as an advocate of "bon sens," must have been disturbed by the excessive influence some advisors, such as Richelieu and Mazarin,[242] men of religion with very temporal ambitions, had exercised over Louis XIV and his predecessor Louis XIII. Equally disturbing to Molière, especially in the light of his experience with the Compagnie du Saint-Sacrement, must have been the influence of "la cabale dévote" which flocked constantly around the Queen-mother, Anne of Austria.[243] This lady, accompanied by her band of zealots, attempted to influence Louis into accepting their "austere programme of conduct"[244] based on bigoted religious principles. To Molière this action must have struck a discordant note. A king should be the king; he should not be influenced in his decisions by anyone seeking to gratify personal desires or ambitions. The king must rule with one primary concern — the welfare of the kingdom. This is his main responsibility, his most important duty. Therefore, the king must not leave the decisions of government to others who may be self-serving. He is king not only by divine right, but as a duty. This is what Molière says implicitly in *Tartuffe*. But, if Molière was, as I believe, presuming to offer a lesson to the King, it had to be so managed that Louis would not see, by any means, that the lesson drawn from the experience of Orgon was intended in part for himself. Molière knew that political discussion was a treasonable offense, and that personal criticism of the King would probably result in loss of favor and worse for himself. Therefore, the lessons had to be incorporated in the play in such terms that Louis would not see that he had himself been a motivational factor in Molière's writing of *Tartuffe* along the lines he did, but that he would perceive the similarity between his folly and Orgon's. Thus Molière presents a bourgeois household, which Louis was not likely to equate with his kingdom, ruled by an ordinary citizen not likely to be equated with the Sun-King. But perhaps, Molière hoped, Louis would see the lesson and take the proper steps to avoid becoming a "dupe" like Orgon, without ever realizing that Molière had been thinking of him (Louis) while creating *Tartuffe*. Molière managed to remove any likelihood of Louis's reaching such a realization by means of the very device which, as we have seen, has met much unfavorable criticism — the *deus ex machina* intervention of Louis himself through the person of his agent, the exempt. By having Louis take part in the action, even though indirectly, but in the role of an omniscient and benevolent ruler, Molière effectively removed any possibility that Louis would see the intended, direct similarity between himself and Orgon, or think that the lesson of Molière's satirical comedy was directed in part at himself. Moreover, if Molière did base the plot and characterizations of *Tartuffe* on the career of Aelius Sejanus, then the *deus ex machina* was an especially brilliant alteration to fit his need. Whereas Tiberius effected the downfall of Sejanus, Molière makes Orgon incapable of such an action, putting the power instead into the hands of the King. The King, therefore, cannot be Orgon, and cannot take offense. An offense would have been due, if the ending were not changed to remove any possibility of an equation between Orgon and Louis, for "if the Roman knight Aelius Sejanus became a menace, it was Tiberius Caesar who made him so."[245] If Tartuffe became a menace to the household of Orgon, it was Orgon who made him so. Accordingly, if Louis were not presented in a favorable light and set in complete opposition to all that Orgon and Tartuffe represent, it would be possible to say that the lesson of *Tartuffe*, when applied to Louis, was that, if men succeeded in menacing the health of the kingdom by exerting malicious or malignant influence, it was the King himself who allowed them to do so.

It must at first seem difficult to accept the possibility that Molière was making comparison of Louis to Orgon or Tiberius. After all, Louis was a generous patron and protector. He had stood godfather to Molière's child. Moreover, in the play itself, Molière makes the veiled reference to Louis XIV: "Nous vivons sous un prince ennemi de la fraude." But Molière was not adverse to pointing his satiric sting at the monarch, as can be seen in the comedy of *Amphityron*, in which Molière mocks Louis himself.[246]

Lionel Gossman notes that in a subtle way the satire of *Le Bourgeois Gentilhomme, L'Avare, Tartuffe* and *Le Misanthrope* can be applied to the King himself. He further makes a direct comparison of Tartuffe to Louis, stating that "the absolute superiority of the monarch with respect to the noblemen of the realm was sustained in mid and late seventeenth-century France by the vanities and rivalries of the noblemen among themselves, rather than by naked force, just as the position of Tartuffe in Molière's play is sustained by the vanity and hidden rivalry of Orgon and Madame Pernelle."[247] It is further notable, since we have looked closely at traditional material which Molière presents through reversals and variations to fit his purpose, that Gossman finds in Alceste "the inverted image of the King himself. He is the King dethroned, the King whose marble columns have come crashing down and who finds himself no longer on the balcony but with the crowd below'' (p. 239). Gossman finds in Molière's comedy, then "a constant unmasking of imposture, a constant process of liberation from the slavery and fear of illusion and falsehood. Nothing is spared, not even the monarchy itself.''[248]

It can be seen, then, that satire directed toward Louis is observable in several of Molière's plays, including *Tartuffe*. It is still difficult, however, to accept the fact that Molière's satiric lesson was intended for the King, whom he respected and to whom he was greatly indebted.

To understand this conflict of meaning, one must look in part at the history of Molière's time, as we have done, and at the events surrounding the production of *Tartuffe*. Molière was, of course, aware of many examples of hypocrisy in France, and especially in Louis's court. What rankled in his heart was the failure of the King to act as an "ennemi de la fraude." This can be seen in the tone of the *Préface* and three *Placets* to *Tartuffe*. Although Molière couches his feelings in terms of honest respect, he is clearly criticizing Louis for his failure to act on his behalf in the matter of the publication of *Tartuffe*. A series of selections from the *Préface* and *Placets* will clarify this point.

In the *Préface*, Molière complains of the fact that the favorable judgment of the King and a number of the members of his court has had no influence:

> Les corrections que j'y ai pu faire, le jugement du Roi et de la Reine, qui l'ont vue, l'approbation des grands princes et de Messieurs les ministres, qui l'ont honorée publiquement de leur présence, le témoignage des gens de bien, qui l'ont trouvée profitable, tout cela n'a de rien servi.

Molière continues his complaint to the King in the first *Placet*, in which he says:

> J'avois eu, Sire, la pensée que je ne rendrois pas un petit service à tous les honnêtes gens de votre royaume, si je faisois une comédie qui décriât les hypocrites, et mît en vue comme il faut toutes les grimaces étudiées de ces gens de bien à outrance, toutes les friponneries couvertes de ces fauxmonnoyeurs en dévotion, qui veulent attraper les hommes avec un zèle contrefait et une charité sophistique. Je l'ai faite, Sire, cette comédie, avec tout le soin, comme je crois, et les circonspections ...

He tells Louis exactly what he has done, exposed hypocrisy, and the reason, as a service to the kingdom. But Molière does not stop with telling Louis that his kingdom contains hypocrites. He goes on to tell the King that there are hypocrites who have found favor with him (Votre Majesté):

> On a profité, Sire, de la délicatesse de votre âme sur les matières de religion, et l'on a su vous prendre par l'endroit seul que vous êtes prenable, je veux dire par le respect des choses saintes. Les Tartuffes, sous main, ont eu l'adresse de trouver grâce auprès de Votre Majesté, et les originaux enfin ont fait supprimer la copie, quelque innocente qu'elle fût, et quelque ressemblante qu'on la trouvât.
> (*First Placet*)

This statement is particularly important in our consideration of Louis as one of the intended recipients of Molière's didacticism. The last sentence makes the point that the hypocrites in Louis's kingdom, who it will be remembered asserted that Molière was attacking true religion, have suppressed *Tartuffe*. When considered in the light of the play, the meaning of the whole passage is that the hypocrites have succeeded by means similar to those by which Tartuffe succeeded with Orgon. According to Molière, then, Louis is intended to profit from the lesson of *Tartuffe*.[249]

Molière writes in the hope that Louis will change, that he will once more begin to function ideally as King and cease to be a foil for the hypocrites. This hope for change is combined with a statement of trepidation at the current circumstance, if it should prevail:

> J'attends avec respect l'arrêt que Votre Majesté daignera prononcer sur cette matière; mais il est très assuré, Sire, qu'il ne faut plus que je songe à faire de comédie si les Tartuffes ont l'avantage, qu'ils prendront droit par là de me persécuter plus que jamais, et voudront trouver à redire aux choses les plus innocentes qui pourront sortir de ma plume.
> (*Second Placet*)

It is obvious that Molière is not above making veiled criticisms and suggestions to Louis XIV. He certainly did so in the *Préface* and *Placets*. It is not unreasonable to state, then, that *Tartuffe* is indeed an extended satiric statement directed toward the enlightenment of Louis so that he would live up to the ideal painted in the last act and expressed in the words "prince ennemi de la fraude."

---

[1] One critic, John Wilcox, in his study, *The Relation of Molière to Restoration Comedy* (New York, 1938), p. 159, has noted this combination of social and ethical satire, but considers it a detriment to a comedy.

[2] These *vitia* should be compared to the seven deadly sins of the Christian tradition: pride, envy, wrath, lust, gluttony, avarice, and sloth. Pride, it should be noted, as the sin of Satan, was the worst. As will be seen in the following discussion of *sophrosyne*, ambition is based on pride and envy, so that of the five *vitia* which are particularly antithetical to virtue, three are found in

the seven Christian sins, with superstition and luxury being the exceptions. We will find that sloth and wrath, although it is possible to find traces of them in Orgon or Tartuffe, are not important elements in their characters.

³Helen North, *Sophrosyne: Self-Knowledge and Self-Restraint in Greek Literature* (Ithaca, New York, 1966), pp. 3-4.

⁴One of the main considerations of the theme of *sophrosyne* in the Greek literature is that related to the happy medium. Niall Rudd comments that "It is implied in other passages of Epicurus, of which the most apposite is perhaps no. 21 of the Kyriai Doxai.

> The man who knows the limits of life realizes that what removes the pain due to want and renders the whole of life complete is easy to obtain; so there is no need for actions which involve competition.

Within these natural limits Horace locates the happy medium—his second main idea. The fullest and most sophisticated treatment of the happy medium is found, of course, in Aristotle's *Nicomachean Ethics*, but it goes back through Plato to Pythagorean and Sicilian researches into music and medicine. And even this is being over-precise, for the ideal of moderation was deeply embedded in the religion of early Greece. The precept 'Nothing too much' Méden Agan was inscribed above the portals of Apollo's temple at Delphi . . ." *The Satires of Horace* (Cambridge, 1966), p. 23.

⁵North, *Sophrosyne*, p. 10.

⁶Plato, *Gorgias* 482b4. North, p. 29 and pp. 150-195.

⁷North, *Sophrosyne*, p. 263. Miss North notes that "the noun *modus* (limit and its numerous derivatives—especially *modestia*, a very ancient abstract noun, *moderatio*, *moderare* and *moderari* — expressed one of the central themes of *sophrosyne* from the very beginning of Latin literature."

⁸*Ibid.*, p. 259.

⁹*Ibid.*, pp. 261-262, 264-265. Although they will not be studied in detail as influences on Molière's comedies, Plautus and Terence have been shown to be sources of several of Molière's comedies. See K. E. Wheatley, *Molière and Terence* (Austin, Texas, 1931); possible influences on the figure of Tartuffe will be considered later in this chapter.

¹⁰*Ibid.*, p. 265. Miss North has noted that such terms as *sobrius, castus, temperans, moderans, continens* all imply restrictions or denial. She further notes that "*verecundus* (etymologically 'full of compunction,' from *vereri*, 'to be afraid') is another early synonym for *sophron*, whose significance is basically negative. For its importance in Cicero, see p. 282 and n. 64. Like *pudor*, *verecundia* is also a common translation of *aidos* or *aidemosyne*. The antonyms to *sophrosyne* that appear during this early period include *ferocia* (*orge*) in Appius Claudius, Frag. I; *confidentia* (*hybris?*) in Pacuvius, Frags. 44, 55; *ignavia* (*malakia?*) in Plautus, *Most.* 137. *Luxuria* (*akolasia*) and *cupido* (*epithymia*) are frequent in comedy."

¹¹*Ibid.*, pp. 290-291.

¹²Tacitus, *Annales*, 3. 65. I.

¹³Although the concept of *sophrosyne* is ubiquitous in Plautus and Terence, it will help to consider a few occurrences of the theme, as listed in North, *Sophrosyne*:

"*Modestus:* Plautus *Trin.* 4. 1. 12.; Terence *Adelphi* 5. 8. 7. *Modeste:* Plautus *Pers.* 3. 1. 18 (*modice et modeste*), *Men.* 5. 6. 5; Terence *Phorm.* 1. 3. 18, *Eun.* 3. 5. 32. *Moderare:* Plautus *Mil.* 2. 2. 115. *Moderari:* Plautus *Curc.* 4. 1, *Truc.* 4. 3. 57. *Modice* (with *verecunde*): Ennius *Hecuba* 214. *Modus:* Plautus *Poen.* 1. 2. 21, *Merc.* 3. 4. 67. In Cato *R. R.* 5, *bono modo* means 'moderately'." (p. 363)

"*Pudicitia:* Plautus *Cist.* 1. 1. 90; *Epid.* 3. 3. 24, *Amph.* 929-30; L. Piso, Frag. 38 Peters (*pudicitiam subversam*). *Pudicitia* as an excellence of the young: Cicero *Pro Caelio* 3-6. *Pudor:* Naevius, Frag. 61; Ennius *ap.* Nonius 2. 696. *Pudor* also translates *aidos* (as in some Latin versions of Herodotus 1. 8; on these, see Bickel, 205, n. 1). *Pudens:* Terence *Heaut.* 1. 1. 78. *Pudicus:* Plautus *Trin.* 4. 2. 104, *Curc.* 1. 1. 51. Manutius (see Fausset on *Pro Cluentio* 12): *pudor animi, pudicitia corporis.* The alliteration common in Roman poetry leads to the coupling of *pudicitia* and *pudor:* Plautus *Amph.* 2. 2. 209. *Proba is linked with pudica by Afranius,* Frag. 8 Ribbeck." (p. 264)

For the employment of the themes of *sophrosyne* in the historians, see North, *Sophrosyne*, pp. 285-292.

[14]The curriculum at a typical Jesuit school following the *Ratio* included these authors and many others so that graduates of the Jesuit colleges were ultimately familiar with nearly all the writers of antiquity. Le P. Camille de Rochemonteix, *Un Collège de Jésuites aux XVIIe et XVIIIe Siècles: Le Collège Henri IV de la Flèche* (Le Mans, 1889), pp. 7-9.

[15]Brander Matthews, *Molière: His Life and His Works* (New York, 1916), p. 53.

[16]Although the emphasis in this study is placed on Stoicism as the basis of satiric concepts of *sophrosyne,* it must be realized, as Helen North stated, that in Horace "both Stoic and Epicurean principles sometimes issue in the same practical advice, even couched in the identical vocabulary of *modus* and *temperantia* . . ." (p. 135)

[17]"The prominence of the topic of *sophrosyne* or moderation . . . in Roman historiography and literature is in part a consequence of Cicero's preoccupation with effect of example in the State and his emphasis on the particular danger presented by the two vices of *avaritia* and *luxuria,* which it is the function of *sophrosyne* to restrain. Livy is the historian who responded most sympathetically to Cicero's influence and put into operation the orator's suggestions about both the style and the moral framework suitable for composing Roman history." North, p. 285.

[18]Clarence M. Mendell, *Our Seneca* (New Haven, 1941), pp. 163-164. (Italics mine.)

[19]See *Satires* I. 1. 106, 2. 25, 6. 68; II. 3., and *Odes* 2. 10. 5-8.

[20]*Epist.* I. 6.

[21]Rudd, *The Satires of Horace,* p. 218.

[22]L. Cazamian, *A History of French Literature* (Oxford, 1960), p. 1 7.

[23]This is a technique followed by many other classical authors as well; notably: Theophrastus; Plautus; and Terence.

[24]*Ad Lucilium Epistulae Morales,* tr. Richard M. Gummere, Loeb Classical Library (London, 1925), III, cx, pp. 267ff. Hereafter cited as *Epistles.*

[25]Seneca, *Epistles* V; Gummere, I, 23.

[26]The Stoics held the concept that "all good actions are absolutely equal in merit, and so are all bad actions." Oskar Seyffert, *A Dictionary of Classical Antiquities,* ed. Henry Nettleship and J. E. Sandys, 7th ed. (1891; rpt. New York, 1961), p. 483.

[27]Horace provides another clue to Tartuffe's character, for he notes the topics of useful discussion for edification and moral improvement:

> We discuss matters which concern us more, and of which it is harmful to be in ignorance—whether wealth or virtue makes men happy, whether self-interest or uprightness leads us to friendship, what is the nature of the good and what is its highest form. *Satires* II. 6. 72-76, tr., H. Rushton Fairclough, Horace, *Satires, Epistles* and *Ars Poetica,* Loeb Classical Library, 2nd ed. (1929; rpt. Cambridge, 1947), pp. 216-217.
>
> These are questions fundamental to ethical philosophy, and which would have been discussed in Roman times by anyone wishing to attain virtue, or to aid someone

else to do so. If Tartuffe had really been concerned, as a director of conscience should, with the spiritual and moral improvement of Orgon and his family in *Christianas costumbres*, he would certainly have discussed similar topics with Orgon. That, however, would have been highly impractical; any attempt at true edification might accidentally have worked, and that would have destroyed Tartuffe's game.

In the remainder of this chapter, except for quotations run into the text, all passages from Horace and Juvenal will be presented in translation, with the original Latin in the footnote, if it is particularly relevant because of its wording. Passages from Latin authors which are more pertinent because of their *Gehalt* than their *Stoff* will be presented only in translation. Translations from Horace will be taken from the Fairclough edition, unless otherwise noted; translations from Juvenal will be taken from G.G. Ramsay, tr., *Juvenal and Persius*, Loeb Classical Library (1918; rpt. New York, 1924), unless otherwise indicated.

[28] Jacques Guicharnaud, *Molière: une aventure théâtrale* (Paris, 1963), p. 29.
[29] *Ibid.*, p. 76.
[30] Paul Stapfer, *Molière et Shakespeare* (Paris, 1905), pp. 217-218.
[31] The effect of Tartuffe on Orgon has been seen not as instilling Orgon with hypocrisy to match his own, but as whetting to a fine edge Orgon's incipient urge for "spiritual health." Ramon Fernandez, *Molière: The Man Seen Through the Plays* (New York, 1958), pp. 133-134.
[32] *Les Luttes de Molière* (Paris, 1925), p. 97.
[33] Judd David Hubert, *Molière and the Comedy of Intellect* (Los Angeles, 1962), p. 95.
[34] *Epistles* CVIII; Gummere, III, 233.
[35] Cf. St. Thomas Aquinas, *Commentary on the Nicomachean Ethics*, tr., C. I. Litzinger (Chicago, 1964), I, 8. The position of St. Thomas in the Jesuit *Ratio* is with Cicero and Aristotle. It is not unlikely that Aristotle was studied in this commentary by those students whose Greek was inadequate to approach the original.
[36] Seneca, *Epistles* LXXV; Gummere, II, 143.
[37] *Satires* II. 3. Juvenal's attitude toward religion will be treated under the theme of hypocrisy.
[38] Ursula Schoenheim, *A Study of the Major Themes of Roman Satire*. Unpublished Doctoral Dissertation (Cornell University, Ithaca, 1958), p. 175.
[39] *Satires* II. 2. 9, 25, 30, 35.
[40] It is possible to see in several characters from Molière's plays examples of the *corruptus iudex*: Arnolphe in *L' École des Femmes;* M. Jourdain in *Le Bourgeois Gentilhomme*; Argan in *Le Malade Imaginaire*; and Harpagon in *L'Avare*.
[41] Although Gilbert Highet suggests that Juvenal was not a Stoic, commenting that "he either did not know or did not accept their basic teaching on certain important matters" *Juvenal the Satirist* (New York, 1954), p. 93, R. Schuetze, in his *Juvenalis ethicus* (Greifswald, 1905), shows the possible extent of the influence of Stoicism on Juvenal by the collection of philosophical commonplaces from his satires. Highet, "The Philosophy of Juvenal," *TAPA,* LXXX (1949), 254-270, suggests that Juvenal was converted to Epicureanism in later life.
[42] Seneca, *Epistles* CVII; Gummere, II, 228-230.
[43] Seneca, *Epistles* LXVI; Gummere, II, 25.
[44] The following passage from Seneca is further verification of this point:

> We have separated this perfect virtue into its several parts. The desires had to be reined in, fear to be suppressed, proper actions to be arranged, debts to be paid; we therefore included self-restraint, bravery, prudence, and justice — assigning to each quality its special function. How then have we formed the conception of virtue?

Virtue has been manifested to us by this man's order, propriety, steadfastness, absolute harmony of action, and a greatness of soul that rises superior to everything. Epistles CXX; Gummere, III, 388-389.

[45] Horace, *Epistles* I. 16. 73-79; Fairclough, p. 357.

[46] *Epistles* VII; Gummere, I, 39-41.

[47] His attacks occur outside the satires proper, for the most part, See, e.g., *Ep.* I. 6, 28-68, on excess in food as a deterrent to virtuous living; also. *Ep.* I. 15. 26-41, on the folly and penalties of gluttony.

[48] This same theme is treated in *Satires* II. 7. 105-111.

[49] See Appendix III for a Senecan treatment of this theme.

[50] North, *Sophrosyne*, p. 27. Inconsistency "was a commonplace, and was recognized as such by Plato, who quotes the saying 'Bad men are never the same and never consistent' (*Lysis* 214c). The proverb suited the philosopher's teaching, for an inconsistent man lacked that steady rational control which unified the personality and fitted it for the good life. This ideal of steadiness, passing down through Aristotle and the Stoics, gave men a center of gravity; it told them not to be unsettled by adversity or prosperity, to show themselves reliable in dealing with others, and to preserve a decent restraint in their social habits."

[51] This satire, which has as its subject the tendency of men to run to extremes and their inability to hold to the golden mean, is illustrated particularly with depictions of sexual indulgence, especially the vice of adultery. The nature of the satire would suggest, then, that if Molière read it, he did not do so in his days at Clermont, but later, perhaps when considering the theme of moderation.

[52] To show the strength of this ideal of consistency in Horace's philosophy one has merely to note that he allows the man who is persistently perverted in his aims a higher position than the man who but now and then aims at the right things (*Satires* II. 7. 6-37).

[53]       nam quis
   peccandi finem posuit sibi? . . .
   quisnam hominum est quem tu contentum videris uno
   flagitio? (*Satires* XIII. 240-244)

[54] It may, however, have a further and more important significance, particularly in view of Dorine's comments in the preceding scene. Molière gives to Tartuffe, as he will in the near future to Don Juan also, a ruddy complexion. the ruddiness perhaps being symbolic of fire, which can be equated with Hell. It is possible that Molière intended symbolically to say that Tartuffe equals Satan, who, one will recall, fell through *pride* and *ambition*. Cf. Jean Meyer, *Molière* (Paris, 1963), 160 ff.

[55] *Les Epoques du théâtre français* (Paris, 1892), p. 125.

[56] Highet, *Juvenal the Satirist*, p. 135.

[57] *Satires* I. 1. 106-107; Fairclough, pp. 12-13.

[58] Cf. *Satires* II. 3. 126-128; *Odes* II. 18. 23-28; III. 24. 36-44, 59-62.

[59] Any of the classical examples of the *prodigus* could have given Molière keys to the character and actions of Tartuffe. A development can be proposed dependent upon the acceptance of Tartuffe's tendency toward excess and his early career as a *prodigus*. Tartuffe was excessively lavish when he had money to waste. Once he had wasted his wealth, he entered new excesses, avarice and covetousness, both directed toward the same object as his prodigality—wealth. And once he gained new wealth, through the benevolent stupidity of Orgon, Tartuffe returned to his former excess—prodigality.

[60] Highet, *Juvenal the Satirist*, p. 51.

[61] Juvenal treats the subject of legacy-hunting in four other satires: I. 33-39, 55-57; II. 58-61; V. 132ff.; and VI. 38-40. The subject is widely treated in other authors as well, as Martial: I. 10; II. 18; V. 39; VI. 63; IX. 48; IX. 88; XI. 4; XII. 10.

⁶²*Satires* XII. 122-126; Ramsay, pp. 244-245.

. . . nan si Libitinam evaserit aeger,
delebit tabulas inclusus cacere nassae
post meritum sane mirandum atque omnia soli
forsan Pacuvio breviter dabit, ille superbus
incedet victis rivalibus.

⁶³Cf. *Epistles* I. 1. 77-80.

⁶⁴It is strongly implied here that the main enemy of the legacy-hunter is not wives, but children. See Rudd, *The Satires of Horace*, p. 226. Women of the higher, and therefore wealthier, class of citizens were no competition to the *captator* till after the time of Horace, since they were prohibited by the Lex Voconia (169 B.C.) from inheriting property. Such restrictions were eased, legally and otherwise, in the period of the Empire. F.H. Marshall, *A Companion to Latin Studies*, ed. J.E. Sandys (Cambridge, 1929), pp. 185-187, 315-316.

⁶⁵An interesting variation on the theme of the successful *captator* is presented in Petronius' *Satyricon* 140-141, where the heirs must eat the body of their dead patron before inheriting his wealth. Due to the corrupt nature of the manuscript, however, Petronius' work is broken off before we behold the humiliation of the legacy-hunters.

⁶⁶J. Calvet, *Molière: est-il chrétien?* (Paris, 1950), p. 78, calls Tartuffe a "directeur captateur de testament."

⁶⁷St. Thomas Aquinas, *Comm. on Nic. Ethics*, I. 125. It is noteworthy that Eugène Rigal, *Molière* (Paris, 1908), states specifically that Tartuffe is "un egoïste" (pp. 238-239) and that "c'est l'égoïsme que Molière raille et combat" (pp. 240-241) in *Tartuffe*.

⁶⁸Aquinas, *Ibid.*

⁶⁹A common concept among philosophers was that a criminal's conscience and fear of discovery were his punishment. Cf. Lucretius, 3. 1011-1123; Seneca, *Epistles* XCVII, CV; Juvenal, XIII.

⁷⁰Cf. Horace, *Epistles* I. 1. 36-40.

⁷¹Horace, when dealing with the problem of ambition, tells a story which has a very interesting analogue. In *Satires* II. 3. 158-223, he deals once more with the question of who is sane and who a fool. Coming to the subject of ambition, he tells of Servius Oppidius, a rich man, who, as he lay dying, divided his property between his two sons, one of whom was a spendthrift, the other a miser. He compels the sons, respectively, to swear an oath, the one not to reduce, the other not to increase, what their father thought enough.

The tale is quite comparable to the parable of the talents told by Christ. But there are noteworthy differences which point up the satiric traditions which Horace is employing in his story. The tale, as told by Horace, puts extra stress on the idea of moderation in all things. This idea is understated in Christ's parable. But what is especially interesting at this point is the fact that Horace employs the story as a lead-in to a lengthy sermon on ambition.

⁷²*Satires* I. 6. 24-29; Fairclough, pp. 78-79. Throughout classical literature there occurs the suggestion that one should live cautiously lest the attention of the gods be attracted; if a man rises to prominence, he may seem to be rivalling the gods, and thus evoke their jealousy and wrath. This is part of the lesson of Horace *Odes* II. 10; and of Aeschylus' *Agamemnon*.

⁷³*Satires* I. 6. 34-37; Fairclough, pp. 78-79.

⁷⁴The importance of the interpretation of Orgon's household as a political microcosm will be discussed more fully in the section of this chapter on Sejanus.

⁷⁵*Satires* VIII. 140-141; Ramsay, pp. 168-169.

⁷⁶Schoenheim, *Major Themes of Roman Satire*, p. 118.

⁷⁷St. Thomas Aquinas, *Comm. on Nic. Ethics*, II, 629.

[78]For a discussion of these terms as renderings of *sophrosyne*, vd. North, *Sophrosyne*, pp. 263-265.
[79]St. Thomas Aquinas, *Comm. on Nic. Ethics*, I. 279.
[80]*Ibid.*, II, 695.
[81]Epicurus discusses this matter in *Sententiae Vaticanae*, 51, where says:

> Provided you don't break the laws or good customs and do not cause annoyance to any of your neighbors or do yourself physical harm or waste your money, you may indulge yourself as you please. But you are bound to encounter one of these obstacles, for sexual pleasure never did a man any good, and he is lucky if it doesn't do him harm. (Translated by Rudd, *The Satires of Horace*, p. 24.)

Lucretius also accepts the necessity of physical pleasures. In *De rerum natura* 4. 1065, 1071, 1073, he suggest that casual intercourse, as opposed to marriage, avoids many of the problems of love.

Molière was doubtless familiar with these teachings of Epicureanism, having himself translated Lucretius.

[82]Rudd, *The Satires of Horace*, p. 24.
[83]*Epistles* I. 1. 41-42; Fairclough, pp. 254-255.

> Virtus est vitium fugere et sapientia prima stultitia caruisse.

[84]North, *Sophrosyne*, p. 293. She also notes a number of odes which are representative of the theme of moderation in Horace: "*Epode* I; *Odes* II. 18. 1-4; III. 1. 45-48; III. 6. 33-34" (p. 294).
[85]Margaret M. Fitzgerald, tr., *The Complete Works of Horace*, ed. C.J. Kraemer, Jr. (New York, 1936), p. 193.
[86]*Satires* I. 6. 82-84. "Need I say more? He kept me chaste— and that is virtue's first grace—free not only from every deed of shame, but from all scandal."

> quid multa? pudicum,
> qui primus virtutis honos, servavit ab omni
> non solum facto, verum opprobrio quoque turpi . . .

[87]Niall Rudd, *The Satires of Horace* (Cambridge, 1966), p. 192.
[88]Basic to this issue is the problem of the truly free man. "Who, then, is free? The wise man, who is master of himself, who is undaunted by poverty, death, or bonds, who bravely defies his passions and despises positions of power, who is complete in himself, smooth and round, so that no foreign element can adhere to his polished surface, and who always causes Fortune to lame herself when she attacks him." Horace, *Satires* II. 7. 83-88. Rudd, *Satires of Horace*, p. 192.
[89]*Satires* II. 7. 68-115.
[90]*Satires* I. 2. 105-119.
[91]*Satires* I. 2. 37-46; Fairclough, pp. 20-23.
[92]This is shown in Horace, *Satires* II. 7. 68-82; Fairclough, pp. 230-231.
[93]*Satires* II. 7. 53-67; Fairclough, pp. 228-231.
[94]A similar occurrence to that in Horace can be found in Juvenal:

> . . . if he, who has long been the most notorious of gallants, who has so often found safety in the corn-bin of the luckless Latinus, puts his head into the connubial noose?

> . . . si moechorum notissimus olim
> stulta maritali iam porrigit ora capistro
> quem totiens texit perituri cista Latini?

(*Satires* VI, 42-44; Ramsay, pp. 86-87.)

[95] *Satires* II. 7. 68-70; Fairclough, pp. 230-232.

[96] Rudd, *The Satires of Horace*, p. 1.

[97] Virtue is the one and only true nobility. *Satires* VIII. 20; Ramsay, pp. 158-159.

[98] Schoenheim, *Major Themes of Satire*, p. 141, refers to Juvenal, *Satire* VIII.

[99] This corruption in Orgon may have first evidenced itself in Orgon's failure to adhere to the law by rather protecting his friend and his secrets than respecting the order of the realm. This action can, however, be seen in a different light, dependent upon the importance one sets on the relationship of friends, a subject which will be considered more fully below. At this point one must accept the failure of Orgon to obey the law of the land as a breach of good judgment.

[100] Guicharnaud, *Molière: une aventure théâtrale*, p. 163.

[101] Daniel M. Crabb, *Tartuffe and Other Plays of Molière* (New York, 1966), p. 37.

[102] Stapfer found this quality of running to opposite extremes rooted deeply in Orgon's character: "L'expérience les contraint-elle à changer d'avis, ils ne font que changer d'exagération; ils ne mettent aucun ménagement, aucune retenue dans leur ardeur à maudire ce qu'ils avaient élevé jusqu'au ciel." *Molière et Shakespeare*, pp. 217-218.

[103] Guicharnaud, *Molière: une aventure théâtrale*, p. 135.

[104] *Ibid.*, p. 132. Cf. also p. 138.

[105] Highet, *Juvenal the Satirist*, p. 140, notes that "the type of fraud Jevenal is here discussing seems to have been quite as common in Greece and in Rome, for it is often mentioned. The Christians of Juvenal's day took a special oath to practice virtue—an oath . . . based on the Ten Commandments; but they included an explicit provision against this action, and swore 'not to deny a deposit.' " See Pliny, *Letters*, with an English translation by W. Melmoth, Loeb Classical Library (1915; rpt. Cambridge, Mass., 1958) II, 402-403. *Epistles* X, xcvi.

[106] The theft of the strongbox and Tartuffe's breaking of faith with Orgon strikes one immediately as a form of treachery. This interpretation depends on the understanding which we have of the ultimate basis of the relationship between Orgon and Tartuffe. According to some theories Tartuffe's actions are not treacherous but rather are faithful to a greater ideal—that of the state. Tartuffe, then, is not betraying Orgon; obedient to a greater obligation and duty, he is protecting the state.

In line with this theory we find that Arnavon, in his book *Molière: notre contemporain*, (Paris, 1929), entitled one chapter "Tartuffe agent secret?." His theory is that Tartuffe is an agent of the secret police, whose mission is to capture the strongbox and thus "get the goods" on Orgon. According to Arnavon, then, Tartuffe is a police officer, who, in his relationship with Elmire, is side-tracked from his mission.

The invalidity of Arnavon's theory can be seen in the play itself. The author reveals Tartuffe's character to us without a doubt when Tartuffe, having made Orgon a virtual prisoner, still persists in playing his role as *dévot*, in language if not in deed:

   Et je suis pour le ciel appris à tout souffrir. (1868)

[107] Seneca, *Epistles* XXXIX; Gummere, I. 263.

[108] It is a poor thing to lean upon the fame of others, lest the pillars give way and the house falls down in ruin. Juvenal, *Satires* VIII. 76-77; Ramsay, pp. 164-165.

[109] Seneca, *Epistles* XCIV; Gummere III, 35.

[110] "But suppose," people retort, "that a man is not the possesor of sound dogmas, how can advice help him when he is chained down, as it were by vicious dogmas?" In this, assuredly, that he is freed therefrom; for his natural disposition has not been crushed, but overshadowed

and kept down. Even so it goes on endeavouring to rise again, struggling against the influences that make for evil; but when it wins support and receives the aid of precepts, it grows stronger, provided only that the chronic trouble has not corrupted nor annihilated the natural man. For in such a case, not even the training that comes from philosophy, striving with all its might, will make restoration. Seneca, *Epistles* XCIV; Gummere, III, 30-33.

111

> ... there are but few who can
> distinguish true blessings from their opposites, putting aside the mists of error.

> ... pauci dinoscere possunt
> vera bona atque illis multum diversa, remota
> erroris nebula.
> *Satires* X. 2-4; Ramsay, pp. 192-193.

[112] ... in avoiding a vice, fools run into its opposite. *Satires* I. 2. 24; Fairclough, pp. 20-21.

[113]Gossman, *Men and Masks*, p. 142.

[114]Although *Tartuffe* is the only one of Molière's plays to present hypocrisy as the main subject of his attack, a brief study shows that hypocrisy of one form or another is often a secondary object for Molière's satiric attack in a number of his other plays. In *Don Juan*, the protagonist uses religious hypocrisy to win his ends. (It is noteworthy that Don Juan, like Tartuffe, does not repent his crime.)

[115]*Webster's Third New International Dictionary* (Springfield, Mass., 1961), p. 115.

[116]*Epistles* XCIV; Gummere, III, 57.

[117]St. Thomas Aquinas, *Comm. on Nic. Ethics*, I. 364. Theophrastus, while giving the characteristic actions of a hypocrite under his heading *Eironeias* (dissembling) does not provide explanations for these actions; he seems to be more concerned with the result than the cause. See *The Characters of Theophrastus*, ed. and tr. J. M. Edmonds (London, 1929), pp. 40-42.

[118]Jacques Guicharnaud, ed., *Le Tartuffe and Le Médecin malgré lui* (New York, 1962), p. 12.

[119]"De Beneficiis," in *Moral Essays*, with an English translation by John W. Basore, Loeb Classical Library (New York, 1932), III, 239-241.

[120]"tu cum sis quod ego et fortassis nequior, ultro/insectere velut melior verbisque decoris/ obvolvas vitium?" *Satires* II. 7. 40-42; Fairclough, pp. 228-229.

[121]Another category of hypocrite will be dealt with under the subheading *Clientela* later in this chapter.

[122]Guicharnaud, *Molière: une aventure théâtrale*, p. 99.

[123]Because woman is so *varium et mutabile* in her nature, man has found through the years that hypocrisy is necessary to win her love. Therefore, the suitor is a prime example of the hypocrite. This is shown repeatedly in Ovid's *Ars Amatoria*, with which Molière may have been familiar, although only the *Metamorphoses* was taught in the Jesuit system.

[124]The Ovidian lover sets the pattern for the courtly lover of the Middle Ages, who then influenced the gallants of the seventeenth century. Thus, Tartuffe's spiel has its very basis in hypocrisy, above and beyond any intention of his own.

[125]absentem qui rodit amicum, qui non defendit alio culpante, solutos qui capat risus hominum famamque dicacis, fingere qui non visa potest, commissa tacere qui nequit: hic niger est, hunc tu, Romane, caveto. *Satires* I. 4. 81-85; Fairclough, pp. 54-55.

[126]Horace considers hypocrisy directed toward the poet in *A. P.* 419-437.

[127] ... detrahere et pellem, nitidus qua quisque per ora cederet, introrsum turpis ... *Satires* II. 1. 64-65; Fairclough, pp. 130-133. The Latin word for hypocrite, *simulator*, is not used by Horace in this satire, although it occurs in *Epistles* I. 9. 9.

[128]*Satires* VI. 343-345. Juvenal's attitude toward religion is considered by E. E. Burriss, "The Religious Element in the Satires of Juvenal," *CW* XX (1926), 19-21; and J. D. Jefferis, "Juvenal and Religion." *CJ* XXXIV (1939), 229-33.
[129]Horace, *Odes* III. 6. 5-6.
[130]*Satires* VIII. 146-162. Exemplary of the same tradition, and written before Juvenal's poem, is Persius' Satire II, in which Persius discusses the fact that men pray openly for worthy objects, but secretly pray for money, inheritances, and the death of their enemies.
[131]*Satires* XIII. 31-33; Ramsay, pp. 248-249.

> nos hominum divumque fidem clamore ciemus, quanto Faesidium laudat vocalis agentem sportula.

[132]*Satires* XIII. 92-94; Ramsay, pp. 252-253.

> Decernat quodcumque volet de corpore nostro Isis et irato feriat mea lumina sistro dummodo vel caecus teneam quos abnego nummos.

[133]*Epistles* I. 16. 57-62; Fairclough, pp. 354-355.

> vir bonus, omne forum quem spectat et omne tribunal quandocumque deos vel porco vel bove placat, "Iane pater!" clare, clare cum dixit, "Apollo!" labra movet metuens audiri: "pulchra Laverna, da mihi fallere, da iusto sanctoque videri, noctem peccatis et fraudibus obice nubem."

[134]Juvenal, *Satires* XIII. 100-105; translated by Gilbert Highet, in *Juvenal The Satirist*, p. 142.

> ut sit magna tamen, certe lenta ira deorum est; si curant igitur cunctos punire nocentes, quando ad me venient? sed et exorabile numen fortasse experiar, solet his ignoscere. multi committunt eadem diverso crimina fato: ille crucem sceleris pretium tulit, hic diadema.

[135]*Epistles* CXXIII; Gummere, III, 433.
[136]*Epistles* CVIII; Gummere, III, 253.
[137]*Epistles* XXIX; Gummere, I, 202ff. Lucian, in his *Sale of Philosophies* (Biôn Prasis), accuses the Stoics of establishing a double standard. See *Lucian*, tr. A. M. Harmon, Loeb Classical Library, (Cambridge, Mass., 1960), II, 489-501.
[138]*Satires* II. 9-10. Highet, *Juvenal the Satirist*, p. 249, lists a series of attacks on hypocrites who pretended to virtue but yielded to lust.
[139]*Satires* XIV. 109-110; Ramsay, pp. 272-273. Juvenal here is talking of the hypocrisy of avarice.

> fallit enim vitium specie virtutis et umbra cum sit triste habitu vultuque et veste severum . . .

[140]It is a frequent theme in Horace also. Cf., *Sat.* II. 2. 23-30, 35; *Ep.* I. 6. 28-56; *Ep.* I. 16. 40-49; *Ep.* I. 19. 12-14.
[141]Orgon should also have been familiar with Christ's teachings on the same subject, in Matthew 6:1-15, which deals specifically with the prayers of hypocrites. Cf. also Horace, *Epistles* I. 16. 57-62, on which I have commented above.

It is possible that Molière was familiar with the charges of hypocrisy brought against Seneca, as found in Tacitus. A certain Suilius, who had fallen into disfavor in 58 A.D., attacked Seneca for his excesses in sexual and financial matters, both very much at odds with Stoic preachments. (*Ann.* XIII. 42.) Similar charges of excessive acquisition of wealth were brought against Seneca in 62 A.D., as well as charges that he had effected the poisoning of two of his freedmen (*Ann.* XIV. 52-54 and 65). Therein is also his rejoinder to such charges (XIV. 54): that he could endure wealth, whereby he meant that it was not hypocritical of him to possess worldly goods, since, were they to be taken from him, he would not miss them.

[142]*Epistles* CIII; Gummere, III, 188-189.

[143]Seneca repeats this advice in a fuller statement earlier in the *Epistles*: " 'The knowledge of sin is the beginning of salvation.' This saying of Epicurus seems to me to be a noble one. For he who does not know that he has sinned does not desire correction; you must discover yourself in the wrong before you can reform yourself. Some boast of their faults. Do you think that the man has any thought of mending his ways who counts over his vices as if they were virtues? Therefore, as far as possible, prove yourself guilty, hunt up charges against yourself; play the part, first of accuser, then of judge, last of intercessor. At times be harsh with yourself." *Epistles* XXVIII; Gummere I, 203.

[144]Moore, *Molière*, pp. 64-65, asks: "Can the master of irony go farther than to convict a criminal out of his own mouth . . . " He continues by noting that "the principle at work here is dramatic irony."

[145]Seneca, *Epistles* XX: Gummere, I, 133-135. See also *Epistles* CXIV, on the consistency of one's character and soul.

[146]Palmer, *Molière*, pp. 133-35, 145, 226, 246, 257, 285, 324.

[147]*Molière*, pp. 133-135.

[148]G. E. Duckworth, *The Nature of Roman Comedy* (Princeton, 1952), p. 266.

[149]Lancaster, *Fr. Dram. Lit.*, III, ii, 628.

[150]There were two different periods of clientage in Rome. The first, which occurred in the time of the Kings and the early Republic, had ceased to exist with the advance of the plebian class to civil rights. The second, which was connected to the first only by name, was the product of Rome's days of Empire, when the "nouveaux riches" sought to gain a reputation by the size of their retinue. It is the latter period which is important here.

[151]The client could also be expected to attend the patron throughout the day, and even on long journeys. Mary Johnston, *Roman Life* (Chicago, 1957), p. 182, notes that "new clients came in with the upstart rich, who considered a long train of dependents as necessary to their position as a string of high-sounding names, or a mansion loaded with slaves. These dependents were merely needy men, or women, usually obscure, who toadied to the rich and great for the crumbs that fell from their tables. There were among them occasionally men of talent - philosophers, or poets like Martial or Statius - but for the most part they were a swarm of cringing, fawning, timeserving flatterers and parasites."

[152]*Epistles* IV; Gummere, I. 19.

[153]For a consideration of the development of this theme from its Greek origins down to Horace, see Fiske, *Lucilius and Horace*, pp. 162-165, and L. R. Shero, "The Cena in Roman Satire," *Classical Philology* XVIII (1923), 126-143. Highet, *Juvenal the Satirist*, pp. 262, 278-279, considers the sources and analogues of this theme. Perhaps the most noteworthy *cena* of classical literature is the "Cena Trimalchionis" in Petronius' *Satyricon*.

[154]Highet, *The Anatomy of Satire*, pp. 221-223, notes that Horace, *Satires* II. 8, is the earliest of this particular genre. He also notes that Régnier's Tenth Satire, which Molière likely had read, is of this type, being in part an adaptation of Horace.

[155]Rudd, *The Satires of Horace*, p. 223. It is possible to see in the opening scenes of Act IV of *Le Bourgeois Gentilhomme* a variety of painful dinner.

[156]Erich Auerbach, *Mimesis* (New York, 1957), p. 318.

[157]Lionel Gossman, *Men and Masks* (Baltimore, 1963), p. 110. For a more complete discussion of the reasons for the union of Tartuffe-Orgon, see pp. 102-113.

[158]A somewhat similar reversal takes place in Horace, *Satires* II. 7. There, the time being the Saturnalia when slaves have unusual freedom, Horace's slave Davus presumes to lecture him on virtue and vice, actually going so far as to criticize his master. A more similar reversal was

discussed above in the section on *Sophrosyne* dealing with adultery. There Horace's actions as adulterer were contrasted with Tartuffe's.

[159]Virro will be studied more exactingly in his relationship to the figure of Orgon in the Appendix. It will be seen that his character may be even more complex than that presented in Juvenal's Fifth Satire, for Virro will be seen again in Juvenal's Ninth Satire, this time not just as a patron, but as a practicing homosexual.

[160]Seneca's *Apocolocyntosis* is another example of a perversion of normal order which Molière may have known. It presents a ruler, Claudius, who yielded excessive power at his court to freedmen. Claudius is repeatedly shown to be a silly ass (the idea of the title).

Gilbert Bagnani, *Arbiter of Elegance* (Toronto, 1954), asserts that the *Ludus de Morte Claudii*, which has been widely considered the *Apocolocyntosis*, is not the work of Seneca, but of Petronius (pp. 43-45). Concerning the *Ludus*, he does follow the belief that it is a work attacking Claudius and the advisory council that deified him (43).

[161]Highet, *Anatomy of Satire*, p. 52.

[162]VII. 20; IX. 10. 4.

[163]Highet, *Juvenal the Satirist*, p. 72. The material on the *Graeculus* is developed partially from the outline of Vincent Pascucci, as provided by Highet, p. 325.

[164]Juvenal, *Satires III. 73-74;* Ramsay, pp. 36-37. For further consideration of clientship, see X. 44-46, XIII. 32-33.

[165]The parallel here is not to a Greek, but to a woman caught in the act. (VI. 284-285).

[166]Guicharnaud, *Molière: une aventure théâtrale*, pp. 39-41.

[167]There may seem to be some difficulty in aligning the forementioned tendency toward self-aggrandizement with Orgon's desire to serve, or at least stand in a subordinate and less responsible position. This should not be a problem, however, for one has but to think of the numerous examples in our society in which a man puts himself in a secondary position for the very purpose of gaining credit from the results or reputation of his superior. A man can reveal desires which are discordant to one another, yet are integral parts of that man's character. This is certainly part of Molière's genius in creating Orgon and Tartuffe: they are both combinations of character traits which are extraordinary when combined in a figure of drama.

[168]Guicharnaud, *Molière: une aventure théâtrale*, pp. 41-42.

[169]Gossman, *Men and Masks*, p. 110.

[170]This reversal occurs in verse 194 in Molière: Et s'il vient à roter, il lui dit: "Dieu vous aide?" which is a variation on Juvenal, III. 106-107, "Laudare paratus si (dominus) bene ructavit." It is noteworthy that Alméras, *Le Tartuffe de Molière* (Paris, 1928), p. 50, says "C'est un hypocrite . . . que Juvénal montre . . ."

[171]Here Maecenas is contrasted with the people who are dazzled by titles and busts of great ancestors (15-17).

[172]Schoenheim, p. *Major Themes of Roman Satire*, 157.

[173]Rudd, *The Satires of Horace*, p. 48.

[174]*Epistles* I. 17. 43-51; Fairclough, pp. 364-365.

[175]*Epistles* I. 18. 1-36; Fairclough, pp. 368-369.

[176]*Epistles* I. 18. 37-38; Fairclough, pp. 370-371.

[177]*Epistles* I. 18. 39-66; Fairclough, pp. 370-373.

[178]Guicharnaud, *Molière: une aventure théâtrale*, pp. 48 and 79. For the centrality of Orgon, see pp. 46ff.

[179]Gossman, *Men and Masks*, p. 110.

[180]*Epistles* I. 18. 39.

[181]*Epistles* I. 18. 72-73; Fairclough, pp. 374-375.

[182]*Satires* III. 109-112; Ramsay, pp. 40-41.

[183]Donohue, *Jesuit Education* (New York, 1963), p. 131.

[184]Palmer, *Molière*, p. 361.

[185]Seneca, *Epistles* IX; Gummere I, 43ff. In the Stoic philosophy wisdom and virtue were inseparable. One of the best treatments of friendship, and a work which Molière may have read is Cicero's *De Amicitia*. The requisites for choosing a friend are in sections XVIII-XX.

[186]Horace, *Satires* I. 6. 44-64; Fairclough, pp. 80-81.

[187]A variation on this idea occurs in Horace, *Satires* I. 3. 38-54; Fairclough, pp. 34-37; but the main statement thereof is *Satires* I. 3. 69-72; Fairclough, pp. 38-39.

[188]*Satires* I. 3. 30-34; Fairclough, pp. 34-35.

[189]"De Beneficiis" IV, *Moral Essays*; Basore, III, 281. I have abbreviated the story as told by Seneca.

[190]Seneca, *Epistles* LXXXVI. 32; Gummere, II, 167.

[191]Seneca, *Epistles* LXXXIX. 18; Gummere, II. 211.

[192]Seneca, *Epistles* XCV.; Gummere, III. 82-84.

[193]Juvenal, *Satires* XIII. 199-208; Ramsay, pp. 260-261.

[194]Highet comments on this occurrence, especially among Christians, *Juvenal the Satirist*, p. 140.

[195]*Epistles* XCIV; Gummere, III, 47. A similar tradition may be found in Terence's *Adelphi* where the reformed father, Demea, says that the golden mean lies in a young man's liberty being duly checked by his father's advice and correction (985-995).

[196]*Epistles* XXV; Gummere, I. 185; *Epistles* XCIV; Gummere, III, 47.

[197]*Epistles* LII; Gummere, I, 349.

[198]*Epistles* XI; Gummere, I, 63-65.

[199]A discussion of Cleanthes as a proponent of *sophrosyne* is provided by Helen North, *Sophrosyne*, pp. 216-217. It is interesting that she immediately follows material on Cleanthes with that on Aristo, whom Cléante classed among the truly devout (386).

[200]*Epistles* CVIII; Gummere, III, 229ff.

[201]*Satires* I. 6. 81-84; Fairclough, pp. 82-83.

> Ipse mihi custos incorruptissimus omnis circum doctores aderat. Quid multa? pudicum qui primus virtutis honos, servavit ab omni non solum facto verum opprobrio quoque turpi . . .

[202]A similar version of the *custos* is found in Terence's *Adelphi*, where Demea fulfills the role for his own son Ctesipho.

[203]*Satires* I. 4. 115-120; Fairclough, pp. 58-59.

> 'sapiens, vitatu quidque petitu sit melius, causas reddet tibi: mi satis est si traditum ab antiquis mores servare tuamque, dum custodis eges, vitam famamque tueri incolumem possum; simul ac duraverit aetas membra animumque tuum, nabis sine cortice.'

[204]Lionel Gossman, *Men and Masks: A Study of Molière* (Baltimore, 1963), p. 102.

[205]*Mimesis* (New York, 1953), p. 318.

[206]Donna Gerstenberger and Frederick Garber, *Microcosm* (San Francisco, 1969), p. 1.

[207]*Ibid.*, p. 1.

[208]*Comedy* (London, 1950), in *Comedy: Meaning and Form*, ed. R. W. Corrigan (San Francisco, 1965), pp. 211-212.

[209]Potts, in Corrigan, *Comedy*, p. 212.

[210]Guicharnaud, *Molière*, pp. 45-46. An understanding of the tendency of the Renaissance man to make such analogies of the microcosm to macrocosm may be gained from E. M. W. Tillyard's *The Elizabethan World Picture* (New York, 1943). Although not concerned with Molière, Tillyard's book can be applied indirectly to Molière.

[211]*Molière*, p. 117.

[212] Eugène Despois and Paul Mesnard, eds., Œuvres, by Molière, Les Grands Ecrivains de la France, (Paris, 1889), IV, 345.

[213] *Moralia*, with English translation by Benedict Einarson and Phillip H. Delacy, Loeb Classical Library (Cambridge, Mass., 1967), XIV, 275-295. The inventory of Molière's possessions taken after his death reveals a copy of Plutarch's *Moralia* as well as a two-volume Seneca. See Madeline Jurgens and Elizabeth Maxfield-Miller, eds., *Cent Ans de Recherches sur Molière* (Paris, 1963), pp. 560-561. One will also recall that Molière's mother owned a Plutarch. See Eudore Soulié, *Recherches sur Molière et sur sa famille* (Paris, 1868), p. 13.

[214] The only other occurrence of the figure of Sejanus that I have found is in Ben Jonson's *Sejanus: His Fall*, which seems to have had no direct connection with the work of Molière.

[215] Lancaster, *Fr. Dram. Lit.*, II, ii 587.

[216] *Ibid.*, II, ii, 587.

[217] *Ibid.*, 589-590.

[218] Lancaster, II, ii, 590.

[219] *Ibid.*

[220] The plot of the *Séjanus* has been summarized by Lancaster, II, ii, 590, as follows:

Livia informs her *confidente* that she is willing to marry Drusus, son of Germanicus, if he will help her plot against Sejanus. She is told by the latter of his arrangements for dethroning Tiberius. Apicata comes to appeal to the emperor on the question of her divorce, but meets her husband and gets no satisfaction from him. Livia tells her plans to Drusus and bids him prepare the emperor's mind for her revelations. Meeting Apicata, she is accused of having murdered her husband and become the mistress of Sejanus, but she rebuffs her by pretending that the charges are true, while telling her that she is too insignificant for her to punish. Tiberius is convinced by Livia and Drusus of Sejanus' crimes, while the latter is unable to answer their charges. Tiberius has him arrested and sends him to the Senate for judgment. Before leaving the palace, Sejanus meets his wife and daughter with Térence, asks pardon, and expresses fear of conviction. Tiberius is deaf to the women's appeal, but clears Térence of conspiring with Sejanus, notwithstanding the boldness of his speech. Condemned to death, Sejanus commits suicide. The mob attacks his friends, kills the members of his family, but is quieted by Drusus, sent in haste by Tiberius. As a reward, the emperor consents to the marriage of Drusus and Livia.

[221] *Ibid.*, 586-587, 651.

[222] *Ibid.*, 496. It is further interesting that we have already considered the relationships of *Fourberies* to the classical tradition of the parasite, especially in Roman comedy.

[223] *Ibid.*, 591, notes the comparison of Agrippine to Livia. The following passages from *Agrippine* are cited by Lancaster, III, i, 170-171.

[224] The plot of *Agrippine* is immediately very dissimilar to that of *Séjanus* or *Tartuffe*, for the spotlight shifts from the villainous protagonists to the heroine. "In Cyrano's tragedy, Agrippina, to avenge Germanicus, offers to marry Sejanus if he will kill Tiberius, and secretly hopes subsequently to murder her accomplice. Tempted, Sejanus abandons his mistress, Livilla (Livia), widow of Drusus. The emperor makes several attempts to prove that Agrippina is plotting against him. At last the conspiracy is revealed by Lavilla, who, as well as Sejanus, is executed, while Agrippina, allowed to live, will be kept in constant fear of death." Lancaster, *Ibid.*, 171.

[225] For Tartuffe as a despiser of the gods, see the earlier section of this chapter on Hypocrisy.

[226] La Monnoye, in notes to the *Ménagiana* of 1715 (II, 25), cited by Lancaster, *Ibid.*, 169. Lancaster also notes that there had been atheists on the French stage before Séjanus; he refers the reader to Mairet's *Chryséide*, Du Ryer's *Scévole*, and Jobert's *Balde*.

[227] It will be remembered that Tacitus was read, according to the *Ratio Studiorum*, at the Collège de Clermont. The works of Tacitus and Juvenal do not include the account of Juvenal's

fall from power. At Book V. 5 of the *Annales*, Tacitus' manuscript contains a lacuna, with more than two years being omitted. The history of the intervening period can be partly reconstructed from the account of Dio Cassius in his *Roman History*, LVII and LVIII. See also, Suetonius, "Tiberius," in the *Vita Caesarum*.

[228] An interesting comparison with Sejanus and Tartuffe is provided by the figure of Maecenas, whom Horace depicted as an ideal patron. Maecenas was of an old Etruscan house and rose to be the adviser of an emperor, in his case, Augustus. But from this point on he and Sejanus stand in contrast, for Maecenas again represents an ideal, while Sejanus is a perversion of all the traditional values. Maecenas never tried to rise above the rank of knight to which he had been born; he was always modest in his demeanor and way of life. But Sejanus was continually arrogant and tyrannical. Maecenas was a skilled politician, who capably maneuvered himself into a position of high favor with Augustus by such ingratiating moves as his attempted enlistment of Horace to write an epic commemorating Augustus' deeds. (*Odes*, II, 12.) While Sejanus put himself into a position from which he intended to rise to supremacy, Maecenas remained loyal to Augustus and willing to remain in his secondary position.

[229] Ronald Syme, *Tacitus* (Oxford at the Clarendon Press, 1958), I, 420, states that "it was clear that the ruler underwent a change," for that change is shown by a dichotomy in the reign of Tiberius which is reflected in the facts. Although Roman literature reveals little or no character development, Tacitus' presentation of Tiberius has been explained by Syme: "The way of thought of the ancients was prone to conceive a man's inner nature as something definable and immutable. A change in observed behavior was therefore not a change in essence, but only a manifestation of what was there all the time . . ." (p. 421)

[230] Tacitus, *The Annals*, ed. Moses Hadas (New York, 1942), IV. 1, p. 144. The italicized portions are my own, and indicate the areas in which Tartuffe parallels Sejanus.

> . . . mox Tiberium variis artibus devinxit, adeo ut obscurum adversus alios sibi uni incautum intectumque efficeret, non tam sollertia (quippe isdem artibus victus est) quam deum ira in rem Romanam, cuius pari exitio viguit ceciditque. Corpus illi laborum tolerans, animus audax; sui obtegens, in alios criminator; iuxta adulatio et superbia; palam compositus pudor, intus summa apiscendi libido, eiusque causa modo largitio et luxus, saepius industria ac vigilantia. . . .

[231] B. Walker, *The Annals of Tacitus*, 2nd ed. (Manchester University Press, 1952), p. 36.
[232] Ronald Syme, *Tacitus* I, 413.
[233] *Annales*, IV. 71.
[234] *Annales*, VI. 51.
[235] *Annales*, XV. 63; cited by Syme, *Tacitus*, I, 345.
[236] *Annales*, IV. 3; Hadas, *The Annals*, p. 145.

[237] Highet, *Juv. the Sat.*, p. 81. It is interesting when one recalls Arnavon's suggestion that Tartuffe functions as an agent of the secret police, "Tartuffe: Agent Secret?" in *Molière: Notre Contemporain* (Paris, 1929), that Highet continues this statement by saying: "In effect, therefore, they were a high-level Gestapo . . ." Although Arnavon's theory is disproven by the final act of *Tartuffe*, where it is shown Tartuffe is certainly not an agent of the Prince, a possible similarity between the *delator* and Tartuffe is pointed up by Arnavon's suggestion. The subject of *delatio* does not bulk large in the works of Horace and Juvenal, occurring only in five poems: Horace, *Sat*. I. 4. 65-67; *Ep*. I. 15. 26-41; Juvenal, *Sat*. IV. 109-110, 113-116; *Sat*. VII. 13-16; *Sat*. XII. 121-130.

[238] This is the version which most historians transmitted, according to Tacitus, *Annales*, IV. 57.
[239] *Annales*, IV. 39.
[240] Syme, *Tacitus*, I, 255.

[241] Percy A. Chapman, *The Spirit of Molière*, p. 176.
[242] Gossman, *Men and Masks*, p. 119.
[243] Antoine Adam, *Histoire de la littérature française au XVIIe siècle* (Paris, 1962), III, 307-309.
[244] *Ibid.*, p. 308.
[245] Syme, *Tacitus*, I, 404.
[246] Gossman, *Men and Masks*, p. 235.
[247] *Ibid.*, p. 236.
[248] *Ibid.*, p. 241.
[249] Respectful didacticism directed to an emperor or king is not unheard of among artists of stature. Vergil, for instance, intended Augustus to profit from the example of Aeneas. See Kenneth Quinn, *Vergil's Aeneid* (Ann Arbor, 1968), p. 54. Shakespeare, too, presented a lesson in his plays, and there is little doubt that the didacticism was directed in part to Elizabeth I. See O. J. Campbell, *Shakespeare's Satire* (New York, 1943), 89ff.; also L. B. Campbell, *Shakespeare's Histories* (San Marino, Calif., 1947), pp. 3-17.

## IV

## CONCLUSION

I stated at the outset that my purpose was to study the extent to which Molière's *Tartuffe* reflects the traditions of classical literature in order to provide a better understanding of Molière's play. The results of this study reveal that it is hardly possible to appreciate *Tartuffe* without an understanding of the traditions which had become a part of the classical heritage of Western literature, and upon which either directly or indirectly Molière based part of his plot and characterizations.

As a young man, Molière attended the Collège de Clermont, where he followed the *Ratio Studiorum*, a plan of studies intended to imbue the students with "Christianas costumbres." The education provided by Jesuit schools was particularly designed to prepare young scholars in self-knowledge *(Nosce teipsum)* and self-control *(Vince teipsum)*. The lessons were taught largely through the exacting study of classical authors, especially the Latin, among whom were Horace, Juvenal and Seneca.

In classical literature there was an extended tradition of character-writing, seen especially in the works of Theophrastus, which merged with other traditions, notably those of moral or ethical literature and of satire. Thus there was available to Molière and other authors of later times in the many Latin writers (e.g., Plautus, Terence, Cicero, Horace, and Juvenal) who used these traditions, a source book of methods and materials for revitalizing moral lessons.

Molière tells us implicitly in his *Préface* of 1669 that his method in writing *Tartuffe* has been *renverser* (to present the inversions or reversals of) institutions and ideals which are normally innocent, salutary and good. The particular ideals and institutions which Molière depicts as reversed are those of *sophrosyne, sapientia*, clientage, and friendship, all of which are presented by the satirists as perverted and misused in their own times. The result was that the satirists, and Molière after them, portrayed the perversions of those institutions and the antitheses of those ideals: parasitism and hypocrisy, dementia and intemperance.

Molière also tells us his purpose in writing *Tartuffe*. Following the predominant literary theory of his day, which stated that art should not merely please, but should profit as well, Molière asks in his *Préface* of 1669 if the function of comedy is not to correct the vices. But he does not stop there, for Molière even tells us indirectly who it is that he intends to correct. Molière says that hypocrites have found favor with Louis XIV *(Premier Placet)*. It is Louis XIV himself, then, toward whom the lesson of Molière's satire is directed. But Molière was too politically aware of the dangers of so rash an act as the writing of satire openly directed to the King. Therefore he masterfully veiled his attack in the structures of comedy.

A study of *Tartuffe* reveals that the satire in Molière's play reflects the same two traditions, ethical-writing and the character, which were merged inseparably in the satiric works of Horace and Juvenal. There are, then, two satirical aspects of Molière's *Tartuffe*: the ethical, expressed in the themes of virtue and evil, and explicitly revealed in Molière's concepts of *le juste milieu* and *bon sens*; and the social, represented by the type characters who appear in the comedy of manners. Molière's concepts of *le juste milieu* and *bon sens* are clearly reflections of the classical ideals of *sophrosyne* (moderation), and *sapientia* (wisdom), especially as seen in the Stoic sage, the *sapiens* (wise man), who realizes that there are *vitia* (sins) to be avoided in this life, among the most destructive to goodness being *luxury, ambition, avarice, lust,* and *superstition*.

Molière was no doubt familiar with the concepts of *sophrosyne* and *sapientia* from the works of the historians Livy and Tacitus, from the comedies of Plautus and Terence, but most of all from the satires of Horace and Juvenal, and the philosophic writings of Seneca, all of whose works were included in his personal library. It was particularly the Stoic philosophy which influenced Roman satire and impressed on it its concept of virtue, which was attainable only by the exercise of self-control *(sophrosyne)* and the avoidance of vices. The ideal of *sophrosyne* was translated into Latin by Horace, who used the term *aurea mediocritas* to express the Greek concept of moderation and the avoidance of all excesses.

Molière says in his *Préface* of 1669 that the *scélérat* in his play would be identifiable by certain "marcs." Those "marcs" are the variations on the themes of *sophrosyne* and *sapientia*, which were part of the literary heritage of the seventeenth century, and with which the audience of his plays would likely be familiar. Among those "marcs" are the inconsistency and lack of self-control that Tartuffe is shown to exhibit. Molière in his characterization of Tartuffe and, to a lesser extent, Orgon, follows the method of Horace and Juvenal, who usually accomplished their didactic tasks by a satiric inversion, showing the negative side of ideals such as *sapientia* and *sophrosyne*; he presents one after another the excesses which are depicted by the Roman satirists in particular and classical literature in general as antithetical to *sophrosyne: luxury; avarice; ambition; sex; superstition;* and *inconsis-*

*tency*. Each of these is a recurring theme in Roman Satire, and the depiction of Tartuffe reflects their treatment in Horace and Juvenal.

The opening scenes of *Tartuffe*, which foreshadow all that is to come, present the conflict of Tartuffe with the family of Orgon. Since the family represents the norm and *bon sens*, Tartuffe is seen to be against *bon sens*, or wisdom (that leads to virtue and *honnêteté*); being against wisdom, Tartuffe must be a *demens*, a fool. Orgon who backs Tartuffe in his tyrannical actions must also be in conflict with wisdom, and thus a fool. This is shown particularly by the fact that Orgon does not have the faculty of right understanding, of discerning good from evil, which ability the Stoics point out as the mark of a wise man. Similarly, Tartuffe is shown to be a fool by the fact that, although he has the ability to tell right from wrong, he chooses the wrong. The perversions of judgment which Orgon and Tartuffe reveal are further reflections of Stoic philosophy — particularly the concept of *morbi mentis*, diseases of the mind. This is shown by the fact that they strive after things which have little or no value — position, power, wealth, and sexual love. Horace's *corruptus iudex* is an example of the man of diseased mind, who is contrasted with the *sapiens*, who can see through to the truth, even when it is disguised. Orgon is a *corruptus iudex* in that he cannot see through to the truth about Tartuffe. This is emphasized by Act III, scene vi, where Orgon cannot see what Tartuffe is even when Tartuffe tells the truth about himself. Tartuffe's status as a fool is further indicated by his establishment of a double standard, one for Orgon's family and one for himself. The wise man, as depicted in Roman literature, is one for whom virtue is a habit, and whose actions are all equal in merit to one another. Since his actions and counsel are always congruous, he is never ambivalent.

The Orgon-Tartuffe relationship develops from Orgon's and Tartuffe's personal needs. Orgon is attracted by the excessive religious behavior of Tartuffe, not by his religion. Orgon wanted a religious man, yes, but one with a flair for the spectacular, so that his deep desire to be recognized, to achieve self-aggrandizement, even if only on a secondary level through association with a spectacularly devout man, could be attained. Orgon's association with Tartuffe, moreover, brings him to choose a life of asceticism to which he has no right, because, as *paterfamilias*, head of his household, Orgon has obligations which require him to act in this world rather than contemplate the next. The choice of an ascetic life is further proof of Orgon's *dementia*. Revealing clearly his warped sense of values is the fact that Orgon's religiosity leads him into very unchristian actions toward his family. Molière uses Orgon's religion as one of the extremes (all in opposition to moderation) which constitute his character.

Both Horace and Juvenal present strong arguments against those desires which run contrary to Juvenal's concept of *mens sana in corpore sano*, a sound mind in a sound body. Molière especially follows Horace in his treatment of these *vitia*, incorporating into his depiction of Tartuffe not just one element of the classical tradition of *sophrosyne*, but every important theme. This follows the Stoic teaching, found also in Horace, that all vices are equally bad and, therefore, equally to be avoided. Horace especially advises the man who would be virtuous and wise to *nil admirari*, to be undisturbed in spirit. Here we see further proof of the *dementia* of Tartuffe, for, although both Tartuffe and Orgon are offenders against the ideal of *sophrosyne*, Tartuffe is the consummate exception to all the advice of Horace. He is "disturbed in spirit" by all the wrong things (precisely those noted by Horace): he is ambitious, else he would not try to gain control in Orgon's house; he desires wealth, else he would not seek and win the fortune of Orgon.

Tartuffe is motivated in all his actions by pride. Pride leads him into ambition and the belief that he is worthy of great things. The great things Tartuffe desires are not, however, part of his lot in life. Therefore he must attain them through fraud and deceit. Tartuffe especially desires three things: power; money; and sex. These are the most magnetic forces in his life, and the ones that will lead to his destruction. Ambition, the desire for power and money, had led many men to the giddy heights, and a fall. It is certainly these that bring Tartuffe to the heights of success; but it is sex that brings him to his fall. Tartuffe, disturbed by his sexual desires, exhibits lust directed toward Elmire. His failure to temper his passions, especially his desire for Elmire, precipitates Tartuffe into all his troubles. He has been guilty of many forms of incontinence, but these have not caused his downfall. It is the repeated rash act of attempting adultery that crumbles Tartuffe's world. Lust is employed as Tartuffe's most destructive flaw in accordance with classical tradition, which had established that even the consideration of an illicit sexual act was proof that the character is flawed and not really virtuous. There can be little doubt that Molière was aware of this fact, and that he created Tartuffe by employing those vices with which he was most familiar, and which he thought appropriate to his depiction of a creature of consummate vice.

Tartuffe clearly reflects the classical concept of the *demens*, but so does Orgon. This can be observed especially in the fifth act, where Orgon fails to act against Tartuffe at a time when decision is crucial to the welfare of his family. When he does react to the crimes of Tartuffe, it is with anger, not intelligence, for he condemns all religious men because one has proved false to him. Orgon still does not have the ability to see the truth. His character is bound up in excess — a fact that Cléante sums up in these words: *Et toujours d'un excès vous vous jetez dans l'autre* (1610). Orgon makes a classic mistake: by trying to avoid one vice, he runs in the opposite direction, and into a vice equally as bad as that which he is fleeing. This action is precisely that which Horace had said was typical of the fools of the world: *dum vitant stulti vitia, in contraria currunt* (Sat. I. 2. 24). In Orgon's very last speech (1957-1962) we are given hope that he has come to his senses and that he will thereafter act rationally and wisely. This is the immediate implication of the closing scene of the play. Molière's other plays as well as the lessons of classical literature, however, leave one with a sense of foreboding. Molière's great comic figures do not suffer a sudden reformation or repentance. Moreover, classical tradition would observe in the sudden rationality of Orgon another of the "leaps" into a different direction which are typical of his tendency toward excess. One is left to wonder how long it will be before Orgon "leaps" from his temporary (as all his previous allegiances have been) allegiance to the Prince and the ideal of *bon sens*.

The foolishness of Orgon and his continuing tendency toward excess are pointed up by the figures of Cléante and the Prince. Throughout the play Cléante has exhibited *bon sens* and moderation. When Orgon is about to attack Tartuffe, it is Cléante who restrains him, at the same time expressing his hope for Tartuffe's moral recovery. Moreover, the contrast between the actions of the Prince, who forgives Orgon for his treason, and Orgon, who cannot forgive Tartuffe his treason, underlines the continued *dementia* of Orgon.

In *Tartuffe*, Molière is attacking both the hypocrites and those who accept them. In the classical tradition he found three types of hypocrites, all of whom employed a virtuous guise to win their ends. These were the philosopher, the client, and the friend. All of these, of course, have their good representatives; more prominent in the works of Horace and Juvenal, however, are the bad examples, the perversions of the ideals. Thus, the social satire in Molière's *Tartuffe* can be seen particularly in the depiction of Tartuffe and Orgon as variations on these type characters who had been the subjects of criticism since classical times. It is virtually impossible to divorce these types from the ethical satire which we have considered as a recurrent element in Molière's comedy. This is typically so of the hypocrite, whose hypocrisy is usually a product of his foolish desires for the antitheses (power, etc.) of *sophrosyne*. There are many reasons for hypocrisy which can be considered applicable to Tartuffe. One is that, as Aristotle's *blatopanurgi*, he takes pleasure in his game; he gains a feeling of superiority by being the tricker. Also, although Orgon's religious interests must have been a strong factor in Tartuffe's choice of religious hypocrisy as his way to power and riches, it is evident that Tartuffe sees in religion something desirable. True religion, however, conflicts with his temporal desires, so that Tartuffe must make a choice: that choice is his desires, but under the pretense of religion and virtue, in which he sees something respectable.

Tartuffe is, first of all, the clever con-man, the user of words to achieve his ends. Hypocrisy is Tartuffe's main device, and resultantly it becomes his primary vice. Tartuffe the hypocrite, however, is inseparable from Tartuffe the proud, ambitious, gluttonous, and lustful. Molière keeps intensifying the classical idea that a man subject to one vice is subject to all vices.

There were many kinds of hypocrites in ancient Rome, but the hypocrites who particularly caught the attention of the satiric poets Horace and Juvenal and the Stoic philosopher Seneca were the philosopher-hypocrites; these are clearly reflected in Molière's characterization of Tartuffe. There were also religious hypocrites, who flaunted their foolish desires in the faces of the gods, men such as Juvenal's fat Lateranus (VIII. 146-162), who were driven by a desire for wealth. Among the most obvious classical forerunners of Tartuffe were the philosopher-hypocrites, especially those who presented themselves in the guise of the Stoic, who used philosophy as a "trade" with which to enrich themselves, who indulged their appetites in every imaginable way, while preaching asceticism. Tartuffe, just as the false Stoic, put on the appearance of virtue to hide his real nature. His real nature — inconsistent, excessive, vicious — should have been recognized by Orgon, but Orgon was a fool, without the ability to tell good from bad.

We have already seen how the stress which the Jesuits placed on the concepts of *Nosce teipsum* and *Vince teipsum*, which were presented through the medium of classical literature especially, found voice in Molière's *Tartuffe* in his concepts of *bon sens* and *juste milieu*, which are variations of the classical concepts of *sapientia* and *sophrosyne*. Emphasis was also placed at the Collège de Clermont on human relations, on the idea that all men are neighbors. Molière's life as well as his education suggest that he would have taken a strong interest in certain human relationships, and this is proven by *Tartuffe*: three particular relationships, each with its own satiric tradition in classical literature, are reflected in Molière's play — parasitism, clientage, and friendship.

The parasite of Roman satire was largely the product of clientage, a system in which a patron insured his prominence by surrounding himself with clients, to whom the patron owed one meal a day. Tartuffe resembles the typical parasite of Roman literature in his love of good food and his desire for free meals. At that point, however, the resemblance of Tartuffe to the typical parasite-client ends. Clients usually were humiliated by their patrons, willingly suffering any debasement for a piece of bread. This is obviously not Tartuffe. *Tartuffe* presents an inversion of the normal relationships between patron and client. It is Tartuffe, the nominal client, who humiliates the family of Orgon, and ultimately Orgon himself, the nominal patron. The immediate reason for this is that Molière is presenting a comic and satiric inversion of the normal situation. It is also possible that Molière was thinking of the one type of client who was capable of achieving such a reversal of roles — the *Graeculus esuriens*, the hungry Greekling. The Greek, as depicted by Juvenal (Satire III), was, like Tartuffe, quick-witted and silver-tongued, able to play any role, a parasite, but most of all a hypocrite; his one goal was to become master in his patron's house.

Although Roman satire presents its lesson particularly through negative examples, there are also numerous positive models for one to profit from. Such is the case with the patron-client, for Horace presents his own relationship with Maecenas as an ideal situation, in which each man maintained his proper position. Horace's relationship with Maecenas, a truly great man in the early Empire, is comparable to that of Molière with Louis XIV. Maecenas, as depicted by Horace, and Louis, Molière's ideal king and *prince ennemi de la fraude*, are *sapientes*, who search through the false appearances to get to the truth. Molière's last act depicts his own patron, Louis XIV, then, as a good leader, but good particularly in that he embodies those positive virtues which are typical of all wise men.

I have pointed out that one of the concepts that was impressed on Molière in his days at Clermont was that of the neighbor-function of mankind. In *Tartuffe*, Molière treats a concept which was part of classical and Christian ethical teaching, friendship, following the same method he used for the concepts and institutions of *sophrosyne, sapientia* and clientage: he perverts the ideals, presenting their negative or antithetical aspects. For Tartuffe, friendship is not an ideal and virtuous relationship, but one which can serve him in his quest for attainment of his worldly desires. Just as he perverted every ideal which he would embody if he were a truly devout man, Tartuffe turns friendship and neighborliness into perversions.

The general category of friendship includes a classical parallel for Tartuffe's position as lay director of conscience to Orgon: this is Seneca's *custos*. The *custos* is a guardian of one's moral life, whose job it is to point out what things are to be sought and what avoided. One's *custos* must be a man of *true* wisdom and virtue. Such a moral guardian was Horace's own father (*Sat.* I. 6. 81-84); he was incorruptible, he honored virtue, especially chastity, and his primary purpose was to protect his ward. Horace presents his father as an ideal *custos*.

Tartuffe, by comparison with the Senecan and Horatian concepts of the *custos*, is obviously the reverse of the ideal, another perversion in the continual procession of perversions which constitute his character and prove that he is truly a *demens*, a fool. By his acceptance of Tartuffe as spiritual advisor, as a *custos*, for himself and his family, Orgon too is revealed as a *demens*. Orgon did not choose Tartuffe on the basis of wisdom and virtue; for Orgon Tartuffe was especially a means to flaunt his religiosity and to tyrannize and torment his family.

# CONCLUSION

Molière's *Tartuffe* clearly reflects the traditions of classical literature as we have seen in the study of parallels in theme and subject matter. There is, however, one parallel which is most noteworthy — that of the careers and characters of Aelius Sejanus and Tartuffe. The plot and political setting of Molière's play can both be explained if Molière used Sejanus as a model for Tartuffe.

The consideration of *Tartuffe* as a reflection of the character and career of Sejanus depends on the acceptance of Orgon's household as a microcosm in which Orgon is the nominal ruler, who has been corrupted by a self-seeking hypocrite. Such words as "usurper" and "tyrannique" especially serve to reenforce the suggestion of a political microcosm. Once this condition is accepted, it can be observed in the study of Molière's *Tartuffe* and the figure of Sejanus, as depicted by Tacitus in the *Annales*, that every major action of Tartuffe has a parallel in the career of Sejanus. Although some of the obviously "pure comic" scenes (the *dépit amoureux* in Act II) have no basis in Tacitus' depiction of Tartuffe, they are evidence of the perverse and divisive effects of Tartuffe on the household. It is not just the close resemblance of Tartuffe to Sejanus, however, that suggests a conscious adaptation of Sejanus by Molière. It is also the remarkable similarity between the figure of Orgon and the Emperor Tiberius.

The suggestion that Molière used Sejanus as the basis for *Tartuffe* gains further emphasis from the figure of Elmire. Her dissimulation, pretending to love Tartuffe in order to thwart his schemes, parallels the actions of two heroines of French drama, Livia, in Jean Magnon's *Séjanus*, and Agrippine, in Cyrano de Bergerac's *La Mort d'Agrippine*, both of whom pretend to love Séjanus in order to bring about his destruction. It is further noteworthy, since Molière was familiar with the works of both Magnon and Cyrano, that Cyrano's Séjanus was not merely a political hypocrite, but a despiser of the gods as well, thus possibly providing Molière with an element of character — an attitude toward religion — which he could have elevated in importance to make it the primary aspect of his hypocrite, Tartuffe.

A direct comparison of Sejanus as depicted by Tacitus and Tartuffe reveals that the characters of the two were remarkably similar. Each employed clever devices to win the heart of his prospective patron; each masked his true desires, while attacking others; each was proud and imperious, while affecting humility; each lusted after supremacy; each was sometimes lavish and luxurious, sometimes cautious. The similarities are not limited to character, however, for the actions of Sejanus can provide the bases of Tartuffe's actions in Molière's play. Sejanus and Tartuffe both had as primary obstacles to their accession to power the son of the rulers of their respective worlds— the Roman Empire and the house of Orgon; these obstacles they removed, Sejanus by murdering Drusus, Tartuffe by Orgon's banishment of Damis. Sejanus seduced Livia, Tiberius's daughter-in-law; Tartuffe attempted to seduce Elmire, Orgon's young wife. Sejanus induced Tiberius to leave Rome; Tartuffe tried to evict Orgon from his home by force. The fall of each man came at a moment when he was expecting a confirmation of his power. These are but a few of the remarkable similarities between Sejanus and Tartuffe.

Equally noteworthy are the similarities in the characters and actions of Tiberius and Orgon. Tiberius is the leader of the state religion, and is a devotee of astrology; Orgon is religious (in his own way). Tiberius was a cruel tyrant and an abettor of cruelty; Orgon exercises his tyranny through Tartuffe, being cruel himself as well as abetting Tartuffe's cruelty. Tiberius wanted to be relieved of the burdens of rule; Orgon relieved himself of the burdens of rule by putting the power into Tartuffe's hands.

The remarkable similarity in character and action of Sejanus-Tiberius and Tartuffe-Orgon along with the actions of Livia and Agrippine in Magnon's and Cyrano's plays may be merely fortuitous. If so, it is indicative of the verisimilitude of Molière's plot and characters. If not, however, the meaning of Molière's play is strikingly altered, for *Tartuffe* ceases to be merely a satirical comedy written against the most odious vices of humanity, among which hypocrisy ranks first, becoming a pointed object lesson directed at a man of Molière's acquaintance whose situation was closely parallel to that of both Orgon and Tiberius, in that he too was being influenced by self-seeking hypocrites. This man was Louis XIV himself. Furthermore, although the meaning of *Tartuffe* would be enhanced if it could be shown without doubt that Molière was thinking of Sejanus and Tiberius when he created Tartuffe and Orgon, the lesson of the foolishness of the man who yields the reins of power to a hypocrite remains implicit in the play, particularly through the contrast of Orgon with the "prince ennemi de la fraude." Molière presents in *Tartuffe* a picture of Louis XIV both as he is (Orgon) and as he should be (Prince). *Tartuffe*, then, although it is an extended lesson on the wisdom of moderation and virtue, is especially designed as a lecture on the obligations of kingship for the temporarily errant King, Louis XIV.

The writing of *Tartuffe* as a satirical comedy in which the lesson is intended for the King of France may immediately appear to be an act of disloyalty. This was, however, not the case for Molière. Molière wrote *Tartuffe* as his supreme act of loyalty, with the loftiest of purposes, for he saw in Louis a king worthy of respect and loyalty, who had temporarily fallen prey to the forces of evil. Molière makes an extended statement on the importance of wisdom and virtue so that a ruler may avoid corruption. The lesson was not conceived haphazardly or fortuitously, but with a serious and important purpose in the mind of Molière — the rectification of the temporarily ineffective King. *Tartuffe* was written with the patriotic hope to see

France once more healthy and strong under the power of a wise and benevolent leader.

The career of Sejanus parallels the plot of *Tartuffe*, and Sejanus and Tiberius are reflected in the characters of Tartuffe and Orgon. But it is in his utilization of the material found in the character-moral writings of the satirists that any understanding of Molière's play and characters lies. Molière constructed, whether on the frame of Sejanus or not, a Tartuffe who contains almost every major fault considered in the works of Horace, Seneca, or Juvenal. In a comparison of Sejanus and Tartuffe, it is obvious that the only fault not shared by both is the self-serving religious hypocrisy of Tartuffe, which was more immediately meaningful to Molière from his personal experiences. But even Molière's depiction of religious hypocrisy contains numerous elements of political hypocrisy as well. Tartuffe is, moreover, the epitome of all that is traditionally vicious according to the satirists, who base their conceptions largely on Stoic doctrine. Not only is Tartuffe a model of vice, but he is the antithesis of the good. Whenever a desirable model for behavior is proposed by one of the satirists, one can be sure that Tartuffe's actions will be exactly the opposite, unless the character of Orgon calls for him to adapt to that role. Orgon follows the same pattern: every ideal of the wise and benevolent ruler is far from a model of Orgon. He strives, as does Tartuffe, only for his own pleasure or satisfaction. But this is more blameworthy in the case of Orgon, since he has responsibilities beyond the immediate sphere of self.

Tartuffe and Orgon fail time and again. Their failure is in *bon sens*. The evidence of *Tartuffe* shows that Molière propounds the belief that extremes of any kind are to be avoided, and that the exponent of vice can be overcome by the forces of reason and moderation. Molière doubtless drew this philosophy in part from the Stoic concepts of virtue, the *sapiens*, and *sophrosyne*, as promulgated in the satiric and moral writers, Horace, Seneca, and Juvenal. These concepts were combined with many others drawn from all that Molière read, saw, or heard, including the themes of the hypocrite, the parasite, the client, and the guardian-friend, to create the characterizations of Orgon and Tartuffe.

## APPENDIX

Additional Parallels Between *Tartuffe*
and Classical Literature

### I

Tartuffe's actions upon entering the household of Orgon find a parallel in Juvenal. In his Sixth Satire (511-526), Juvenal describes the entrance into a household of a band of frenzied worshippers of Bellona and Magna Mater. Their leader, an enormous *semivir*, imposes his will on the mistress of the household, from whom he demands not only ritual purification for her, but also a payment (a cloak) for himself (520-521). We find that the woman is willing to go to any lengths to propitiate the gods, who, she believes, have spoken to her directly or through the *semivir* (523-530). Juvenal's comment at this point is again very meaningful for an understanding of Tartuffe:

en animam et mentem cum qua di nocte loquantur (531)

Here we find, in a religious atmosphere, actions which parallel those of Tartuffe. Both he and the *semivir* exert a strong influence over a household and, in the process, manage to come out ahead on their own accounts. The main difference is particularly significant: whereas Juvenal's *semivir* holds sway over the mind of a woman, Tartuffe projects his influence over the mind of a man. This, however, is precisely the point that Molière is implying in his depiction of Orgon: not only that he is a *demens*, as we have seen, but that his mind is that of a woman in that it reveals aspects of a feminine nature. Thus, it is suitable to say of Orgon, after consideration of his relationship with Tartuffe and other (in-) actions, *en animam et mentem cum qua di loquantur*. Here we see reemphasized the fact that Molière's depiction of Orgon reflects the concept of the *demens*, wherein the irrationality of the fool's thoughts and actions would make him an unlikely man to be conversant with the gods. Instead, he would be a likely target for the opportunistic hypocrite. It is the feminine aspect of Orgon, as seen in his tendency toward religion, which is traditionally more woman's business, that is pointed out by these parallel passages.

## II

In Act I, scene iii, there is revealed an aspect of the Orgon-Tartuffe relationship which is inseparable from the patron-client concept, which I considered in Chapter Three. There it is shown that Orgon is not just under the influence of Tartuffe; he is inspired with a passion for Tartuffe which can be compared with love, especially when seen in the terms with which Dorine presents it:

> Il le choie, il l'embrasse; et pour un maîtresse
> On ne sauroit, je pense, avoir plus de tendresse ...(189-190)

This aspect of their relationship has elicited comment from more than one scholar. Guicharnaud states: "Suggérée par les comparaisons amoureuses dont se sert Dorine, l'interprétation d'Orgon comme personnage à valeur féminine est tout à fait légitime."[1] Gifford P. Owen goes into this subject at some length. He notes, in regard to Orgon, that "he is at a critical age when sexual aberrations may well occur, and he is an entirely plausible candidate. Still dominated by Mme. Pernelle, indifferent to both wife and children, he is a pathetic figure seeking some release or prop in religion." Considering Dorine's words (above), Owen continues by stating: "These are damning words, so specific and unvarnished in their import that they can scarcely be construed as indicating admiration only for his guest's putative saintliness. Orgon's intense concern for Tartuffe's health to the exclusion of any interest in his wife's indisposition (I, 5) ... is comic only in that it indicated a lover's preoccupation with the beloved."[2]

Certainly the evidence of the play shows a feminine side of Orgon's character: he desires to exist in a secondary relationship, the servant to the master, avoiding all responsibility; affectionate and loving completely and whole-heartedly, well beyond the wont of normal men, to the extent of having a blind admiration for the one loved. After consideration of Owen's proposition, however, we may, on the evidence of the play, remove any idea that the homosexual aspect of the Orgon-Tartuffe relationship did exist.[3] The feminine aspect of Orgon is present, however, and it may reveal a potential for homosexuality; but this potential never becomes fact. Orgon's way of "loving" Tartuffe is a reflection of his feeling for religion. Both are extreme, and both are more appropriate to a woman. At the most, one may see in Orgon a latent homosexual attraction for Tartuffe, but it can as well be seen as another evidence of his lack of *bon sens*.

Resemblances to this suggested side of the Orgon-Tartuffe relationship can be found in the traditions of the hypocrite, parasite, and patron-client. Since we have considered each of these, it will also be profitable to compare the treatment of this idea within the context of these three themes with that presented in Molière's *Tartuffe*. Specifically, homosexuality is found in Juvenal's Ninth Satire. There a homosexual relationship somewhat similar to that seen by Owen in Molière's play is revealed in no uncertain terms. There are also a number of significant differences. A parasite, Naevolus, has been living with a corrupt millionaire named Virro. Naevolus has been the husband in the relationship and Virro the wife. Naevolus' reason for taking part in such an affair is made very clear — money. He is not the type to try working. Rather parasitism has been his solution — a particularly repulsive type of parasitism. Now Naevolus has been kicked out, left to his devices. Naevolus in some respects parallels Tartuffe, who, by mastering Orgon, plays somewhat the same role as Naevolus. The difference in Naevolus and Tartuffe is the same as that between Tartuffe and other clients in the satirists: Tartuffe becomes virtual master of the entire household so that he ejects the nominal patron Orgon, and not the reverse, as befalls Naevolus. The reason for this difference in fates is the difference in the character of the two patrons.

Juvenal depicts Naevolus' patron, Virro, as a man of vicious and perverted character. He is very likely the same Virro whom Juvenal showed in Satire V, taking cruel pleasure in tormenting and humiliating his clients. He is subject to four particular vices:[4]

> First, lust. He is what the Greeks and Romans call a pathic: as soon as he sees a strong young man he showers him with love-letters and slobbers with longing to become his "wife."

It is Tartuffe who is subject to lust: but this lust is not directed toward Orgon. Rather its object is Elmire. On the other hand, Orgon takes the woman's role; even if he does not physically complete the role, in his desire to be mastered and avoid all responsibility, Orgon takes on the feminine aspect of the pathic.

> Then, weakness. He cannot even make love to his own bride on the wedding night; he cannot become the father of his own child, although he registers and boasts of its birth. His wife has to be married and his children begotten for him by his dependent Naevolus, while he stands snivelling at the door.

This aspect of Virro can also be seen in Orgon, although not to the same extent. Orgon is weak; weakness is one of his primary characteristics in fact. This weakness has caused him to shun his obligations as ruler of his household. Tartuffe has performed a twofold function for the pathetic Orgon: he has relieved him of his burden of responsibility; and he has exerted a masculine dominance over Orgon. Actually, by extending his domination over the rest of the family as well, Tartuffe has effectively satisfied Orgon's desires by one action.

From the text of the play, it is impossible to say that Orgon has not consummated his marriage with Elmire. He did father children by his first wife, so he is not impotent. One wonders, therefore, why he has not begotten children by his second marriage. One possible answer is that Orgon is not the same man he was. After all, in the past Orgon has nobly acquitted himself in the service of the Prince, but he now serves Tartuffe. His interests and ideals changed with the passing of time. Perhaps the real Orgon, who had been concealed in those earlier days, had come to the fore. Perhaps time had perverted his judgment. In any case, the influence of Tartuffe manifests itself so that all that Orgon should, according to nature, consider important is of no interest to him. He has a new interest, religion, and he has an embodiment of that interest, Tartuffe. He no longer has any reason to take interest in sex.[5] What does Orgon do, then, but follow the example of Virro and put his wife into the hands of his dependent Tartuffe, who promptly does his best to perform the husband's role, just as Naevolus did before him. Assuredly, Orgon's purpose is markedly different from Virro's, since Orgon thinks Tartuffe, as a director of conscience, should be a good influence on and a trusted guardian for his young wife. The results, however, as far as Orgon's family is concerned, are almost disastrously similar. All the time Tartuffe is trying to seduce Elmire (second attempt), Orgon lies under the table in the same room, incapable of action. He may not whimper, but Orgon is definitely drawn in the same tradition as Virro and at this point is intended to elicit a sneer of contempt more than a laugh of amusement. One can hardly imagine Virro evoking laughter, unless it is that of disgust.

> Third, secretiveness and vindictiveness. His discarded donkey Naevolus must not be thought to have described their amours; for Virro is quite capable of having him murdered, violently or cunningly. His catlike secrecy and vengefulness are the obverse of his softness and weakness.

Secretiveness is the basis of Tartuffe's ploy, for what is a mask but a secret? It is Orgon's secretiveness, however, which equates more closely with Virro's, for Orgon makes the same mistake Virro did — he tells his dependent an incriminating secret. But here again the character of the two patrons causes a reversal in the action. In Juvenal, the patron vindictively plagues his former dependent with silent threats of murder and violence. In Molière's play, however, the vindictiveness is directed toward the patron by the client Tartuffe, almost as if he were "scorning the base degrees by which he did ascend." Tartuffe may have played the "tener" for a while, but once his position is firm, in his opinion at least, Tartuffe removes his mask of secrecy and reveals in no uncertain terms his vindictiveness.

Orgon, however, makes a show of vindictiveness, too. This is directed toward his family when they question his decision no longer to determine the fate of the family, but to leave that up to Tartuffe. He objects to his family's questioning his prerogative to surrender the authority he does not want. For this imposition he cruelly torments his family as if they were clients and he were their patron.[6]

Fourth, meanness.

This is the classical fault of *sordes*, or stinginess. It is the action which Orgon perpetrates upon his family when he treats them with unconcern as to their needs while giving Tartuffe every consideration, especially that which Tartuffe is most interested in — Orgon's wealth. Meanness is also shown by Tartuffe in the restrictions he places on the family of Orgon, while he heads into one excess after another.

It is obvious that Molière does not base his depiction of the Tartuffe-Orgon relationship directly or solely on that of Virro-Naevolus. However, the construction of the characters of Tartuffe and Orgon clearly reflects the same satiric tradition. The satire in *Tartuffe* seems magnified by the variations in character and actions which are presented therein from that of the version of Juvenal. Each point of variation intensifies the malignity and destructiveness of Tartuffe, while it further clarifies the *dementia* of Orgon. Molière draws his characters on variations of traditional guidelines, but his depictions of Tartuffe and Orgon are new and different for one important reason: his admixture of traditional ingredients is in novel proportions. The old and familiar takes on new meaning. His treatment of relationships is exemplary of this. He has added elements of the patron to the dependent, and elements of the dependent to the patron. His combination is more comical than before, because it is more incongruous; but at the same time it maintains its satiric force.

III

The lesson of moderation in drink is a commonplace in classical literature. Perhaps the best brief discussion, and one which is quite applicable to the character of Tartuffe, is the following passage from Seneca:

> Drunkenness does not create vice, it merely brings it into view; at such times the lustful man does not wait even for the privacy of a bedroom, but without postponement gives free play to the demands

of his passions; at such times your cross-grained fellow does not restrain his tongue or his hand. The haughty man increases his arrogance, the ruthless man his cruelty, the slanderer his spitefulness. Every vice is given free play and comes to the front.[7]

It is obvious from the dialogues of the first and second acts that Tartuffe is incontinent in both food and drink. Not only the assertion that he eats as much as six men, but also his corpulence and ruddy complexion serve as proofs of his lack of temperance. That Tartuffe is intemperate in drink is shown by Dorine's speech in Act I, scene v, where she states that he had had four large draughts of wine for breakfast the day before. Taking wine for breakfast at all was rare, but drinking that amount was the act of a man who was highly immoderate.

Although any such term as alcoholic must be reserved for later times than those of Molière, since the concept of alcoholism is a modern one, it is possible to see in Tartuffe a man who drinks to excess. Assuming that this is so, and that the lustful passions, as Seneca noted, when continued over a period of time, become habits, then an answer can further be offered to the problem of the gross and self-endangering temperance shown by Tartuffe in attempting to seduce Elmire. Although the play itself provides no definite evidence, Dorine's statement supplying the idea that Tartuffe drinks to excess and the quotation from Seneca can supply an answer to this problem. Tartuffe has had a "few too many" on the day of his first attempt at the seduction of Elmire. What Tartuffe does is precisely what Seneca suggested as the result of drunkenness: his vice is "brought into view"; he "does not await the privacy of a bedroom"; he "gives free play to the demands of his passions" (or at least attempts to do so); he "proclaims his malady"; and he "does not restrain his tongue or his hand." This is an exact description of Tartuffe's actions toward Elmire in Act III, scene iii. Therefore one definite possibility of an explanation for this precipitous action by Tartuffe is that he attempted to fulfill his most secret desires at a time when he was somewhat under the influence of alcohol, and thus freed of his normal inhibitions in the face of so obvious a danger to his career.

The actions of Tartuffe toward Elmire, however, are not the only reason why, according to Seneca, we should suspect him of being in a state of intoxication. Tartuffe, when confronted by Damis with accusation of his activities, increases his "arrogance," his "cruelty" (which functions indirectly, through the decisions of Orgon), and his "spitefulness." He boldly admits the truth, that he is guilty, knowing that Orgon will not believe him, and then has Damis ejected from the house and his hereditary rights. His spitefulness does not stop, however, until Orgon has been expelled from his own house and has been betrayed to the King.

¹*Une Aventure Théâtrale*, pp. 43-44.
²"Tartuffe Reconsidered," *French Review*, XLI (Oct., 1967), 614
³Paul A. Mankin, in a letter to the editor, *French Review*, XLII (Oct., 1968), p. 121, takes issue with Owen's article. He notes quite correctly that "Molière would not 'incorporate casually' a trait presumably as flagrant as the one shown by an aggressive homosexual with side-penchants for attractive young wives."

There would appear to be an immediate conflict between the suggestion that there may be a homosexual aspect to the Tartuffe-Orgon relationship and the fact that Tartuffe is clearly depicted as motivated by a heterosexual, and illicit, love for Elmire. These of course are two distinct vices. There should, however, be no difficulty in resolving the apparent conflict between Tartuffe's relationship with Orgon and his desire for Elmire, if one sees that there is no opposition between the two. Any part which Tartuffe takes in his relationship with Orgon is not the product of a "love" for Orgon, but of his desire to fulfill his own passions for food, money, power, and sex. His sexual passions are directed toward Elmire, to whom he has gained entrance by means of his relationship with Orgon. Orgon, then, is one of Tartuffe's means to his ends.

⁴The categorization of these four vices is drawn from Highet, *Juvenal the Satirist*, pp. 119-120. The following inset quotes are all from this source.

⁵Indicative of this fact is Orgon's statement:

> De toutes amitiés il détache mon âme;
> Et je verois mourir frère, enfants, mère et femme,
> Que je m'en soucierois autant que de cela. (277-279)

⁶His cruelty may be seen particularly in the quotation in the preceding footnote. From such feelings his actions toward his family spring.

⁷*Epistles* LXXXIII; Gummere, II, 270-271.

Non facit ebrietas vitia, sed protrahit; tunc libidinosus ne cubiculum quidem expectat, sed cupiditatibus suis quantum petierunt sine dilatione permittit; tunc inpudicus morbum profitetur ac publicat; tuc petulans non linguam, non manum continet. Crescit insolenti superbia, crudelitas saevo, malignitas livido. Omne vitium laxatur et prodit.

SELECTED BIBLIOGRAPHY

A. Editions and Translations of French Authors

Boileau. *Boileau*. Ed. Pierre Clarac. Paris: Mellotte, 1936.
Molière. *Le Tartuffe and le Médecin malgré lui*. Ed. Jacques Guicharnaud. New York: Dell, 1962.
Molière. *Le Tartuffe; ou l'Imposteur*. Ed. Burt Edward Young. New York: Oxford University Press, 1918.
Molière. *Œuvres complètes*. Ed. Eugène Despois and Paul Mesnard. Les Grands Ecrivains de la France. 13 vols. Paris: Hachette, 1873-1893.

B. Editions and Translations of Classical Authors

Gifford, William, tr. *Juvenal's Satires*. New York: E.P. Dutton, 1954.
Horace. *Satires, Epistles and Ars Poetica*. Tr. H. Rushton Fairclough. Cambridge: Harvard University Press, 1929. (Loeb.)
Horace. *The Odes and Epodes*. Tr. C.E. Bennett. New York: Putnam, 1921. (Loeb.)
Horace. *The Satires*. Ed. Edward P. Morris. New York: American Book, 1909.
Juvenal. *Juvenal and Persius*. Tr. G.G. Ramsay. New York: Putnam, 1924. (Loeb.)
Lucian. *Lucian*. Tr. A.M. Harmon. 8 vols. Cambridge: Harvard University Press, 1960. (Loeb.)
Petronius. *The Satyricon*. Tr. with introd. by William Arrowsmith. Ann Arbor: University of Michigan Press, 1959.
Plutarch. *Moralia*. Tr. Benedict Einarson and Phillip H. DeLacy. 3 vols. Cambridge: Harvard University Press, 1967. (Loeb.)
Seneca. *Ad Lucilium Epistulae Morales*. Tr. Richard M. Gummere. New York: Putnam, 1922-1925. (Loeb.)
Seneca. *Moral Essays*. Tr. John W. Basore. 3 vols. New York: Putnam, 1929-1932. (Loeb.)
Tacitus. *The Complete Works*. Tr. A.J. Church and W.J. Brodribb. Ed. Moses Hadas. New York: Random House, 1942.
Terence. *Adelphi*. Ed. Sidney Ashmore. New York: MacMillan, 1910.
Theophrastus. *The Characters*. Ed. and tr. John Maxwell Edmonds. London: W. Heinemann, 1929. (Loeb.)

C. Works on Molière and French Literature

Adam, Antoine. "L'Ecole de 1660: Histoire ou légende?" *Revue d'Histoire de la Philosophie*, VII (1939), 215-50.
_____ . *Historie de la littérature française au XVIIe siècle*. 5 vols. (V. III, *L'apogée du siècle: Boileau, Molière.*)
Allier, Raoul. *La Cabale des dévots, 1627-1666*. Paris: Colin, 1902.
_____ . "Le Problème de Tartuffe." *Revue de Genève*, II (1921), 3-26.
Alméras, Henri d'. *"Le Tartuffe" de Molière*. Paris: Sfelt, 1946.

Arnavon, Jacques. *Molière: notre contemporain* Paris: Les Editions de France, 1929.
_____. *Morale de Molière*. Paris: Les Editions Universelles, 1945.
Ashton, H. *A Preface to Molière*. New York: Longmans, Green, 1927.
Auerbach, Erich. *Mimesis: The Representation of Reality in Western Literature*. Tr. Willard Trask. New York: Doubleday, 1957.
Baumal, Francis, *Molière et les dévotes: la genèse du Tartuffe*. Paris: Ed. du Livre mensuel, 1919.
_____. *Tartuffe et ses avatars (de Montufar à Don Juan); histoire des relations de Molière avec la cabale des dévots*. Paris: Nourry, 1925.
Bénichou, Paul. *Morales du grand siècle*. Paris: Gallimard, 1948.
Besant, Walter. "Molière and His Satire." *Temple Bar*, XXXIII (1871), 83-95.
Bishop, Morris. *Studies in Seventeenth-Century French Literature*. Ithaca, New York: Cornell University Press, 1962.
Bray, René. *Molière: Homme de Théâtre*. Paris: Mercure de France, 1954.
Brisson, Adolphe. *Portraits intimes*. Paris: Colin, 1899.
Brisson, Pierre. *Molière: sa vie dans ses œuvres*. Paris: Gallimard, 1943.
Brody, Jules. *Boileau and Longinus*. Geneva: Droz, 1958.
Brunetière, Ferdinand. *Epoques du théâtre français (1636-1850)*. Conférences de l'Odéon. Paris: Calmann Levy, 1892.
_____. *Etudes critiques sur l'historie de la littérature française*. 8 vols. Paris: Hachette, 1896-1907.
_____. "La Philosophie de Molière." *Revue des Deux Mondes*, C (1890), 649-687.
_____. *Tartuffe*. Paris: Hachette, 1892.
Calvet, J. *Molière: est-il chrétien?* Paris: F. Lanore, 1950.
Caspari, Hugo. *Die originalität Molieres im "Tartuffe" und im "Avare."* (Inauguraldissertation, Wurzburg.) Gottingen: Dietrich, 1902.
Cazamian, Louis F. *A History of French Literature*. Oxford: Oxford University Press. 1955.
Chapman, Percy Addison. *The Spirit of Molière: An Interpretation*. Ed. Jean-Albert Bédé; intro. by Christian Gauss. Princeton: Princeton University Press, 1940.
Charlier, Gustave. "L'Original de Tartuffe." *Flambeau*, IX (1926), 319-332.
Charpentier, John. *Molière*, Paris: Société d'Editions et de Publications. 1942.
Chatfield-Taylor, H.C. *Molière: A Biography*. New York: Duffield, 1906.
Chill, Emanuel S. "Tartuffe, Religion, and Courtly Culture." *French Historical Studies*, III (1963), 151-183.
Crabb, Daniel M. *Tartuffe and Other Plays of Molière*. New York: Educational Research Associates. 1966.
Currier, Thomas F., and Ernest L. Gay. *Harvard University Catalogue of the Molière Collection in Harvard College Library*. Cambridge, Mass.: Library of Harvard University, 1906.
Deffoux, Léon. "L'hypocrisie et Tartuffe." *Mercure de France*, CLXVII (1923), 222-225.
Demeure, J. "Les Quatre Amis de Psyché." *Mercure de France*, CC (Jan. 15, 1928), 331-66.
_____. "L'Introuvable Société des quatre amis (1664-1665)," *Revue d'Histoire Littéraire de la France*, XXXVI (1929), 161-180, 321-36.
Domecq, l'abbé Jean Baptiste. "Molière: *Tartuffe*; analyses, morceaux choisis, étude littéraire." In his *Cours de littérature*. Tours: Cuttier, 1926.
Edelman, Nathan. *The Seventeenth Century* ("Molière" pp. 226-43). Vol III of *A Critical Bibliography of French Literature*. Ed. David Cabeen and Jules Brody. Syracuse: Syracuse Univeristy Press, 1961.
Emard, Paul. *Tartuffe; sa vie, son milieu, et la comédie de Molière*. Paris: Droz, 1932.
Estrée, Paul. "Une Origine possible de Tartuffe." *Moliériste*, X (1888-89), 121-122.

Faguet, Emile. *En lisant Molière; l'homme et son temps, l'écrivain et son œuvre.* Paris: Hachette, 1914.
Falk, Eugene H. "Molière the Indignant Satirist: *Le Bourgeois gentilhomme,*" *Tulane Drama Review*, I (1956), 73-88.
Fernandez, Ramon. *Molière: The Man Seen Through the Plays.* Tr. Wilson Follett. New York: Hill and Wang, 1958.
Gossman, Lionel. *Men and Masks: A Study of Molière.* Baltimore: Johns Hopkins Press. 1963.
Grimarest, Jean Leonor le Gallois, de. *La Vie de M. de Molière.* Ed. Georges Mongrédien. Paris: Brient, 1955.
Guicharnaud, Jacques, ed. *Molière: A Collection of Essays.* Englewood Cliffs, N.J.: Prentice Hall, 1964.
Guicharnaud, Jacques. *Molière: une aventure théâtrale.* Paris: Gallimard, 1963.
Gutkind, Kurt. *Molière und das komische Drama.* Halle: Niemeyer, 1928.
Hall, H. Gaston. *Molière: "Tartuffe."* London: Edward Arnold, 1960.
Hémon, Félix. *Cours de Littérature.* 9 vols. Paris: Librairie Delagrave, 1889-1919.
Hubert, Judd David. *Molière and the Comedy of Intellect.* Berkeley: University of California Press, 1962.
Huszar, Guillaume. *Molière et l'Espagne.* Paris: Librairie Honore Champion, 1907.
Jurgens, Madeleine, and Elizabeth Maxfield-Miller, eds. *Cent Ans de Recherches sur Molière.* Paris: Imprimerie nationale, 1963.
Lacour, Louis. *Etudes sur Molière: Tartuffe par ordre de Louis XIV.* Paris: Claudin, 1877.
Lancaster, Henry Carrington "Additional sources for Molière's *Avare, Femmes savantes,* and *Tartuffe.*" *Modern Language Notes*, XLV (1930), 154-157.
⸻. *A History of French Dramatic Literature in the Seventeenth Century.* 9 vols. Baltimore: Johns Hopkins Press, 1929-1942.
Lawrence, Francis L. "The Norm in Tartuffe." *Revue de l'université d'Ottawa*, XXXVI (1966), 698-702.
⸻. "The Roots of Molière." *Tennessee Studies in Literature*, X (1965), 151-164. 151-164.
Lewis, D.B. Wyndham. *Molière: The Comic Mask.* New York: Coward-McCann, 1959.
Livet, Charles-Louis, "Quelques observations sur le personnage de Tartuffe." *Moliériste*, III (1881-82), 45-51.
Magendie, Maurice. "Une source inconnue du Tartuffe." *Revue des Deux Mondes*, LI (1929), 929-936.
Mangold, Wilhelm. *Molieres "Tartuffe": Geschichte und Kritik.* Oppeln: Franck, 1881.
Martinenche, E. *Molière et le Théâtre espagnol.* Paris: Hachette, 1906.
Matthews, Brander. *Molière: His Life and His Works.* New York: Scribner's, 1910.
Mercader, Albert. "L'hypocrisie et Tartuffe." *Mercure de France*, CLXVI (1928), 289-315.
Meyer, Jean. *Molière.* Paris: Librairie Académique Perrin, 1963.
Michaut, Gustave. *La jeunesse de Molière.* Paris: Hachette, 1922.
⸻. *Les débuts de Molière.* Paris: Hachette, 1923.
⸻. *Les Luttes de Molière.* Paris: Hachette, 1925.
Moland, Louis. *Molière et La Comédie Italienne.* Paris: Didier, 1867.
Mongrédien, Georges. *La Vie Littéraire au XVIIe Siècle.* Paris: Tallandier, 1947.
Monval, Georges. "Madame Pernelle, Flipote et Monsieur Tartuffe dans un roman de Charles Sorel." *Moliériste*, X (1888-9), 97-108, 129-140.
Moore, Will G. *French Classical Literature.* London: Oxford University Press, 1961.
⸻. *Molière: A New Criticism.* Oxford: Oxford University Press, 1949.
⸻. "Tartuffe and the Comic Principle in Molière." *Modern Language Review*, XLIII (1948), 47-53.

Mornet, Daniel. *Molière*. Paris: Boivin, 1943.
Owen, Gifford P. "Tartuffe Reconsidered." *French Review*, XLI (1968), 612-13.
Palmer, John L. *Molière: His Life and Works*. New York: Brewer and Warren, 1930.
Perry, Henry Ten Eyck. *Height of French Comedy: Molière*. Cambridge: Harvard University Press, 1939.
Peyre, Henri. *L'influence des littératures antiques sur la littérature française moderne. Etat des travaux*. New Haven: Yale Univeristy Press, 1941.
Rigal, Eugene. *Molière*. 2 vols. Paris: Hachette, 1908.
Roy, Emile. *La vie et les œuvres de Charles Sorel*. Paris: Hatchette, 1891.
Saintonge, Paul, and Robert W. Christ. *Fifty Years of Molière Studies: A Bibliography, 1892-1941*. Baltimore: Johns Hopkins Press, 1942.
———. "Omissions and Additions to *Fifty Years of Molière Studies*: . . *Modern Language Association*, LIX (1944), 282-5.
Soulié, Eudore. *Recherches sur Molière et sur sa famille*. Paris: Hachette, 1863.
Stapfer, Paul. *Molière et Shakespeare*. Paris: Librairie Hachette, 1905.
Tilley, Arthur. *Molière*. Cambridge: Cambridge University Press, 1921.
Turnell, Martin. *The Classical Moment: Studies in Corneille, Molière and Racine*. London: H. Hamilton, 1963.
Wilcox, John. *The Relation of Molière to Restoration Comedy*. New York: Columbia University Press, 1938.

### C. Works on Satire and Comedy

Allen, Charles A., and George D. Stephens. *Satire: Theory and Practice*. Belmont, California: Wadsworth, 1962.
Anderson, William S. "Recent Work in Roman Satire (1937-55)." *Classical World*, L (1956), 33-40.
———. "Recent Work in Roman Satire (1955-62)." *Classical World*, LVII (1964), 293-301; 343-348.
———. "Recent Work in Roman Satire (1962-68)." *Classical World*, LXIII (1970), 181-194; 199.
Barnet, Sylvan, Morton Berman, and William Burto. *An Introduction to Literature*. New York: Little Brown, 1956.
Bergson, Henri. *Laughter: An Essay on the Meaning of the Comic*. Tr. Cloudesley Brereton and Fred Rothwell. New York: MacMillan, 1921.
Calderwood, James L., and Harold E. Toliver. *Perspectives on Drama*. New York: Oxford University Press, 1968.
Campbell, O.J. *Shakespeare's Satire*. New York: Oxford University Press, 1943.
Cook, Albert. *The Dark Voyage and the Golden Mean*. Cambridge: Harvard University Press, 1949.
Cooper, Lane, *An Aristotelian Theory of Comedy*. New York: Harcourt, Brace, 1922.
Cornford, F.M. *The Origin of Attic Comedy*. London: Edward Arnold, 1914.
Corrigan, R.W., ed. Comedy: *Meaning and Form*. San Francisco: Chandler Publishing Co., 1965.
———, ed. *Greek Comedy*. New York: Dell, 1965.
Dobrée, Bonamy. *Restoration Comedy, 1660-1720*. Oxford: Oxford University Press, 1924.
Drew, Elizabeth A. *Discovering Drama*. New York: Norton, 1937.
Duckworth, George E. *The Nature of Roman Comedy: A Study in Popular Entertainment*. Princeton, N.J.: Princeton University Press, 1952.

# SELECTED BIBLIOGRAPHY

Duff, J. Wight. *Roman Satire: Its Outlook on Social Life*. Hamden, Conn.: Archon, 1964.
Elliot, Robert C. *The Power of Satire: Magic, Ritual, Art*. Princeton: Princeton University Press, 1960.
Feibleman, James. *In Praise of Comedy*. London: Allen and Unwin, 1939.
Feinberg, Leonard. *Introduction to Satire*. Ames: Iowa State University Press, 1967.
_____ . *The Satirist: His Temperament, Motivation, and Influence*. Ames: Iowa State University Press, 1963.
Fiske, George C. *Lucilius and Horace: A Study in the Classical Theory of Imitation*. Madison: University of Wisconsin Press, 1920.
Herrick, Marvin T. *Comic Theory in the Sixteenth Century*. Urbana: University of Illinois Press, 1964.
Highet, Gilbert. *Anatomy of Satire*. Princeton: Princeton University Press, 1962.
_____ . *Juvenal the Satirist*. New York: Oxford University Press, 1961.
_____ . "The Philosophy of Juvenal." *Transactions of the American Philological Association*, LXXX (1949), 254-70.
Kernan, Alvin B. *The Plot of Satire*. New Haven: Yale University Press, 1965.
Kronenberger, Louis. *The Thread of Laughter*. New York: Knopf, 1952.
Lejay, P. *Horace: "Satires."* Paris: Hachette, 1911.
Nicoll, Allardyce. *The Theory of Drama*. London: Harrap, 1937.
Nybakken, O.E. "An Analytical Study of Horace's Ideas." *Iowa Studies in Classical Philology*, V (1937).
O'Hara, Frank H., and Margueritte H. Bro. *Invitation to the Theater*. New York: Harper, 1938.
Rand, E.K. "Horace and the Spirit of Comedy." *The Rice Institute Pamphlet*, XXIV (1937), 39-117.
Rooy, C.A., Van. *Studies in Classical Satire and Related Literary Theory*. Leiden: Brill, 1966.
Rudd, Niall. *The "Satires" of Horace: A Study*. Cambridge: Cambridge University Press, 1966.
Schoenheim, Ursula. "A Study of the Major Themes of Roman Satire." Diss., Cornell University, 1958.
Shero, L.R. "The Cena in Roman Satire." *Classical Philology*, XVIII (1923), 126-143.
Smith, Robert Metcalf. *Types of Social Comedy*. New York: Prentice-Hall, 1928.
Sullivan, J.P. "Critical Essays on Roman Literature". Volume II: *Satire*. London: Routledge and Kegan, 1963.
Sypher, Wylie, ed. *Comedy*. Garden City: Doubleday, 1956.
Watts, Helena W. *The Satiric and the Didactic in Ben Jonson's Comedy*. Chapel Hill: North Carolina University Press, 1947.
Witke, Edward C. "Latin Satire: The Classical Genre and Its Medieval Development." Diss., Harvard University, 1960.

### D. Works on Classical Literature and Culture

Alton, John Francis, D'. *Horace and His Age*. New York: Longmans, Green, 1917.
Aquinas, Thomas, St. *Commentary on the Nicomachean Ethics*. Tr. C.I, Litzinger. 2 vols. Chicago: Henry Regnery, 1964.
Aristotle. *On the Art of Poetry*. Tr. Lane Cooper. Ithaca: Cornell University Press, 1947.
Bagnani, Gilbert. *Arbiter of Elegance: A Study of the Life and Works of C. Petronius*. Toronto: University of Toronto Press, 1954.
Boak, Arthur E.R. *A History of Rome to 565 A.D.* New York: MacMillan, 1921.
Boyce, Benjamin. *The Theophrastan Character in England to 1642*. Cambridge: Harvard University Press. 1947.

Dalzell, A. "Maecenas and the Poets." *Phoenix*, X (1956), 151-162.
DeWitt, Norman W. "Epicurean Doctrine in Horace." *Classical Philology*, XXXIV (1939), 127-134.
Duff, J. Wight. *A Literary History of Rome from the Origins to the Close of the Golden Age*. Ed. A.M. Duff. New York: Barnes and Noble, 1964.
Edelstein, Ludwig. *The Meaning of Stoicism*. Cambridge: Harvard University Press. 1966.
Fraenkel, Edward. *Horace*. Oxford: Clarendon Press, 1957.
Furley, D.J. "The Purpose of Theophrastus's Character." *Symbolae Osloenses*, XXX (1953), 60.
Grant, Mary A. *The Ancient Rhetorical Theories of the Laughable*. Madison: University of Wisconsin Press, 1924.
Grube, G.M.A. "Theophrastus as a Literary Critic." *Transactions of the American Philological Association*, LXXXIII (1952), 60.
Guthrie, William K.C. *A History of Greek Philosophy*. 2 vols. Cambridge: University Press, 1962.
Hadzsits, George D. *Lucretius and His Influence*. New York: Cooper Square, 1963.
Highet, Gilbert. *The Classical Tradition*. New York: Oxford University Press, 1949.
Lord, Louise E. *Aristophanes: His Plays and His Influence*. New York: Cooper Square, 1963.
Marmier, Jean. *Horace en France au XVIIe Siècle*. Université de Rennes. Faculté des lettres et Sciences Humaines Publications, XXIII, 1962.
Mendell, Clarence. *Our Seneca*. New Haven: Yale University Press, 1941.
North, Helen. *Sophrosyne*. Ithaca: Cornell University Press, 1966.
Quinn, Kenneth. *Virgil's Aeneid*. Ann Arbor: University of Michigan Press, 1968.
Rand, Edward K. *Ovid and His Influence*. Boston: Marshall Jones, 1925.
Saintonge, P.F., L.G. Burgevin, and H. Griffith. *Horace: Three Phases of His Influence*. Chicago: University of Chicago Press, 1936.
Sandys, J.E., ed. *A Companion to Latin Studies*. 3 vols. Cambridge: Cambridge University Press, 1906-1910.
Showerman, Grant. *Horace and His Influence*. New York: Cooper Square, 1963.
Syme, Ronald. *Tacitus*. 2 vols. Oxford: Clarendon Press, 1958.
Walker, Bessie. *The Annals of Tacitus*. Manchester: Manchester University Press, 1950.
Walsh, Patrick Gerard. *Livy: His Historical Aims and Methods*. Cambridge: Cambridge University Press, 1967.
Wheatley, Katherine E. *Molière and Terence: A Study in Molière's Realism*. Austin: University of Texas, 1931 (Diss., Chicago).
Whitman, Cedric H. *Aristophanes and the Comic Hero*. Martin Classical Lectures, XIX. Cambridge: Harvard University Press, 1964.

E. Miscellaneous

Aldridge, A. Owen. *Comparative Literature: Matter and Method*. Chicago: University of Illinois Press, 1969.
Campbell, L.B. *Shakespeare's Histories*. San Marino, California: Huntington Library, 1947.
Donohue, John W. *Jesuit Education*. New York: Fordham University Press, 1963.
Dupont-Ferrier, Gustave. *Du Collège de Clermont au Lycée Louis-le-Grand*. 2 vols. Paris: E. de Brocard, 1921-22.
Farrington, Frederic Ernest. *French Secondary Schools: An account of the Origin, Development and Present Organization of Secondary Education in France*. London: Longmans, Green, 1910.

# SELECTED BIBLIOGRAPHY

Fouquéray, Henri. *Histoire de la Compagnie de Jésus en France des origines à la suppression (1528-1762)*. 5 vols. Paris: Alphonse Picard, 1910-25.

Ganss, George E. *Saint Ignatius' Idea of a Jesuit University*. Milwaukee: Marquette University Press, 1956.

Gerstenberger, Donna, and Frederick Garber, eds. *Microcosm: An Anthology of the Short Story*. San Francisco: Chandler, 1969.

Gifford, William. *Comparative Literature: Method and Perspective*. Carbondale: Southern Illinois University Press, 1961.

Gilbert, Allan H. *Literary Criticism, Plato to Dryden*. Detroit: Wayne State University Press, 1962.

Rochemonteix, Camille de, S.J. *Un Collège de Jésuites aux XVIIe et XVIIIe Siècles: Le Collège Henri IV de la Flèche*. 4 vols. Le Mans: Leguicheux, 1889.

Sandys, J.E. *A History of Classical Scholarship*. 3 vols. New York: Hafner, 1967.

Schimberg, André. *L'Education Morale dans les Collèges de la Compagnie de Jésus en France sous L'Ancien Régime*. Paris: Honore Champion, 1913.

Schwickerath, Robert, S.J. *Jesuit Education*. St. Louis: B. Herber, 1903.

Sicard, L'abbé Augustin. *Les études classiques avant la Révolution*. Paris: Perrin, 1887.

Tillyard, E.M.W. *The Elizabethan World Picture*. New York: MacMillan, 1943.

# STUDIES IN THE ROMANCE LANGUAGES AND LITERATURES
Distributed by: The University of North Carolina Press
Box 2288 Chapel Hill, N.C. 27514

## Recent Publications

Dana Drake. *Don Quijote (1894-1970): A Selective Annotated Bibliography - Volume I.*

Judith Rothschild. *Narrative Technique in the Lais of Marie de France: Themes and Variations.*

John F. Winter. *Visual Variety and Spatial Grandeur: A Study of the Transition from the Sixteenth to the Seventeenth French Century.*

Florence Yudin. *"The Vibrant Silence" in Jorge Guilleu's Aire Nuestro.*

Antoinette Knapton. *Mythe et psychologie chez Marie de France*

Rob Roy McGregor. *The Lyric Poems of Jehan Froissart: A Critical Edition.*

Arthur Askins. *The Hispano-Portuguese Cancionero of the Hispanic Society of America.*

Ruth El Saffar. *Distance and Control in Don Quioxte: A Study in Narrative Technique.*

Rafael Osuna. *Los Sonetos de Calderón en sus obras dramáticas: Estudio y Edición.*

Shirley B. Whitaker. *The Dramatic Works of Alvaro Cubillo de Aragón.*

Ann Turkey Harrison. *Charles D'Orléans and the Allegorical Mode*

Laurence Romero. *Molière: Traditions in Criticism*

Ruth Lee Kennedy. *Studies in Tirso, I.*

Karin Ciholas. *Gide's Art of the Fugue: A Thematic Study of "Les Faux-Monnayeurs."*

J. B. Avalle-Arce. *Las Memorias de Gonzalo Fernández de Oviedo, Vol. I.*

J. B. Avalle-Arce. *Las Memorias de Gonzalo Fernández de Oviedo, Vol. II.*

Joseph R. Danos. *A Concordance to the Roman de la Rose*

J. B. Avalle-Arce. *Los Narradores Hispanoamericanos de Hoy.*

Andrew Debicki and Enrique Pupo-Walker. *Estudios Hispanoamericanos en Honor of J. J. Arrom.*

Aldo Scaglione. *Francis Petrarch, Six Centuries Later*

Francisco Rico. *Vida u obra de Petrarca.*

John J. McCann. *The Theater of Arthur Adamov.*

Mary G. Hauer. *Luis Velez de Guevara: A Critical Bibliography.*

Karlis Racevskis. *Voltaire and the French Academy.*

Ernesto G. Caserta. *Giacomo Leopardi: The War of the Mice and the Crabs.*

Joan Stewart. *The Novels of Mme Riccoboni.*

Marcia L. Welles. *Style and Structure in Gracián's "El Criticón."*

Ursla Franklin. *An Anatomy of Poesis: The Prose Poems of Stéphane Mallarmé.*

Eugene Weinraub. *Chrétien's Jewish Grail.*

Merlin H. Forster. *Fire and Ice: The Poetry of Xavier Villaurrutia.*

Annette Thau. *Poetry and Antipoetry: A Study of Selected Aspects of Max Jacob's Poetic Style*

Edouard Morot-Sir, Howard Harper, and Dougald McMillan. *Samuel Beckett: The Art of Rhetoric.*

G. Lohmann-Villena. *Un Tríptico del Perú Virreinal: El Virrey Amat, El Marqués de Soto Florido y La Perricholi.*

Christopher Kleinhenz. *Medieval Manuscripts and Textual Criticism.*

Jerry Nash. *Délie. Concordance.* 2 vols. Xerox On-Demand Printing. Ann Arbor, Michigan.

Nathaniel B. Smith. *Figures of Repetition in the Old Provençal Lyric.*

Patricia Willet Cummins. *A Critical Edition of Le Regime tresutile et tresproufitable pour conserver et garder la santé du corps humain.* Xerox On-Demand Printing. Ann Arbor, Michigan.

Richard Howard Stamelman. *The Drama of Self in Guillaume Apollinaire's "Alcools".*

Edward Joseph Gallagher. *A Critical Edition of "La Passion Nostre Seigneur."*

The Department of Romance Studies Digital Arts and Collaboration Lab at the University of North Carolina at Chapel Hill is proud to support the digitization of the North Carolina Studies in the Romance Languages and Literatures series.

www.ingramcontent.com/pod-product-compliance
Lightning Source LLC
Chambersburg PA
CBHW022021220426
43663CB00007B/1161